CISTERCIAN STUDIES SERIES: NUMBER FORTY-SEVEN

D1559995

pachomian koinonia

Volume Three

Instructions, Letters, and Other Writings
of Saint Pachomius and his Disciples

pachomian koinonia

the Lives, Rules, and Other Writings of Saint pachomius and his disciples

CISTERCIAN STUDIES SERIES: NUMBER FORTY-SEVEN

pachomian koinonia

volume three

Instructions, Letters, and Other Writings of Saint Pachomius and his Disciples

Translated, with an introduction,
by
Armand Veilleux
Monk of Mistassini

Cistercian Publications Inc.
Kalamazoo, Michigan

© Cistercian Publications, Inc., 1982
Kalamazoo, Michigan 49008

Publication of this volume was assisted by a grant from the
Publications Program of the National Endowment for the Humanities
an independent federal agency.

Translation of the works contained in this volume
was made possible in part by a translator's grant from the
National Endowment for the Humanities,
Washington, D.C.

Typeset by the Carmelites of Indianapolis

Library of Congress Cataloging in Publication Data

Main entry under title:

Instructions, letters, and other writings.

   (Pachomian koinonia; v. 3)   (Cistercian studies series; 47)
   Bibliography: p. 299
   Includes index.   1. Christian literature, Early — Collected works.
I. Veilleux, Armand. II. Series. III. Series: Cistercian studies series; 47.

      BR1720.P23P3 vol. 3 [BR60.A62]   271'.12s [271'.8]   81-10140
ISBN   (hardcover)   0-87907-847-2 (v. 3)
      (paperback)   0-87907-947-9

Typeset and printed in the United States of America

To the memory of
Father Basilius Steidle, osb,
(1903–1982),
my dearly remembered professor,
who first introduced me to monastic studies.

CONTENTS

CRITICAL EDITIONS

of the texts translated in this volume

WRITINGS OF PACHOMIUS:

Instructions: L.T. Lefort, *Oeuvres de s. Pachôme et de ses disciples*, CSCO 159. Louvain, 1956, pp. 1-26.

Letters: Coptic text: Hans Quecke, *Die Briefe Pachoms. Griechischer Text der Handschrift W. 145 der Chester Beatty Library eingeleitet und herausgegeben von Hans Quecke. Anhang: Die koptischen Fragmente und Zitate der Pachombriefe. Textus Patristici et Liturgici 11.* Regensburg, 1975, pp. 111-118. Letter 11b has been translated from a photocopy of MS Bodmer P. XXXIX.

Greek text: *Ibidem*, pp. 99-110.

Latin text: A. Boon, *Pachomiana latina. Règle et épîtres de s. Pachôme, épître de s. Théodore et 'Liber' de s. Orsiesius. Texte latin de s. Jérôme, Bibliothèque de la Revue d'histoire ecclésiastique 7.* Louvain, 1932.

Fragments: L.T. Lefort, *Oeuvres* ..., pp. 26-30 and 80.

WRITINGS OF THEORDORE

Instructions: L.T. Lefort, *Oeuvres*, ..., pp. 37-60.

Letters: Latin: A. Boon, *Pachomiana latina* ..., pp. 105-106.

Coptic: H. Quecke, 'Ein Brief von einem Nachfolger Pachoms, (Chester Beatty Library Ms Ac 1486)' *Orientalia* 44 (1975), pp. 430-432.

Fragments: L.T. Lefort, *Oeuvres* ..., pp. 60-62.

WRITINGS OF HORSIESIOS:

Instructions: L.T. Lefort, *Oeuvres* ... pp. 66-79.

Letters: I and II: *Ibidem,* pp. 63-65.
III and IV: MS Chester Beatty Library Ac 1494
and 1495.

Fragments: L.T. Lefort, *Oeuvres* ..., pp. 81-82.

Testament: A. Boon, *Pachomiana latina* ..., pp. 109-147.

introduction

IN THIS THIRD VOLUME of our *Pachomiana* in English we have collected all those writings of Pachomius, Theodore, and Horsiesios that were not parts of the *Life* and did not belong to the *corpus* of the Rules.

Most of these documents were unknown until very recently, and they bring important new light on pachomian spirituality. All of them—with the exception of one, translated in 1913—are here translated into English for the first time.

writings of pachomius

A. Instructions

The *catechesis*, instruction on the Holy Scriptures, was a very important feature of pachomian cenobitism. The housemaster delivered it to the monks of his house twice a week, on the fast days, and the superior of the local monastery three times a week, on Saturday evening and twice on Sunday. Pacomius and his successors at the head of the *Koinonia* gave also other instructions, either when they were visiting the brothers of the various monasteries or on special occasions like the celebration of the Passover at Phbow or the second general gathering of all the brothers at the end of the year. Some of these instructions have been used by the biographers and can be found in the *Life*. The manuscript tradition has also preserved some of them as separate documents. It is these that we translate here. Of Pachomius we have two, a long catechesis concerning a spiteful monk, and a shorter one about the six days of the Passover. We did not translate the several fragmentary instructions which we find in the fragments of the *Third Sahidic Life*. They are accretions, the authenticity of which is too doubtful.

INSTRUCTION CONCERNING A SPITEFUL MONK

The Coptic text of this instruction exists only in one manuscript, *British Oriental 7024*, fol. 18r-49v. It was first published by E.A.W. Budge in 1913, with an English translation.[1] L.T. Lefort published a new edition of the Coptic text, with a French translation, in 1956.[2]

There is no doubt that the original language of this text was Coptic;[3] but we have at least two manuscripts of an Arabic translation. One of them was used by L.T. Lefort in editing the Coptic text, and the other has been identified more recently by K. Samir. A complete analysis of all the Arabic collections of manuscripts will probably reveal yet a few more witnesses.[4]

The instruction has integrated a large quotation from an homily by Athanasius.[5] At the same time, from it comes an aphorism attributed to Evagrius Ponticus.[6] The manuscript tradition attributes this instruction to Pachomius. Budge did not question that attribution, and it has been defended by Crum and Lefort. In fact there is no doubt that it comes from a pachomian milieu and that it is, therefore, pachomian in character. But the fact that it contains a large quotation of Athanasius permits us to think that it could be a literary composition by a pachomian monk rather than an instruction actually given in that form by Pachomius himself. A few other elements of the instruction do not fit well into the context of pachomian cenobitism.[7]

The instruction constitutes a good treatise on monastic *ascesis*, stressing the importance of all the monastic values: humility, detachment, simplicity, chastity. It insists especially on the need to forgive the brother who has offended us, and it is directed to 'a brother monk bearing a grudge against another'.

All the brothers of the pachomian *Koinonia* met every year at Phbow to celebrate the Passover together in the Word of God and by fasting. The meeting concluded with the celebration of the Resurrection during the Easter Vigil, when catechumen monks were baptized. The superiors of the *Koinonia* customarily gave instructions during these days. One of these instructions given by Pachomius on the Passover has been preserved, although only fragmentarily. The text of this fragment was published first by E. Amélineau in 1895,[8] and again by L.T. Lefort in 1956.[9]

There is no positive reason to doubt the pachomian character of this document either, although the last part of the text does not fit well in a pachomian context: 'Let the wealthy women lay down their ornaments during these days of sorrow.'[10]

B. *Letters*

The *Pachomiana latina* contain the text of eleven letters of Pachomius, most of them extremely difficult to interpret.[11] Till very recently these letters were known only in the Latin version; but in recent years the Greek and Coptic text of many of them has been discovered and published.

In 1968 the Coptic text of letters 8, 10, and 11a was published and translated in German by A. Hermann (letter 8) and A. Kropp (letters 10 and 11a) among a series of Demotic and Coptic documents from the Cologne collection.[12] These letters were found on two folios of parchment from the fifth-sixth century. Neither the editors nor the reviewers were able at that time to identify these texts as pachomian letters. The identification was made by Hans Quecke in a communication to the eighteenth *Deutscher Oriental-*

istentag in Lübeck in October 1972, where he also announced the discovery in the Chester Beatty Library of a Greek parchment of the fourth century containing the Greek translation of letters 1, 2, 3, 7, and 10.[13] That communication was published only in 1974, but a new translation of letters 8 and 10 from the Coptic text of Cologne was published by Hans Quecke in 1973.[14] In 1974 he published a new discovery: fragments of letters 9a, 9b, 10, and 11b as well as a cryptogram, all from Coptic fragments from the same Chester Beatty Library.[15]

In 1975 Hans Quecke published the Greek text from the Chester Beatty Library (Ms W. 145) with a long and very careful analysis of all the related problems. An appendix gives all the known Coptic fragments.[16] This book, therefore, gathers in a practical format all the documents discovered during the preceding years.

Lately a new Coptic fragment has been discovered among the Bodmer Papyri (n. XXXIX), giving the full text of letter 11b. That text is still unpublished, but Hans Quecke had the kindness to provide us with a photocopy of the manuscript, along with his transcription of the Coptic text and a German translation.

In our translation we have kept the numbering assigned these letters by Jerome; but the Coptic manuscript tradition knows thirteen letters instead of eleven, both Jerome's ninth and eleventh letters being divided in two distinct documents.

Hans Quecke has dedicated a full chapter of his *Die Briefe Pachoms. Griechischer Text . . .* to the question of the authenticity of these letters. They certainly existed in Coptic at a very early stage, for we have a Greek translation preserved on a parchment of the fourth century. From a comparison between Jerome's version and the Coptic and Greek texts, we can deduce that Jerome had before his eyes a Greek text very similar to the one preserved in the Chester Beatty Library, although he paraphrased it at times, as he often did in his other translations. Jerome attributed these letters explicitly to Pachomius, and Hans Quecke does not find any positive reason to doubt that affirmation although none of the letters, either in Greek or Coptic, bears a title attributing it to Pachomius. Personally we consider that one is left here with the same uncertainty as prevails regarding the *Pachomiana latina* in general.

A difficult aspect of these letters is the use that many of them make of a mysterious language, or rather, their mysterious use of the alphabet. All efforts made to decipher them remain unconvincing.[17] Hans Quecke has made a very thorough study of all the aspects of this problem, but has been unable to find any clear answer.

The nature of these letters still escapes us, but it is perhaps much less complicated than we think it is. It probably has something to do with the traditional love of the Egyptians for cryptograms, to which old Egyptian hieroglyphs lent themselves so well. The use of series of vowels and nonsense syllables is not rare either in the gnostic documents discovered in 1946 at Nag Hammadi, near the great basilica of St Pachomius at Phbow, and there could be some similarity or affinity between the two.[18]

In our translation of the letters, we have followed the Coptic text when it existed. When it did not, we have translated from the Greek for the letters existing in Greek. Otherwise we have followed the Latin version of Jerome.

C. Fragments

Two Coptic folios identified by Zoega (CLXXIV) were first published by E. Amélineau.[19] L.T Lefort has made a newer edition.[20] These folios belong to a series of *miscellanea* from an eleventh century manuscript. The third of the three fragments they contain is also found in the collection of *Apophthegmata* in Coptic, Greek, and Latin.[21]

To these three fragments we have added a fourth which has been attributed by L.T. Lefort to Horsiesios, but which must be restored to Pachomius.[22] It is found on the recto of a folio on the verso of which we read the Prologue to the *Praecepta et Instituta* that L.T. Lefort had also attributed to Horsiesios and that was identified by Heinrich Bacht as part of the pachomian Rule.[23]

WRITINGS OF THEODORE

A. Instructions

As is the case with Pachomius, several instructions given by
Theodore were preserved in the Life. Three instructions however
were transmitted as separate documents in the Coptic manuscript
tradition. The first two are extremely fragmentary, but we have a
fairly large section of the third one. They were published by Lefort
in 1956.[24] Apart from one of the nineteen folios that still exist of
the third instruction, nothing of this had been published before.[25]

Although very short, the fragment of the second instruction is
important because it is one of the texts in which the life of the *Koinonia* is explicitly called 'the life of the apostles', and Pachomius is
proclaimed the father of the *Koinonia* after God and the apostles.

The third instruction deals mostly with the theme of the *Koinonia* itself and, along with the Testament of Horsiesios (*Liber Orsiesii*), is one of the two most articulate and most beautiful expressions of pachomian spirituality.

B. Letters

Of Theodore we have two letters, one preserved in Latin and the
other in Coptic. The latter belongs to the handful of pachomian
documents found in the Chester Beatty Library in Dublin.[26] It was
published and analysed by Hans Quecke in 1975.[27] A. de Vogüé
published a French translation accompanied by long and very
useful annotations.[28] There is another manuscript of the same letter soon to be published by M. Krause.

The archbishops of Alexandria used to publish every year a pastoral letter indicating the dates of the fast of forty days and the fast
of the Passover, and convoking believers to the Easter celebration.
The superiors of the pachomian *Koinonia* adopted the same practice. The first letter of Theodore — the one translated into Latin by
Jerome — is one of these Easter letters inviting the brothers to gath-

er together at Phbow for the Passover and exhorting the superiors as well as the brothers.[29] The second letter comes certainly from a successor of Pachomius. H. Quecke found several good reasons to attribute it to Horsiesios, although he did so with some hesitation. But a second manuscript of the same text was later discovered by Krause and it bears a title attributing the letter to Theodore: 'This is the letter from our father Theodore for the Remission'. This title expresses also the occasion of the letter. It is a letter of convocation to the second annual meeting of the pachomian monks, at the end of the year according to the egyptian calendar. It begins exactly like the seventh letter of Pachomius, which was also a letter of convocation to the general assembly of the end of the year.

C. Fragments

The manuscript containing the three first fragments from Pachomius mentioned above gives also a very short fragment from Theodore. It was published first by E. Amélineau in 1895[30] and again by L.T. Lefort in 1956.[31]

WRITINGS OF HORSIESIOS

A. Instructions

From three manuscripts, the folios of which have been spread in various libraries from Paris, London, Vienna, and Leyde to Cairo, L.T. Lefort has published a certain number of fragments which have some chance of being parts of instructions by Horsiesios.[32] We have translated here all of them except the last one, which Lefort attributed to Horsiesios but which must be restored to Pachomius. The first of these texts is an almost complete instruction and is quite in Horsiesios' style. The others are more fragmentary. The seventh, which is a strange diatribe against friendship, does not correspond much to Horsiesios' usual line of thought. Its authenticity remains somewhat doubtful.

B. Letters

Two letters from Horsiesios are found in a manuscript published first by Amélineau[33] and again by Lefort.[34] Two more were discovered among the Coptic codices of the Chester Beatty Library. The last of these letters — all very rich in biblical quotations — is addressed to Theodore. Several of the quotations are found in more than one letter and again in the Testament of Horsiesios. The two letters from the Dublin collection are still unpublished, but they have been translated into French by A. de Vogüé.[35] For our translation of these two letters, we have used a transcription of the manuscript made by Tito Orlandi, with his kind permission. We were also able to check the text of the manuscript itself at the Chester Beatty Library in Dublin.

C. Fragments

From Horsiesios, as in the case of Pachomius and Theodore, Lefort has published some texts from an unclassified folio, under the title 'excerpta'. We have translated them under the title 'fragments'.[36]

D. Testament of Horsiesios

The 'Book of our father Horsiesios' (*Liber Orsiesii*), also called the 'Testament of Horsiesios', is certainly his most important writing. It is also one of the most beautiful pieces of pachomian literature, and a faithful and complete expression of pachomian spirituality. It presupposes a situation of crisis similar to the one caused by Apollonios that obliged Horsiesios to resign as superior of the *Koinonia*. But the end of the text leads us to think that it was written towards the end of Horsiesios' life, and is really his spiritual testament.[37] It is a long call to conversion, to a total renunciation of any form of personal property, in order to arrive at a perfect communion with the brothers.

Although we know this text only through Jerome's translation,[38] its authenticity was never put in doubt. A very good annotated German translation was published by H. Bacht,[39] who had written another good study of the document several years earlier.[40] There is also a French and a Spanish translation available.[41] A few chapters (7-18 and 39-40) have also been translated into German by O. Schuler.[42] As a basis for our own translation, we have used an English version made by Philip Timko, with his kind permission.

CAROUR

At the end of his *Oeuvres de s. Pachôme...* L.T. Lefort has published a kind of apocalyptic text from another disciple of Pachomius called Carour.[43] We did not translate that text, first because it is not representative of the pachomian spirit, and then because its language is so colloquial that both Lefort and Crum (consulted by Lefort) were unable to find the meaning of a great number of passages.

Monita Sancti Pachomii

Neither did we translate the *Monita Sancti Pachomii* published by A. Boon in his *Pachomiana latina*, because although Holstenius published them with the Rules, they are not from Jerome, and still less from Pachomius.[44]

Indices

This volume ends with a series of Indices that cover the three volumes.

The *Biblical Index*, by far the most important, is arranged in such a way that by looking at it the reader can know immediately not only the volume and the page where a biblical quotation or allusion is to be found, but also the document. This system did not seem required for the other *indices*.

The *indices* of the names of persons and of places list only the names mentioned in the pachomian documents themselves, and not those mentioned in the introductions or in the notes. The *analytic index* is very detailed. This is consistent with our intention of providing the reader not only with solid material for spiritual reading but also with a useful tool for further research. And we hope indeed that our contribution to the knowledge of pachomian sources among English-speaking readers will give rise to a new interest in spiritual and scientific research on this beautiful segment of the monastic tradition.

NOTES

[1] E.A.W. Budge, *Coptic Apocrypha in the Dialect of Upper Egypt,* London 1913. text, pp. 146-176; translation, pp. 352-382.

[2] L.T. Lefort, *Oeuvres de s. Pachôme,* text, pp. 1-24; translation, pp. 1-26.

[3] See W.E. Crum in his review of Budge's *Coptic Apocrypha . . .* in *Zeitschrift der deutschen morgenländisch Gesellschaft* 68 (1914) 176-184.

[4] Concerning the Arabic manuscripts of this instruction, see K. Samir, 'Témoins arabes de la catéchèse de Pachôme 'A propos d'un moine rancunier'. (CPG 2354.1)', in *OCP* 42 (1976) 494-508.

[5] This has been shown by L.T. Lefort in 'S. Athanase écrivain copte', in *Muséon* 46 (1933) 1-33.

[6] See L.T. Lefort, 'A propos d'un aphorisme d'Evagrius Ponticus', in *Bulletin de l'Académie Royale de Belgique,* 1950, pp. 70-79.

[7] V.g. ¶18: 'If you wish to live among men . . . . If you wish to live in the desert . . .'.

[8] In *Mémoires publiés pour les membres de la mission archéologique française au Caire,* t. IV, Paris 1895, pp. 612-614.

[9] In *Oeuvres de s. Pachôme,* text, pp. 24-26; translation pp. 26-27.

[10] See ¶4.

[11] A Boon, *Pachomiana latina,* pp. 77-101.

[12] *Demotische und Koptische Texte: Papyrologica Coloniensia* 2 (*Wissenschaftliche Abhandlungen der Arbeitsgemeinschaft für Forschung des Landes Nordrhein Westfalens*), Cologne and Upsala, 1968.

[13] 'Die Briefe Pachoms', in *18. Deutscher Orientalistentag from 1. bis 5. Oktober 1972 in Lübeck. Vorträge. Herausgegeben von Wolfgang Voigt: ZDMG, Supplement* 2, Wiesbaden 1974, pp. 96-108.

[14] 'Briefe Pachoms in koptischer Sprache'. Neue deutsche Übersetzung', in *Zetesis* (*Festschrift E. de Strycker*). Antwerp and Utrecht, 1973, pp. 655-664.

[15] 'Ein neues Fragment der Pachombriefe in koptischer Sprache', *Orientalia* 43 (1974) pp. 66-82.

[16] 'Die griechische Übersetzung der Pachombriefe', in *Studia Papyrologica* 15 (1976) 153-159.

[17] An author of the seventeenth century, Athanasius Kircher, dealt with these letters in several of his works; see references in H. Quecke, *Die Briefe Pachoms.*

Griechisher Text, pp. 33-34. More recently: P.E. Testa, in *Il simbolismo dei Giudeo-Cristiani* (*Pubblicazioni dello Studium Biblicum Franciscanum - 14*), Jerusalem 1962, pp. 78-79, 361, 363-4, 367-9, 375 and 395.

[18] See F. Wisse, 'Language Mysticism in the Nag Hammadi Texts and in Early Coptic Monasticism. I: Cryptography', in *Göttinger Orientforschungen VI. Reihe Hellenistica*, Wiesbaden 1977; *Idem*, 'Gnosticism and Early Monasticism in Egypt', in *Gnosis*. (*Festschrift für Hans Jonas*), Göttingen 1978, p. 438.

[19] *Mémoires*, pp. 616-619.

[20] *Oeuvres de s. Pachôme*, text, pp. 26-30; translation, pp. 27-30.

[21] See references given by L.T. Lefort in *Oeuvres de s. Pachôme, CSCO - 159*, p. VIII.

[22] *Oeuvres de s. Pachôme*, text, p. 80; translation, p. 79. See H. Quecke, *Die Briefe Pachoms. Griechisher Text*, pp. 44-46.

[23] H. Bacht, 'Ein verkanntes Fragment des koptischen Pachomiusregel', in *Muséon* 75 (1962) 5-18.

[24] *Oeuvres de s. Pachôme*, text, pp. 37-60; translation, pp. 38-61.

[25] *Mémoires*, p. 812.

[26] On the pachomian manuscripts in the Chester Beatty Library, see H. Quecke, 'Eine Handvoll Pachomianischer Texte', in *ZDMG*, Supp. III, 1 (1977) 221-229; T. Orlandi, 'Nuovi Testi copti pacomiani', in *Commandements du Seigneur et Libération évangélique*, SA 70, Rome 1977, pp. 241-243.

[27] 'Ein Brief von einem Nachfolger Pachoms', in *Orientalia* 44 (1975) 426-433.

[28] A. de Vogüé, 'Epîtres inédites d'Horsièse et de Théodore', in *Commandements du Seigneur et Libération évangélique*, SA 70, Rome 1977, pp. 244-257; this letter, pp. 255-257.

[29] Text in A. Boon, *Pachomiana latina*, pp. 105-106.

[30] *Mémoires*, pp. 620-621.

[31] *Oeuvres de s. Pachôme*, text, pp. 60-62; translation, pp. 61-62.

[32] *Ibid.*, text, pp. 66-79; translation, pp. 67-79.

[33] *Mémoires*, pp. 622-627.

[34] *Oeuvres de s. Pachôme*, text, pp. 63-66; translation, pp. 63-66.

[35] 'Epîtres inédites', pp. 245-254.

[36] *Oeuvres de s. Pachôme*, text, pp. 81-82; translation, pp. 80-81.

[37] See the quotation of 2 Tm 4:6-8 in ¶56.

[38] Latin text in A. Boon, *Pachomiana latina*, pp. 109-147.

[39] H. Bacht, *Das Vermächtnis des Ursprungs, Studien zum frühen Mönchtum I*, Würzburg, 1972.

[40] H. Bacht, 'Studien zum "Liber Orsiesii"', in *HJ* 77 (1958) 98-124.

[41] P. Deseille, *L'esprit du monachisme pachômien, suivi de la traduction française des Pachomiana latina par les moines de Solesmes, Spiritualité orientale 2*, Bellefontaine 1968; M. De Elizalde, 'Libro de nuestro Padre San Orsisio. Introducción, traducción y notas de Martin de Elizalde', in *Cuadernos monasticos*, Nos. 4-5 (1967) 173-244.

[42] B. Steidle and O. Schuler, 'Der "Obern-Spiegel" in "Testament" des Abtes Horsiesi (nach 387)', in *EuA* 43 (1967) 5-21.

[43] *Oeuvres de s. Pachôme*, text, pp. 100-104; translation, pp. 100-108.

[44] See the explanations given by A. Boon in his Introduction, pp. L-LI.

Instruction concerning a spiteful monk

(Pach. Instr. 1)

INSTRUCTION PRONOUNCED BY OUR MOST EXCELLENT HOLY FATHER, APA PACHOMIUS THE HOLY ARCHIMANDRITE,[1] FOR A BROTHER MONK BEARING A GRUDGE TO ANOTHER. THIS HAPPENED IN THE TIME OF APA EBONH, BY WHOM HE WAS BROUGHT TO TABENNESI. [OUR FATHER] ADDRESSED THESE WORDS TO HIM IN THE PRESENCE, AND TO THE GREAT JOY, OF OTHER ELDER FATHERS. IN THE PEACE OF GOD! MAY HIS HOLY BLESSING AND THAT OF ALL THE SAINTS COME OVER US! MAY WE ALL BE SAVED! AMEN.

1. *My son, listen and be wise*,* accept the true doctrine,[†] for there are two ways.[1]

2. Be able to obey God like Abraham,[1] who abandoned his country,* went into exile, and with Isaac lived in a tent in the promised land as in a foreign country. He obeyed, humbled himself, and was given an inheritance; he was even put to the test over Isaac. He was courageous in trial and offered Isaac in sacrifice to God; and for that *God called him his friend.*[2]

3. ⟨Take the candor of Isaac as an example too. When he heard his father, he submitted to him, even to being sacrificed, like a gentle lamb⟩.[1]

4. Take as an example also the humility of Ja-

Text: CSCO 159: 1-24
Listen, my son
*Pr 23:19.
[†]Cf. Si 6:23; 16:24.
The example of Abraham's obedience
*Heb 11:8-9.

Gn 22.
Jm 2:23.

Isaac's candor

13

Jacob's humility

Gn 35:9-10.
Joseph's wisdom
Gn 41.

Emulate the
lives of the saints
*Cf. Heb 6:12.
†Cf. Pr 6:9.
Pr 6:3.
Eph 5:14.
Cf. 2 Co 4:15.

Be patient

Cf. Heb. 6:15.

1 P 5:4.

Practise all
the virtues

Cf. Mt 6:6;
    Lk 18:1.

In time of trial,
trust in the Lord

Ps 118(117):11.

Is 58:11.

cob, his submission and his steadfastness, through which he became a light seeing the Father of the universe and was called Israel.

5. Take as an example also the wisdom of Joseph and his submission. Do battle in chastity and service until you make yourself a king.[1]

6. My son, emulate the lives of the saints* and practise their virtues. Wake up and do not be negligent.† *Rouse up your fellow citizen for whom you have pledged yourself.[1] Get up, do not stay among the dead; and Christ will shine on you[2]* and grace will blossom within you.

7. It is patience that reveals every grace to you, and it is through patience that the saints received all that was promised them. Patience is the pride of the saints. Be patient, to be admitted to the saints' legion, confident that *you will be given a crown that will never rust.*

8. A thought? Come to terms with it in patience, waiting for God to give you calm. Fasting? Put up with it in perseverance. Prayer? Without letup, in your room between you and God. One single heart with your brother. Virginity in all your members; virginity in your thoughts, purity of body, and purity of heart. Head bowed, and a humble heart; gentleness in the hour of anger.

9. When a thought oppresses you, do not be downhearted, but put up with it in courage, saying, *They swarmed around me closer and closer, but I drove them back in the name of the Lord.* Divine help will arrive at your side immediately, and you will drive them away from you, and courage will compass you round about, and the glory of God will walk with you; and *you will be filled to your soul's desire.* For the ways of God are hu-

mility of heart and gentleness. It is said indeed, *Whom shall I consider if not the humble and the meek?*[1] If you move ahead in the ways of the Lord he will watch over you, will give you strength, and will fill you with knowledge and wisdom. Your remembrance will remain before him at all times. He will deliver you from the devil, and in your dying day he will grant you his peace.

Is 66:2.

Cf. Ps 128(127):1.

Cf. Is 11:2.

Cf. Ps 112(113):6.

10. My son, I ask you to be watchful and to be on your guard,[1] acquainted with those who lie in ambush against you. The spirit of cowardice and the spirit of distrust walk hand in hand; the spirit of lying and the spirit of deceit walk hand in hand; the spirits of greed and trafficking, of perjury and dishonesty, and that of jealousy walk hand in hand; the spirit of vanity and the spirit of gluttony walk hand in hand; the spirit of fornication and the spirit of impurity walk hand in hand; the spirit of enmity and the spirit of sadness walk hand in hand. Woe to the wretched soul in which they make their home and of which they make themselves masters. They hold such a soul far from God, because it is in their power. It sways from side to side till it ends in the abyss of hell.

Be watchful

Cf. 1 P 4:7; 5:8.

Cf. Rv 21:8.

11. My son, obey me. Do not be negligent, *give your eyes no sleep, your eyelids no rest, so that you may break free like a gazelle from the snares.* For, O my son, all the spirits have attacked me often since my childhood. When I was in the desert they afflicted me to the point that I was about to lose heart and I thought I could not resist the threats of the dragon. He tormented me in every possible way. If I showed myself, he bat-

Affliction by evil spirits

Pr 6:4–5.

tled me with flames; if I withdrew, he afflicted me with his insolence. Many a time my heart was in distress, and I turned from side to side and had no rest. When I fled to God with tears, humility, fasts, and vigils, then the enemy and all his spirits grew weak before me, God's courage came into me, and I experienced at once God's help. For in his mercy he makes his strength and goodness known to the sons of men.[1]

Never condemn anyone

Cf. Mt 6:5.

12. My son, never condemn anyone. If you see someone being honored, do not say, 'He already has received his reward.' Guard yourself from such a thought, for it is very bad, and God detests the man who has praise only for himself, scorning his brother. *The one who says to himself that he is somebody, when he is nothing, is fooling himself.*[1] Who can help him in his pride? And when he presents himself after the manner of God, saying, *There is no one like me*, he will hear his censure without delay, *You will go down to hell, you will be thrown in with the dead, rot will be spread over you, you will be covered with maggots.* As for the man who has acquired humility, he has judged himself, saying that his sins are greater than those of any man. He judges no one and condemns no one. *Who are you to judge a servant that is not yours? The Lord can certainly raise up anyone who has fallen.*[2] Keep watch over yourself, my son, condemn no one, taste all the virtues, and guard them.

Cf. 1 Jn 4:20-21

Ga 6:3.

Ex 9:14.

Is 14:11;
Cf. Is 14:15.19.

Rm 14:4.

In your needs, count on God's help

Si 13:24(30).

13. If you are a stranger, stay back, do not have recourse to the people, and do not meddle in their affairs. If you are poor, let nothing discourage you, lest it be said to you, *Poverty is evil in the mouth of the godless.* Nor should you ever

hear, *Starving, you will become frenzied, and you will speak ill of the chief and the elders.* Watch, too, that no one foment battle with you about something you lack, according to the flesh, in the matter of food. Do not become discouraged, be steadfast; surely God has already done something in secret. Think of Habakkuk in Judaea and of Daniel in Chaldea. Although a distance of forty-five stages separated them, and — still more — Daniel, put out as fodder for beasts, was at the bottom of the pit, Habakkuk brought him dinner.*[1] Think of Elijah in the desert,†[2] and the widow at Zarephath. She was overcome by the pangs of famine and the anguish of hunger. In spite of such misery she was not at all fainthearted. On the contrary she fought, she conquered, and she got what God had promised: her house was in abundance during a time of famine.

To give bread in a time of plenty is no generosity and to be discouraged at a time of need is not to be poor. Indeed, it is written of the saints that, *they were destitute, afflicted, maltreated,*[3] but they gloried in their afflictions. If you remain steadfast in the battle according to the Scriptures you will never undergo bondage; as it is written, *No one should deceive you in matters of food and drink or with regard to a festival or a new moon or a sabbath. These are only a shadow of what is to come.*

14. Recite constantly the words of God. Put up with fatigue and *be grateful for everything.*[1]* Shun the praise of men and love the one who, in the fear of the Lord, reprimands you. Let every man be profitable to you so that you may be good to everyone. Persevere in your work, and in lan-

Is 8:21.

*Dn 14:33-39.
†1 K 19.

1 K 17.

Heb 11:37.
Cf. Rm 5:3.

Col 2:16-17.

Serve God faithfully
*1 Th 5:18.

guage be above reproach. Do not take one step forward, then a step backward, that God may not detest you; for the crown shall go to the one who perseveres.[2] Be ever more obedient to God, and he will save you.

Cf. Mt 10:22.

Avoid joking

15. When you are among brothers, do not indulge in jesting. Shadrach, Meshach and Abednego disregarded the jeering of Nebuchadnezzar, and therefore he could not draw them off by the melodies of his instruments or seduce them with the meals at his table. So they put out the flame that climbed forty-nine cubits high.[1] They did not turn crooked with the crooked, but stayed upright with the upright one, that is to say, with God. For this reason, He made them masters of their enemies. Daniel, in his turn, did not obey the evil reasonings of the Chaldeans. So he was specially chosen and found vigilant and prudent, and *he closed the gullet of savage lions.*

Dn 3:46-50.

Cf. Ps 18 (17): 26-27.

Dn 6:14.

Heb 11:33.

Humble yourself

Cf. Ps 62(61):8.

Heb 11:6.

16. And now, my son, if you take God as your hope, he will be your help in the time of your anguish; *for anyone who comes to God must believe that he exists and that he rewards those who search for him.* These words were written for us, that we may believe in God and do battle, great and little, by fastings, prayers, and other religious practices. God will not forget even the saliva that has dried in your mouth as a result of fasting. On the contrary, everything will be returned to you at the moment of your anguish. Only humble yourself in all things, hold back your word even if you understand the whole affair. Do not quietly acquire the habit of abusing; on the contrary, joyfully put up with every trial. For if you knew the honor that results from trials

you would not pray to be delivered from them, because it is preferable for you to pray, to weep, and to sigh until you are saved, rather than to relax and be led off a captive. O man, what are you doing in Babylon? *You have grown old in an alien land*[1] because you did not submit to the test and because your relations with God are not proper. Therefore, brother, you must not relax.

17. Maybe you are a bit forgetful. But your enemies have not fallen asleep, and night and day they do not forget to set traps for you. Do not seek after honors, then, so you will not be humiliated to the great joy of your enemies. Seek rather humility, for *he who exalts himself will be humbled, and he who humbles himself will be exalted.*[1] If you cannot get along alone, join another who is living according to the Gospel of Christ, and you will make progress with him. Either listen, or submit to one who listens; either be strong and be called Elijah, or obey the strong and be called Elisha. For obeying Elijah, Elisha received a double share of Elijah's spirit.

18. If you wish to live among men, imitate Abraham, Lot, Moses, and Samuel. If you wish to live in the desert, all the prophets have led the way there before you. Be like them, *wandering in the deserts, valleys and caves of the earth,* plunged in misery, trials, and affliction. It is said again, *The shadow of the parched and the spirit of the maltreated will bless you.* And then, for the thief on the cross—the one who spoke a word— the Lord forgave his sins and received him into paradise.[1] See what honor will be yours if you have steadfastness in the face of trial or of the spirit of fornication, or the spirit of pride, or any

Ba 3:10.

Do not seek honors

Cf. Lk 14:8-9.
Cf. Ps 38(37):16.

Mt 23:12.

2 K 2:9,15.

Imitate the examples of the saints

Heb 11:38.

Is 25:4.

Lk 23:40-43.

other passion. Do battle against diabolic passions, not to follow them, and Jesus will grant you what he has promised. Keep from negligence; it is the mother of all the vices.[2]

Flee concupiscence
*Cf. Si 5:2.
†Cf. Mt 13:11.

Cf. Mt 10:38;
Lk 9:23;
14:27.

Love God
*Cf. Si 17:25.

Gn 49:8.
Cf. Tb 4:13.

Mt 24:46-47.

Cf. Sg 7:11-13.

19. My son, flee concupiscence.* It beclouds the mind and prevents it from coming to know the mystery of God.† It makes you alien to the language of the Spirit and prevents you from carrying the Cross of Christ.[1] It does not permit the heart to be attentive to honoring God. Keep from the belly's inclination, which makes you alien to the goods of paradise. Keep from impurity, which irritates God and his angels.

20. My son, turn to God,* and love him. Flee the enemy and despise him. May the graces of God come your way and may you inherit the blessing of Judah, son of Jacob. It is said, *Judah, your brothers shall praise you, your hands will be on the back of your enemies, and the sons of your father shall be your servants.* Keep away from pride, for it is the beginning of every evil. And the beginning of pride is keeping your distance from God, and hardening the heart is what follows. If you guard against this, your resting place will be the heavenly Jerusalem. If the Lord loves you and gives you glory, keep from becoming proud; on the contrary, persevere in humility and you will abide in the glory that God has given you. Watch out, be vigilant, for *blessed is the one who is found watching, because he will be set over the possessions of his master,* and he will enter into the kingdom with gladness. The friends of the bridegroom will love him, because they have found him keeping watch over his vineyard.

21. My son, be merciful in all things, for it is

written, *Strive to be presented to God as having come through trial, like a workman who fears no shame.* Approach God as one who sows and reaps, and into your granary you will gather God's goods. Do not pray with much show, in the manner of hypocrites, but give up your whims and do what you do for God, acting thus for your own salvation. If a passion arouses you, whether it is love of money, jealousy, or hatred and the other passions, watch out, *have the heart of a lion,* a strong heart. Fight against them, make them disappear like Sihon, Og, and all the kings of the Amorites. May the beloved Son, the Only-begotten, Jesus the king, fight for you, and may you inherit enemy towns. Still, toss all pride far from your side, and be valiant. Look: when Joshua [son] of Nun was valiant,[1] God delivered his enemies into his hands. If you are fainthearted, you become a stranger to the law of God. Faintheartedness fills you with pretexts for laziness, mistrust, and negligence, until you are destroyed. Be lion-hearted and shout, you as well, *Who can separate us from the love of God?*[2] And say, *Though my outer self may dissolve, still my inner self is renewed from day to day.*

22. If you are in the desert, do battle with prayers, fasting, and mortification. If you are among men, *be wise as serpents and simple as doves.*[1] If someone curses you, put up with him cheerfully, hoping that God will bring about what is best for you. As for yourself, do not curse the image of God.[2] It is he himself who said, *The one who honors me, I will honor, and the one who curses me, I will curse.*[3] If on the other hand someone praises you, do not be happy about it for

Be steadfast

2 Tm 2:15.

Cf. Mt 13:24-30.
Cf. Mt 6:5.

2 S 17:10.

Dt 31:4;
Jos 2:10.

Jos 2:10-11.

Rm 8:35.

2 Co 4:16.

Be indifferent to curses or praise

Mt 10:16.
Cf. Rm 12:14.

Cf. 1 Co 11:7.

1 S 2:30.

Lk 6:26.

Lk 6:22.

Ac 14:14.

Ac 5:41.

it is written, *Woe to you if all praise you.* Furthermore, *Blessed are you when you are snapped at
and hounded, if your very name is cast out as evil.*
Behold, our fathers Barnabas and Paul, too,
when praised, rent their garments and beat
themselves, out of scorn for human glory. Peter
and John, too, when cursed before the Sanhed-
rin, came out rejoicing for having deserved to be
cursed for the Lord's holy name. Their hope was
in the glory of heaven.

Shun the
comforts of
this time

23. As for you, my son, shun the satisfactions
of this age, so as to be happy in the age to come.
Do not be negligent, letting the days pass by till
unexpectedly they come looking for you and you
arrive at the straits of your anguish and the 'horror-faces'[1] surround you and drag you off violent-

*Cf. Jb 10:21-22;
   Zp 1:14-15.
†Cf. Mt 5:11-12.

ly to their dark place of terror and anguish.* Do
not be sad when you are cursed by men;†[2] be sad
and sigh when you sin—this is the true curse—
and when you go away bearing the sore of your
sins.

Scorn vainglory

24. I urge you from my heart to scorn vainglory. Vanity is the devil's own weapon. This was
how Eve was fooled; he told her, *Eat the fruit of
the tree; your eyes will open and you will be like

Gn 3:5.

gods.*[1] She listened, thinking it was the truth. She
ran after the glory of divinity and her very humanity was taken away. If you, too, seek vainglory it will make you a stranger to the glory of
God. As for Eve, no one wrote her to warn her of
this battle before she was tempted by the devil.

Cf. Jn 1:14.

This is why the Word of God came and took flesh
of the Virgin Mary, to free the race of Eve. But
you have been warned of this battle in the Holy
Scriptures, by the saints who have gone ahead of

you. Therefore, my brother, do not say, I have never heard of all this, or, I was not told of this yesterday or the day before yesterday. For it is written, *Their voice goes out through all the earth, their words reach the ends of the universe.* Now then, if you are praised, control your heart and give glory to God; and if you are cursed, give glory to God and thank him that you have been worthy to share the lot of his Son and of his saints. If your Master was called 'imposter',* the prophets 'contemptible',† and others 'madmen',‡ all the more should we, earth and ashes,* not complain when cursed. This is the way to your life.† If you are led by your negligence, then weep and groan, for *Those who were reared in the purple have been covered with dung*, for neglecting the law of God and following their own whims. Now then, my son, weep before the Lord at every hour, for it is written, *Happy the man you have chosen and adopted! You have placed thoughts in his heart in the valley of weeping, the place you have prepared.*

25. Become guileless and be like the guileless sheep whose wool is sheared off without their saying a word. Do not go from one place to another saying, 'I will find God here or there.' God has said, *I fill the earth, I fill the heavens;*[1] and again, *If you cross over water, I am with you*; and again, *The waves will not swallow you up.* My son, be aware that God is within you, so that you may dwell in his law and commandments. Behold, the thief was on the cross, and he entered paradise; but behold Judas was among the Apostles and he betrayed his Lord.* Behold, Rahab was in prostitution, and she was numbered among the saints;†

Ps 19(18):4;
Rm 10:18.

*Mt 27:63.
†Pr 16:21.
‡1 Co 1:23.
*Cf. Si 10:9; 17:32.
†Cf. Ps 16(15):11.

Lm 4:5.

Ps 65(64):4.

Ps 84(83):6-7.

Do not go from one place to another
Cf. Is 53:7; Ac 8:32.
Jr 23:24.
Is 43:2.
Ibid.

Lk 23:43.

*Lk 22:47.
†Jos 6:17; Jm 2:25.

Gn 3:1-6.
Jb 2:8; Jm 5:11.

Gn 3:17-19.
2 P 2:4.

*2 K 2:11;
  Si 44:16; 48:9;
  Heb 11:5.
†Ps 105(104):4.
Gn 22:1-14.
Jm 2:23.
Gn 39:7-13.

Ex 33:11.

Dn 1:17; 6:23.

Dn 3:50.
Jb 42:10.
Dn 13:1-63.

Jdt 13:1-10.

**How long
will you
be negligent**

Cf. Lm 3:41.

Rm 14:10.12;
Cf. 2 Co 5:10.

but behold, Eve was in paradise, and she was deceived.[2] Behold, Job was on the dungheap, and he was compared with his Lord; but behold, Adam was in paradise, and he fell away from the commandment. Behold, the angels were in heaven, and they were hurled into the abyss; but behold Elijah and Enoch who were raised into the kingdom of heaven.*[3] *In every place, then, seek out God; at every moment seek out his strength.*† Seek him out like Abraham, who obeyed God and offered his son in sacrifice to God, who called him 'my friend'. Seek him out like Joseph, who did battle against impurity, so that he was made ruler over his enemies.[4] Seek him out like Moses, who followed his Lord, and He made him lawgiver and let him come to know His likeness. Daniel sought him out, and He taught him great mysteries; He saved him from the lions' gullet. The three saints sought him out, and found him in the fiery furnace.[5] Job took refuge with him and he cured him of his sores. Susanna sought him out, and he saved her from the hands of the wicked.[6] Judith sought him out, and found him in the tent of Holofernes.[7] All these sought him out and he delivered them; and he delivered others also.[8]

26. You too, my son, how long will you be negligent? What is the limit of your negligence? As it was last year, so is it this year; as it was yesterday, so is it today. As long as you are negligent there will be no progress for you. Be watchful, lift up your heart, because you *will have to stand before the judgement seat of God and give an accounting for what you have done* both in private and in public.[1] If you go where the battle—God's battle—is being fought, and if the Spirit of God spurs

you on, 'Do not fall asleep there, because there are ambushes', and if the devil for his part whispers, 'What happened to you the other time?' or 'Even if you have seen this do not be sad', do not give in to his clever talk. [If you should,] the Spirit of God would leave you, and you would become weak and without strength, like Samson, and strangers would put you in chains and lead you off to the mill,* that is, to the *grinding of teeth.*† You would be for them the object of their mockery, that is, they would laugh at you; you would not know the way to your city because they would have gouged out your eyes, for you have opened your heart to Delilah, that is, to the devil, who has taken you by wile, because you have neglected the counsels of the Spirit. You have also seen what befell a man as strong as David; fortunately he quickly repented concerning the wife of Uriah.[2] It is also written, *You have seen my sores; be afraid.*

*Jg 16:21.
†Mt 8:12.

Cf. Jg 16:21.
Jg 16:17.

2 S 11-12.
Jb 6:21.

27. Behold, you have learned that he spares not the saints.[1] Watch out, then, keep your promises in mind, shun haughty airs, tear yourself away from him, lest he tear away the eyes of your understanding and leave you blind, no longer to know the way to your city, to the place of your dwelling. Again, get to know the city of Christ; give him glory, for he died for you.

Tear yourself away from the devil

28. When a brother hurls his word at you, why do you get angry, why become a beast toward him? Do you not remember, then, that Christ died for you? But when your enemy, the devil, whispers to you, you cock your ears in his direction for him to pour in filth; you open your heart to him and absorb the poison he throws your way.

Put up cheerfully with insults

Cf. Rm 5:8;
1 Co 15:3.

O wretch! This is the time for you to become a
beast, or to become a flame and consume all his
malice, to become nauseated and vomit up the
stinking evil, lest the poison spread through and
kill you! O man, you did not put up with a tiny
word hurled at you by a brother, but when the

Cf. 1 P 5:8.

enemy wants to devour your soul, what do you
do? You show him patience! No, beloved, we
should not have to mourn for you because *instead
of wearing a golden headdress your head will be*

Is 3:24.

shaved on account of your works. But watch
yourself, put up cheerfully with the one who in-

Cf. Eph 4:32.

sults you, be merciful to your brother, do not fear
the suffering of the flesh.

Be confident

29. Pay attention, my son, to the words of the
wise Paul when he says, *There are chains and
trials awaiting me in Jerusalem, but I do not
justify my soul by any word on how to accomplish*

Ac 20:23-24.

my course, and, *I am ready to die at Jerusalem*

Ac 21:13.

for the name of my Lord Jesus the Christ.[1] For
neither suffering nor trial prevented the saints
from reaching the Lord. Confidence, then, and
courage! No more devilish timidity! Run instead,
after the courage of the saints! My son, why do
you flee from Adonai, the Lord of Hosts, and run
straight into Chaldean captivity? Why do you
give your heart to eat in the company of demons?

**Keep away from
fornication**
*Cf. Tb 4:12;
1 Th 4:3.
†1 Co 6:15.

30. My son, keep away from fornication;* do
not corrupt the members of Christ. Do not obey
demons. *Do not make the members of Christ the
members of a prostitute.*† Keep the anguish of
punishments in mind; set the judgement of God
before you. Flee every lust; *put off the old man*

Col 3:9.

and his works, dress yourself in the new man;[1]
keep in mind the anguish of the moment in which
you will take leave of the body.

31. My son, flee to God, for it is he who created you; it was for you that he underwent these sufferings. For he said, *I gave my back to the whips and my cheek to the slaps; I did not turn my face away from the shame of spittle.* O man, *What is the good of your going to Egypt, to drink the water of the Geon* which is turbid?[1] What good is it for you to have these troublesome thoughts so that you undergo these sufferings? Rather convert and weep over your sins, for it is written, *If you make an offering for your sins, your souls will see a long-lived posterity.*[2]

Flee to God

Is 50:6.

Jr 2:18.

Is 53:10.

32. You have seen then, man, that transgression is evil, and that sin brings about suffering and anguish. Quick, man, flee from sin, think at once of death, for it is written, *The prudent man treats sin harshly,* and, *The face of ascetics will shine like the sun.* Remember too that Moses *preferred to suffer with the people of God rather than enjoy the passing pleasures of sin.*[1] If you love the sufferings of the saints, they will be your friends and intercessors before God. He will grant all your proper requests, because you carried your cross and followed your Lord.[2]

Flee from sin

Pr 29:8.
Mt 13:43;
Dn 12:3.

Heb 11:25.

Cf. Mt 10:38;
Lk 9:23; 14:27.

33. Do not look for a throne of human glory,* that God may shelter you against winds you do not know and set you up in his metropolis, the heavenly Jerusalem. *Try everything and keep what is good.*[1] Likewise, do not be overbearing towards the image of God. Watch also over your youth so that you may be able to watch over your old age, lest you have shame and regret in the valley of Josaphat, where all the creatures of God will see you and reproach you saying, 'We thought all along you were a sheep, and here we see you are a wolf!'[2]

Ponder the day of judgement
*Cf. Si 7:4.

1 Th 5:21.

Cf. Si 25:3.

Cf. Jl 4:12.

Now, into the gulf of hell with you; now fall into
Is 14:15. *the belly of the earth!'* Oh what a terrible disgrace! In the world you went about praised as one
of the elect, and when you arrive in the valley of
Josaphat, the place of judgement, you are found
Cf. 2 Co 5:3. naked,[3] and all see your sins and ugliness laid
bare to God and men. Woe to you at that mo-
ment! Where will you turn your face? Will you
open your mouth? To say what? Your sins are
etched into your soul which is as black as a hair-
Cf. Si 25:17;
Rv 6:12. shirt. What will you do at that moment? Weep?
There will be no one to accept your tears. Pray?
No one to accept your prayers, for those to whom
Cf. Pr 17:11. you are handed over are pitiless.[4] How awful the
moment when you hear the terrible, cutting
Ps 9:17. voice, *Sinners, go to hell,* and, *Depart from me,
you damned, to the eternal fire prepared for the*
Mt 25:41. *devil and his angels,* and again, *I have detested*
Ps 101(100):3. *those who transgress.*[5] *I must wipe out of the city*
Ps 101(100):8. *of the Lord all who commit iniquities.*

**Make careful use
of this world**
*Cf. 1 Co 7:31. 34. Now then, my son, make careful use of this
world;* go on counting yourself as nothing; follow
the Lord in all things, to have confidence in the
valley of Josaphat. Be considered in the world as
Cf. Lk 6:22. one of its rejected and discover yourself clothed
with glory on the day of judgement! Entrust your
heart to no one for the gratification of your soul,
but *throw all your cares to the Lord, and he will
Ps 55(54):22. feed you.*[1] Consider Elijah who entrusted himself
to Him at the torrent of Cherith, and He fed him
1 K 17:5-6. by means of a raven.

**Keep away from
fornication**
*Cf. Tb 4:13;
1 Th 4:3.
†Cf. Si 42:12. 35. Keep well away from fornication,* for it has
hurt and brought many low. Do not make friends
with a youth. Do not run after a woman.† Flee
bodily satisfactions, for friendship blazes up like a

flame. Do not run after any flesh, because if stone falls upon steel, flame blazes up and consumes many a substance. Run at all times to the Lord, sit in his shadow; for *he who dwells in the protection of the Most-High will dwell in the shadow of the God of heaven,** and *will not waver for ever.*[†] Think of the Lord and the heavenly Jerusalem;[‡1] if it comes to your mind, you will be under heavenly blessing, and the glory of God will carry you away.

36. Guard your body and your heart in all watchfulness; *seek out the peace and purity**[1] that are knit together, and you will see God.*[2] Do not be at enmity with anyone, because he who is at enmity with his brother is an enemy of God; and he who is at peace with his brother is at peace with God. Have you not learned by now that nothing is preferable to peace, which makes each person love his brother?[3] Even if you are free of all sin, [yet] being your brother's enemy you are a stranger to God, for it is written, *Seek out peace and purity*, for they are knit together. It is also writtten, *If I had the faith necessary to move mountains, if I did not have charity of heart, it would profit me nothing.** *Charity is constructive.*[†] *What will be purified of foulness?*[‡] If you have hatred or enmity in your heart, where is your purity? The Lord says in Jeremiah, *He talks to his neighbor with words of peace, and enmity is in his heart; he speaks considerately with his neighbor, and enmity is in his heart, or he thinks enmity; and shall I not be angry with the likes of these, says the Lord; shall my soul not have its revenge on such a Gentile?* It is as though he said, 'The man who is an enemy of his brother is the

Cf. Si 9:8

*Ps 91(90):1.
[†]Ps 125(124):1;
Cf. Ps 112(111):6.
[‡]Cf. Heb 12:22.

Seek peace
and purity
*Heb 12:14.

Heb 12:14.

*1 Co 13:2-3.
[†]1 Co 8:1.
[‡]Si 34:4.

Jr 9:5-9.

Gentile,' because the Gentiles walk in darkness,
Cf. Eph 4:17-18. not knowing the light. It is the same with a man
who hates his brother. He walks in darkness and
does not know God because, with the hatred that
Cf. 1 Jn 2:11. comes from enmity blocking his eyes, he does not
Cf. 1 Co 11:7. see the image of God.[4]

Love your brother

37. The Lord has ordered us to love our ene-
mies, to bless those who curse us, and to do good
Cf. Mt 5:44. to those who persecute us.[1] What danger we are
in then, when we hate one another, when we hate
our co-members, one with us, sons of God, bran-
Cf. Jn 15:5. ches of the true vine, sheep of the spiritual flock
Cf. 1 P 2:25; gathered by the true shepherd,[2] the Only-Begot-
Jn 10:14. ten son of God who offered hmself in sacrifice for
Cf Eph 5:2. us! The Living Word underwent these sufferings
for so great a work, and you, man, hate it through
jealousy and vainglory, or avarice, or contempt
— things for which the enemy has ensnared you,
to make you a stranger to God. What defence will
you present before Christ? He will say to you, 'Inasmuch as you hate your brother I am he whom
Cf. Mt 25:45. you hate,'[3] and you will go off to eternal torment[†]
[†] Mt 25:41. because you are inimical to your brother. As for
your brother, he will enter into eternal life
because, for Jesus, he humbled himself before
you.

Think of the Day of Reckoning

38. Before we die, then, let us seek out the
remedy for this evil. Beloved, let us turn to the
Gospel of the true law of God the Christ, and we
shall hear him say, *Do not condemn to avoid con-*
Lk 6:37. *demnation; pardon, and you will be pardoned.*[1]
If you do not forgive, neither will you be forgiven.
If you are at enmity with your brother, get ready
to be chastised for your faults, your transgressions, your fornications committed in secret, your

lies, your obscene language, your evil thoughts, your avarice, your evil actions. You *will give an account* of these *at the judgement seat of Christ*[2] while the whole of God's creation looks at you, and the whole army of angels is present with swords unsheathed to force you to give an account and to confess your sins. Your clothing will be soiled, your mouth will be mute, you will be prostrate with not a word to say! Wretched man, of how many things will you have to give account? Of many impurities which are gangrene to the soul, desires of the eyes, evil thoughts that are the distress of the Spirit and the sadness of the soul, slips of speech, the bragging tongue that fouls the whole body, silliness, bad jokes, slander, jealousy, hatred, mockery, insults to the image of God, condemnations, desires of the belly that have cut you off from the goods of paradise, passions, blasphemies too shameful to mention, evil thoughts about the image of God, anger, disputes, impudence, arrogance of the eyes, wicked plans, irreverence, vanity. All these will be demanded of you, because you had misunderstandings with your brother and did not, as you should have done, resolve them in the love of God. Have you never heard it said, *Charity covers a multitude of sins.* and, *This is the way your Father in heaven will act towards you, if you do not pardon one another in your hearts?*[3] Your Father who is in heaven will not forgive your sins.

Rm 14:10-12;
Cf. 2 Co 5:10.

Cf. 1 Jn 2:16.

Cf. Jm 3:6.

1 P 4:8;
Cf. Pr 10:12.

Mt 18:35.

39. Beloved, behold, you know that we have put on Christ,*[1] who is good and the friend of men. Let us not put him off through our evil deeds. Having promised God purity, having promised the monastic life, let us carry out its

Let us be
faithful to our
promises
*Cf. Rm 13:14;
Ga 3:27.

deeds: fasting, unceasing prayer, purity of body
and purity of heart. If we have promised God
purity, may we never be found in fornication, of
which there are several forms. It is said indeed,

Ez 16:26.

They prostituted themselves in a number of ways.
My brothers, may no one ever catch us in deeds of
this kind, may no one ever find us fallen below
every [other] man.

Let us mortify
ourselves

40. We have also promised ourselves to be disciples of Christ. Let us mortify ourselves because
mortification deals roughly with impurity. Here
we are in combat; let us not run off, lest we

Heb 12:1.

become slaves of sin. We have been set up as a

Cf. Mt 5:14.

light for the world;[1] let no one be scandalized be-

Cf. Rm 14:13.

cause of us.[2] Let us put on silence, for to it many
owe their salvation.

Let us not
make demands
on one another

41. Watch over yourselves, brothers. Let us
not reckon with one another, lest we be reckoned
with in the hour of chastisement. Whether you
are virgins, or renunciants[1] or anchorites, [God]
will still say to us: Give me back my goods with in-

Cf. Mt 25:27.

terest. He will reprimand us and say, 'Where is

Cf. Mt 22:11-12.

the wedding garment, where is the light from the

Cf. Mt 5:15-16.

lamps? *If you are my son,* ⟨*where is my glory? If*

Ml 1:6.

you are my servant,⟩[2] *where is my fear?*[3]If you
have hated me in this world, *depart from me,* for

Mt 7:23.

I do not know you. If you have hated your
brother, you are an alien in my kingdom. If you
have had a misunderstanding with your brother,
if you have not pardoned him, they will *tie your
hands*[4] *behind your back—and your feet also—
and throw you into the darkness outside where*

Mt 22:13.

there will be weeping and grinding of teeth. If
you have hit your brother, you will be handed

Cf. Pr 17:11.

over to pitiless angels and you will be chastised in

torments of fire for all eternity. You have not re-
spected my image, you have insulted me, you
have scorned me and dishonored me. Therefore,
I shall have no concern for you in the depth of
your anguish. You have not made peace with
your brother in this world; I shall not be with you
on the day of the great judgement. You insulted
the poor; it was I whom you insulted. You struck   Cf. Jm 2:6.
the unfortunate; you are the accomplice of him
who struck me in my humiliation on the Cross.   Cf. Mt 27:30-31.

42. 'Did I leave you in want when I came to   Let us remember
stay in the world? Did I not bless you with my   what Jesus
body and blood as a food of life?*[1] Did I not taste   did for us
death because of you,[†] to save you? Did I not re-   *Cf. Jn 6:56;
veal to you the heavenly mystery,[‡] to make you   [†]Cf. Heb 2:9.
my brother and my friend? Did I not give you *the*   [‡]Cf. Col 1:26.
power to tread underfoot serpents and scorpions
and the whole strength of the enemy?[2] Did I not   Lk 10:19.
give you several medicines of life, so that you   Cf. Si 6:16.
could save yourself? My miracles, my prodigies,
and my wonderworking, I put on here in the
world as my military armament; I have given   Cf. Eph 6:11-13.
them to you as your equipment for knocking
down Goliath, that is, the devil. What is lacking   Cf. 1 S 17:50-51.
to you now, that you should have become a
stranger to me? Your negligence alone has cast
you into the gulf of hell.'

43. Now then, my son, these things, and worse   Let us practise
still, shall we hear if we are negligent and do not   what we have
obey [the precept] to pardon one another. We   been taught
must watch ourselves and realize what are the vir-   Col 3:13.
tues of God that will be helpful to us on the day of
death, that will be our guide in the midst of the
hard and terrible battle and that raise souls from
the dead. First, we were given faith and the knowl-   Cf. 1 Co 6:14.

edge of being able to cast out unbelief. Then we were given prudence and wisdom, to be able to recognize the devil's thought so as to flee from it and to hate it. We were preached fasting, prayer, and continence, which ought to give calm and restraint to the body in the passions. We were given purity and watchfulness, through which God will dwell in us. We were given patience and mildness. If we observe all this we shall inherit the glory of God.

Charity, joy, prayer

44. We were given charity and peace, which are powerful in battle; for the enemy cannot approach the place they have occupied. In the matter of joy we have our orders to use it to fight sadness. We have also been taught generosity and goodness. We have been given holy prayer and steadfastness, which fill the soul with light. We have been given candor and simplicity, to disarm wickedness. We have it in writing to abstain from judging, so that we may conquer lying, that shabby vice which is in man. For if we do not judge, we shall not be judged on the day of judgement. We have been given endurance in the face of suffering and injustice, not to be struck by weariness.

Mt 7:1.

The example of our fathers
*Cf. 2 Co 11:27

†Cf. Pr 23:31; Si 19:2; Eph 5:18.
‡Cf. Si 31:29-30.

45. In fact, our fathers passed their lives in hunger, thirst, and great mortification,* by which they acquired purity. Above all they fled the wine habit, which is full of every evil.† Troubles, tumults, and disorders are caused in our members through the abuse of wine;‡ this is a passion full of sin, it is sterility and the withering of fruit. For sensuality in unquenchable thirst stupefies the understanding, makes conscience overbold and snaps the rein on the tongue. Total joy is when we do not *grieve the Holy Spirit,* [1] or become de-

Eph 4:30.

ranged by sensuality. As it is said, *The priest and the prophet were deranged by wine. Wine is licentious, drunkenness is bold; the person who indulges in them will not be exempt from sin.* Wine is a good thing if you drink it with moderation; *if you set your eyes on cups and goblets you will walk naked as a pestle.* Therefore, all who have prepared to become disciples of Jesus should abstain from wine and drunkenness.

Is 28:7.

Pr 20:1

Cf. Si 31:28.

Pr 23:31.

46. In fact, knowing the great amount of harm caused by wine, our fathers abstained from it. They drank very little of it and only in case of illness. If, indeed, that great worker, Timothy, was given a little of it, it was because his body was full of infirmities. But what shall I say to the man who is bubbling over with vice and in the prime of youth, weighed down under the impurities of passions? I am afraid to tell him not to drink at all, for fear that some one, mindless of his salvation, might murmur against me. For this language is painful for many nowadays. Nevertheless, beloved, it is good to be on your guard; and mortification is useful. For the man who mortifies himself will save his ship in the good and holy port of salvation, and will be filled with the good things of heaven.

Let us keep from wine

1 Tm 5:23.

Ps 107(106):9.

47. Above all this, we have been given humility, which watches over all the virtues and is that great holy strength with which God clothed himself when he came into the world. Humility is the rampart of the virtues, the treasury of works, the saving armor and the cure for every wound. When they made the fine linens, the wrought gold, and all the fittings of the Tabernacle, they covered them with sackcloth.* Humility is least among

Let us practise humility

Cf. Ph 2:8.

Cf. Eph 6:11.

*Ex 27:9-16; Jdt 4:11.

men, but precious and glorious before God. If we
acquire it we shall *trample the whole force of the*

Lk 10:19.
enemy underfoot. It is said, *Whom shall I con-*
Is 66:2.
sider, if not the humble and meek?

Let us give our
heart no rest
48. Let us not give our hearts rest in time of
famine. For boasting and self-conceit have increased, gluttony has also increased, fornication
reigns through the gratification of the flesh, pride
prevails. The juniors no longer obey the elders; the
elders no longer care for the juniors, and everyone
goes along according to his own whims.[1] Now is
the time to cry with the prophet, *Woe is me, O my*
soul, the pious man has disappeared from the
earth, and he who is upright among men does not
exist according to Christ, that is, does not exist at
Mi 7:1-2.
all. Everyone has crushed his neighbor.[2]

Lamentation
49. Struggle, my beloved, for the time is near
Mt 24:22.
and the days have been shortened.[1] There is no
Cf. Jr 31(38):34
father who instructs his children, there is no child
*Cf. Mi 7:6.
that obeys its father;[2]* good virgins are no longer;†
†Cf. Am 8:13.
the holy fathers have died on all sides; the mothers
and the widows are no longer, and we have be-
Cf. Lm 5:3.
come like orphans; the humble are crushed un-
Cf. Am 4:1.
derfoot; and blows are showered upon the head
Cf. Am 2:7.
of the poor. Therefore there is little to hold back
Cf. Zp 2:2.
the wrath of God from grieving us, with no one to
Cf. Ps 69(68):20.
console us. All this has befallen us because we have
not practised mortification.

Let us struggle
50. Let us struggle, my beloved, so that we
*Cf. 2 Tm 4:8;
may receive the crown now prepared.[1]* The
1 Co 9:25.
throne is readied.† The door of the kingdom is
†Cf. Lk 22:30.
open.‡ To the one who conquers shall I give the
‡Cf. Is 26:2.
secret manna. If we struggle against, and conquer,
Cf. Rv 2:17.
the passions we shall reign eternally. But if we are

conquered we shall have regrets and weep bitter
tears. Let us do battle with ourselves while penance is within our grasp. Let us put on mortification, that we may be renewed in purity. Let
us love men, that we may be friends of Jesus,
friend of men.

Cf. Eph 4:23-24.

51. If we have promised God the monastic
life, ⟨let us carry out the works of monastic life,
which are fasting, purity, silence, humility, self-
effacement,⟩[1] love, virginity not only of body, but
the virginity that is an armor against every sin. For
in the Gospel some virgins were sent back because
of their laziness, while those who kept courageous
watch entered into the wedding chamber.[2] May
everyone then enter there for ever![3]

Let us carry out
what we have
promised

Cf. Mt 25:1-13.

52. We are assailed by [the temptation of] the
love of money. If you wish to acquire riches—they
are the bait on the fisher's hook[1]—by greed, by
trafficking, by violence, by ruse, or by excessive
manual work that deprives you of leisure for the
service of God—in a word by any other means—if
you have desired to pile up gold or silver, remember what the Gospel says, *Fool! They will snatch
away your soul during the night! Who will get your
hoard?* Again, *He piles up money without
knowing to whom it will go.*[2]

Against the love
of money

Lk 12:20.
Ps 39(38):6.

53. Struggle, my beloved, fight the passions
and say, I will act like Abraham, *I will raise ⟨my
hand⟩[1] to God the Most High, who made heaven
and earth; not to take anything that is yours, from
a thread to a shoe lace;*[2] those are great
goods for a humble stranger. And, *The Lord loves
the proselyte, to provide him with bread and
clothing.* The same holds true in the matter
of soft living, about which we are challenged with,

To fight the
passions

Gn 14:22-23.

Dt 10:18.

Si 18:25.

Dt 28:17.

Jm 5:3.

1 K 8:61.

Cf. Ps 30(29):10.

*Cf. Ps 119(118):
34.
†Cf. Is 48:18.
‡Cf. 2 K 2:12;
13:14.

*Cf. Ez 8:1-18.
†Cf. Ba 4:25.
‡Cf. Eph 6:12.

*Jos 5:13-14.
†Cf. Ex 15:4;
Ps 135(134):15.
‡Cf. Ex 14:22;
Ps 136(135):
13-14.

Cf. Ps 35 (34):8.

*Cf. Ps 69:31.
†Cf. Ac 7:22.

Greeting

**Another call to
watchfulness**

Stock up for almsgiving and for your needs. Remember what is written, *Your granaries and all they contain shall be cursed.* As to gold and silver we have the words of James, *Their rust will be your witness; rust will devour your flesh like a flame.* And, *First place goes to the just man who has no idols*[3] and sees their foolishness. Cleanse yourself from the curse before the Lord calls you, for you have set your hope on God, as it is written, *May your hearts be pure and perfect before God.*

54. Beloved, I greet you in the Lord. Indeed, you have taken God as your support, you have become dear to him, you have set out with all your heart to walk according to God's orders.* May God bless you. May your springs become rivers, and your rivers a sea.† Indeed you are a chariot, you are a charioteer‡ of continence, the lamp of God burns before you who reflect the hidden light of the Spirit, and you make careful use of language. God bless you with the endurance of the saints; may no idols be found in your town,* may your foot rest on the neck† of the prince of darkness;‡ may you see the commander of the Lord standing* at your right side; may you drown Pharaoh and his troops;† may you lead your people‡ through the salty sea, that is this life! Amen!

55. After this I urge you again not to relax your heart, for the demons' pleasure is when man relaxes his heart and they can lead him off towards ambush before he notices it. Do not be negligent, then, about learning the fear of the Lord. Progress like young plants and you will please God, like a young bull thrusting horn and hoof.* Be a man strong in action and words, too.†

Do not pray in the way of hypocrites for fear your lot will be put with theirs.[1] Do not lose a single day of your existence, and be aware of what you will give God each day. Sit alone by yourself like a prudent general; sift your thoughts whether you are an anchorite or live with others. In a word, judge yourself each day. For it is better for you to live with a thousand people in all humility than alone with pride in an hyena's den.[2] It is stated of Lot that in the middle of Sodom he was a good, faithful man, while we learn of Cain who was alone on the earth, with only three other human beings, that he was a wicked man.[3]*

56. Now, then, here is the struggle that is proposed to you.* Ponder daily whatever happens to you,[†] to see whether you are on our side or on the side of those who fight against us. Only, demons come to you from the right, while to all other men they clearly come from the left. Truly in fact, they attacked me from the right, too. They dragged the devil to me trussed up like a wild donkey. But the Lord helped me. I did not trust them and did not release my heart to them. Many a time was I tried by the actions of the devil at my right, and he went ahead of me as I walked. He even dared to tempt the Lord, but He made him disappear, him and his tricks.*[1]

57. Now, my son, put on humility.* Take Christ and his good Father as your counsellors. Be the friend of a man of God, having the law of God in his heart. Be like a poor man carrying his cross and loving tears. You too mourn,[1] with a shroud on your head. May your cell[2] be a tomb for you till God raises you and gives you the crown of victory.

Cf. Mt 6:5.
Cf. Mt 24:51.

Cf. 2 P 2:7-8.
*Cf. Gn 4:8;
1 Jn 3:12.

Beware of the demons' attacks
*Cf. Heb 12:1-2.
†Cf. 1 Th 5:21.

Cf. Pr 4:27.

Cf. Ps 54:5.

*Mt 4:1-17;
Heb 2:18.

Put on humility
*Cf. Col 3:12.

Ps 37(36):31.

1 Co 15:52.

Take refuge
in God
58. If you ever have a disagreement with a brother who has caused you to suffer by a word, or if your heart wounds a brother by saying, 'He does not deserve that', or if the enemy hints to you of someone that, 'He does not deserve that praise', if you agree with this suggestion and thought of the devil, if the warfare of your thoughts increases, if you are in dispute with your brother, knowing that, *There is no balm in Gilead or doctor in your company*, without delay take shelter in solitude with the conscience of God, weep alone with Christ, and the Spirit of Jesus will speak to you through your thoughts. He will convince you of the fullness of the commandment. For what need is there of your struggling alone, making yourself like a beast, as if this venom were in you?

Jr 8:22.

Forgive your
brother
59. Remember that you, too, have fallen often. Have you not heard Christ say, *Forgive your brother seventy times seven*?[1] Have you not often wept while praying, *Forgive me the great number of my sins*?[2] Now then, if you insist on the little your brother owes you, the Spirit will immediately set judgement and the fear of chastisement before your eyes. Remember also that the saints deserved to be mocked; remember that Christ was mocked, insulted, and crucified because of you. Then he immediately fills your heart with mercy and fear, and you fall on your face weeping and saying, 'Forgive me, my Lord, for I have made your image suffer'. Immediately in the consolation of repentance you get right to your feet and run to your brother with an open heart, a happy face, a joyous mouth, radiating peace. And smiling at your brother you say, 'Forgive me,

Mt 18:22.

Ps 25(24):18.

Cf. Mt 5:25.
Ac 5:41.

1 P 2:21-24.

brother, because I made you suffer'. Your tears flow; a great joy comes from the tears, peace leaps into place between you, and the Spirit of God for his part shouts with joy, *Blessed the peacemakers, for they shall be called sons of God.* When the enemy hears the sound of this voice ring out he is made ashamed, God is glorified, and you are the object of a great blessing.

Mt. 5:9.

60. Now then, my brother, let us do battle against ourselves, for darkness falls on different sides. The churches are filled with quarrellers and wrathful people; monastic communities have become ambitious; pride reigns; there is no one left who is dedicated to his neighbor; on the contrary, *Every man has crushed his neighbor.* We are plunged into suffering. There is neither prophet nor gnostic. No one wins over another, for hardness of heart abounds. Those who understand keep silence, for the times are evil. Each one is his own lord. They are contemptuous men taking unseemly actions.

Lamentation

Mi 7:2.

Cf. Am 5:13.

61. Now then, my brother, be at peace with your brother. Pray for me, too, for I can do nothing, but I am tormented by my desires. As for you, be watchful in everything, toil, do the work of a preacher, be steadfast in trial. Stay in the combat of the monastic life right to the end, with humility, mildness, and trepidation at the words you will hear, keeping your virginity, avoiding lack of moderation, and those wretched strange words; abiding not without the writings of the saints, but firm in faith in Christ Jesus our Lord. Through whom glory to him, to his good Father, and to the Holy Spirit for ever and ever! Amen! Bless us!

Be at peace with your brother

Cf. 2 Tm 4:5.

Cf. 1 P 5:9.

Notes to the First Instruction of Pachomius

(Pach. Instr. 1)

Pach. Instr. 1- ¹The title 'archimandrite' is not found in any early pachomian document either in Greek or in Coptic, except in late title-headings of a few Coptic documents. The title is given to Pachomius in H.L., in Draguet Fragm. I, and in the two late liturgical hymns in Bohairic published by Lefort in the *appendix* to the Bohairic life (see VB, pp. 218, 24 and 221, 21). D.J. Chitty believed that the term comes from Syriac, where the monastic enclosure was frequently called μάνδρα, a 'fold'; see *The Desert a City*, p. 41, note 68.

Pach. Instr. 1-1 ¹On the doctrine of the two ways, cf. the *Didachè*, c. 1-6; the *Epistle of Barnabas*, c. 18-20 and Hermas' *Shepherd*, n. 6.

Pach. Instr. 1-2 ¹It seems that all the following examples are expressions of the first of the two ways.
²See the same reference below, ¶25.

Pach. Instr. 1-3 ¹This short section is found only in Arabic; we translate it from the Sahidic text restored by L.-T. Lefort.

Pach. Instr. 1-5 ¹The patriarch Joseph is often given as example to the brothers; see G¹ 62-63 (his chastity and prudence); Pach. Letter 8: 2ff (his purity and his constancy in persecutions).

Pach. Instr. 1-6 ¹Pr 6:3 is quoted also in Pach. Letter 3: 13 and in Hors. Test. 9.
²This text is quoted also in G¹ 62 and in Theod. Instr. 3:29 and 37.

Pach. Instr. 1-9 ¹Is 66:2 is quoted again below, ¶47.

Pach. Instr. 1-10 ¹The allusion to 1 P 5:8 is frequent; see below, ¶28; G¹ 135 and Hors. Test. 6.

Pach. Instr. 1-11 ¹See examples of Pachomius' temptations in the Life: SBo 21 (= G¹ 18, 19 and 22).

Pach. Instr. 1-12 ¹In G¹ 135 Theodore uses this text in his teaching about visions.
²This text is quoted also in Hors. Test. 24.

Pach. Instr. 1-13 ¹There is also a reference to this text in S² 6.
²Elijah's being fed by a raven is mentioned below, ¶34.
³The vivid description of the sufferings of the saints taken from Heb 11:37-38 is quoted twice by Theodore (Instr. 3: 5 and 30). We find it also in SBo 16 (= G¹ 13). Heb 11:38 is quoted below, ¶18.

Pach. Instr. 1-14 ¹1 Th 5:18 is applied to Pachomius in SBo 98 and is also quoted by Theodore in SBo 180.
²Hors. Test. 50 uses the same text in a similar context referring to fatigue and trials.

Pach. Instr. 1-15   [1] There are several other references to the children in the furnace; for example: Theod. Instr. 3: 33; Hors. Letter 4: 4; and here below, ¶25.

Pach. Instr. 1-16   [1] This text is found also in Hors. Test. 1. Baruch is quoted mostly by Horsiesios.

Pach. Instr. 1-17   [1] Mt 23:12 is quoted by Pachomius in SBo 97 in referring to Theodore after his great penance.

Pach. Instr. 1-18   [1] The 'good thief' on the cross is mentioned again below, ¶25.
[2] The Sahidic word *cerêt* is a *hapax* (see Crum, *Coptic Dictionary*, p. 829A). We understand 'vices' with E.A.W. Budge (p. 359) and L.-T. Lefort (p. 7).

Pach. Instr. 1-19   [1] The carrying of the cross is one of the central themes of pachomian spirituality. See, v.g., SBo 201; G^1 7, 74, 108; and here below, ¶32, etc. On this theme in Horsiesios, see H. Bacht, 'Vexillum crucis sequi', p. 242.

Pach. Instr. 1-21   [1] In our Coptic texts Joshua son of Nun is always called Jesus son of Nave. The figure of Joshua, Moses' assistant, is applied to Theodore in SBo 78 and Hors. Letter 4: 5, and to Horsiesios in SBo 132 (= S^5 126).
[2] In Theod. Instr. 3: 6, we find the same recommendation to follow Paul's example, and a more complete quotation of Rm. 8:35.

Pach. Instr. 1-22   [1] This text is quoted also in Hors. Test. 19.
[2] The 'image of God' means a fellow-man. See below, ¶36, and cf. SBo 106, n. 2.
[3] This text is quoted often; see SBo 150; G ^{1} 99; Hors. Reg. 52.

Pach. Instr. 1-23   [1] These 'horror-faces' are the servants of Abaddon, the angel of death (Rv. 9:11); they have the mission of making the soul of the dying man come out by frightening him with their terrifying aspect. (See L.-T. Lefort, *Oeuvres*, [CSCO - 160], p. 7).
[2] Mt 5:11 is quoted also in SBo 186 (= G^1 142) and in Theod. Instr. 3: 32.

Pach. Instr. 1-24   [1] Quoted also in Paral. 37 (cf. 39).

Pach. Instr. 1-25   [1] We find the same notion of the omnipresence of God, and the same quotation, in Pach. Letter 3: 13 and in Theod. Instr. 3: 34.
[2] See above ¶24, n. 1.
[3] About Enoch and Elijah, see SBo 55 (= G^1 82) and Paral. 37.
[4] The patriarch Joseph is often given as an example of purity; see above, ¶5; G^1 62-63 and Pach. Letter 8: 2ff.
[5] See above, ¶15, n. 1.
[6] The figure of the chaste Susanna is mentioned again in Hors. Letter 1:1.
[7] Judith is also given as example, along with Susanna, in Hors. Letter 1: 1.
[8] See P. Tamburrino, 'Les saints de l'Ancien Testament dans la Ière catéchèse de saint Pachôme', in *Melto* 4 (1968): 33-44.

Pach. Instr. 1-26   [1] The same text is quoted is quoted below, ¶38; in Hors. Reg. 5; and Hors. Test. 10. See also Hors. Reg. 31 and Hors. Test. 11 and 17.

[2]David's repentance and God's mercy toward him are mentioned also in Hors. Reg. 12.

Pach. Instr. 1-27   [1]It is not absolutely clear who it is who 'spares not the saints'. Lefort's translation supposes that it is God; but the whole context—especially the preceding paragraph—seems to require 'the devil' as subject of the verb 'he spares not'.

Pach. Instr. 1-29   [1]Quoted also in Theod. Instr. 3: 6.

Pach. Instr. 1-30   [1]Quoted also in G[1] 65 and Theod. Instr. 3: 19.

Pach. Instr. 1-31   [1]*Geon*, i.e. the Nile.
[2]The same text is quoted by Theodore in SBo 142.

Pach. Instr. 1-32   [1]Heb 11:25 is quoted by Theodore in an Instruction, in SBo 145.
[2]See above, ¶19, n. 1.

Pach. Instr. 1-33   [1]We find the same allusion to Si 7:4 in remarks made by Antony to his own disciples about Pachomius' monks; see SBo 129.
[2]Cf. *Didachè*, c. 16, 3.
[3]The same imagery is used in Theod. Instr. 3: 8: '. . . at Christ's tribunal before the angels and all the saints, while we shall be naked.'
[4]About these pitiless angels, see the long vision that Pachomius had of the punishments reserved to sinners after their death (SBo 88). See also here below, ¶41 and Hors. Instr. 1: 5.
[5]The same text is quoted also in Hors. Test. 43.

Pach. Instr. 1-34   [1]This text is used in SBo 192 to describe Theodore's attitude.

Pach. Instr. 1-35   [1]In Hors. Fragm. we find the same connection established between avoiding impure thoughts and entering the heavenly city.

Pach. Instr. 1-36   [1]Heb 12:14 is quoted again below, in the same ¶, and twice by Horsiesios: Hors. Letter 3: 4 and Hors. Instr. 7: 11.
[2]The text borrowed from Athanasius begins here. See our Introduction.
[3]In the Sahidic text, read *pefson* in the place of *pefsop*.
[4]On the meaning of the 'image of God', see above ¶22, n. 2.

Pach. Instr. 1-37   [1]Mt 5:44 is quoted also in SBo 186 (= G[1] 142) and in Pach. Letter 7: 3.
[2]We find the same quotation in G[1] 135 and in Pach. Instr. 2: 2.
[3]The same doctrine occurs below in ¶41. Mt 25:45 is quoted also in Hors. Test. 15.

Pach. Instr. 1-38   [1]Lk 6:37 is quoted also in Pach. Letter 7: 3. We find it also in Draguet Fragm. 1: 5 among two series of texts about pardon.
[2]See above, ¶26, n. 1.
[3]This text is quoted also in Pach. Letter 7: 3.

Pach. Instr. 1-39   [1]We find the same quotation in Am. Letter 6.

Pach. Instr. 1-40   [1]In G[1] 120 the brothers visiting Antony apply this text to him. [2]We find the same preoccupation of not scandalizing the brothers in Theod. Instr. 3: 5.

Pach. Instr. 1-41   [1]In the Coptic documents, the monk is often called an *apotaktikos;* see SBo 185 (VB p. 166, 10-11). Renunciation (ἀπόταξις - ἀποταγή) is one of the most fundamental aspects of monastic life. To become a monk is 'to renounce the world' (see Pr. 49) or simply 'to renounce'. See G[1] 24 Halkin, p. 15, 3): τῷ κόσμῳ ἀποτάξωνται; G[1] 39 (Halkin, p. 24, 9-10): τῶν μοναχῶν ἀποτασσόμενος; Am. Letter 23 (Halkin, p. 111, 17-18): τῇ πενίᾳ τῶν γονέων ἀποταξάμενος; Theod. Intr. 3: 20: 'having renounced all they had for this vocation'.
     [2]A few words were omitted by haplography in the Sahidic text.
     [3]Ml 1:6 is quoted also by Horsiesios in a similar context dealing with fraternal charity, in Hors. Test. 47.
     [4]There is a play on words in the Sahidic text: 'If you have had a misunderstanding (*esčeakmour*) with your brother . . . they will tie (*senamour*) your hands . . . .'

Pach. Instr. 1-42   [1]Theodore also speaks of Jesus as 'him who deigned to give his body to men and be eaten because of his boundless divine love' (Theod. Instr. 3: 2).
     [2]In SBo 98 Pachomius instructs the brothers not to lose confidence if they tread on snakes, scorpions and other wild beasts. In Paral. 12 Pachomius explains that it is the fear of God which prepares someone to tread serpents and scorpions underfoot; and in Paral 24, the demons themselves acknowledge that Pachomius received that power from the Word of God. See also G[1] 21.

Pach. Instr. 1-45   [1]The same text is used in G[1] 101, Am. Letter 23 and Hors. Test. 19 and 53.

Pach. Instr. 1-48   [1]'The juniors . . . the elders'; lit.: 'the little ones . . . the great ones'. The phrase 'everyone goes along according to his own whims' has an almost identical parallel in Pach. Letter 3: 9: ἕκαστος ἔτρεχεν μετὰ τῆς ἑαυτοῦ ψυχῆς (H. Quecke, p. 104, 2-3).
     [2]In Hors. Test. 13, this text is quoted in connection with Pachomius' teaching: 'Our father used to impress this on us continually and he used to warn us, so that this saying might not be fulfilled in us, *each man oppresses his neighbor'*.

Pach. Instr. 1-49   [1]Here Pachomius makes an adaptation of Athanasius' words. Athanasius' text clearly referred to the era of the martyrs. See L.-T. Lefort, 'S. Athanase écrivain copte', *Muséon* 46 (1933) p. 22 and *Oeuvres*, (CSCO - 160) p. 21, n. 36.
     [2]Mi 7:6 is also quoted as a complaint in Hors. Test. 31.

Pach. Instr. 1-50   [1]1 Co 9:25 is quoted also in SBo 201. 2 Tm 4:8 is used in SBo 82 and Hors. Test. 56.

Pach. Instr. 1-51   [1]The Sahidic text is lacunose and the Arabic version allows us to restore it. We translate this short addition from the French translation given by L.-T. Lefort in *Oeuvres*, (CSCO - 159), p. 20, n. 54.

[2] We find in Horsiesios several references to the wise and the foolish virgins: Hors. Reg. 3; Hors. Letter 3: 1 and 4: 4; Hors. Test. 20.
[3] Athanasius' text ends here.

Pach. Instr. 1-52   [1] With L.-T. Lefort (*Oeuvres* ... p., 22, n. 55) we read m̄pouôhe instead of m̄pkôht.
[2] Horsiesios also quotes Lk 12:20 and Ps 39:6 together (but in the reverse order) and in a similar context; see Hors. Test. 27.

Pach. Instr. 1-53   [1] Word omitted in the Sahidic text.
[2] The phrase 'from a thread to a shoe lace' is quoted twice by Horsiesios, in different contexts: Hors. Reg. 30 and Hors. Test. 21.
[3] This is a quotation of the apocryphal *Letter of Jeremiah* v. 73. We find it again in Hors. Letter 4, 2, but with the right ending: ' . . . no idols; indeed, he will keep himself far from their [reproach]'.

Pach. Instr. 1-55   [1] The same text is used also in Hors. Test. 14.
[2] L.-T. Lefort has pointed out the similarity of this saying to a sentence of Evagrius in *The Mirror of the Monk*, ed. Gressman, p. 153, ¶9. See L.-T. Lefort, 'A propos d'un aphorisme d'Evagrius Ponticus', *Bull. Acad. roy. de Belgique*, (1950) 70-79; *Idem, Oeuvres,* (CSCO - 160) p. 23, n. 79.
[3] Cain's fratricide is mentioned also in Paral. 37; 1 Jn 3:12 is quoted again in Hors. Test. 55.

Pach. Instr. 1-56   [1] Mt 4:1ff is quoted also in Theod. Instr. 3: 19; and Heb 2:18 in SBo 191.

Pach. Instr. 1-57   [1] With L.-T. Lefort (*Oeuvres*, [*CSCO* - 160], p. 24, n. 90) we correct the Sahidic text, following the Arabic translation.
[2] The Coptic man̄šope means 'dwelling place' in general; but in our pachomian documents it is one of the technical names for the monastic cell.

Pach. Instr. 1-59   [1] Mt 18:22 is quoted in Draguet Fragm. 1: 5; and there is a clear reference to it also in Hors. Test. 54.
[2] The same quotation occurs in SBo 107 and G[1] 85.

INSTRUCTION ON THE SIX DAYS OF THE PASSOVER

(pach. instr. 2)

APA PACHOMIUS THE ARCHIMANDRITE OF TABENNESI, ON THE SIX DAYS OF THE HOLY PASSOVER.[1]

Text: CSCO 159
pp. 24-26

1. Let us struggle, my beloved, during these six days of the Passover, for they are given to us each year for the redemption of our souls, that we may spend them in the works of God. For it was during six days, from the beginning of the creation of heaven and earth, that God worked at his creation until it was completed.[2] *And on the seventh day he rested from all his works.»*

These six days are given us for our redemption

2. God has created these days so that we, too, should labor at the works of God during these six days, each one according to his way of life: silence,* manual labor,[†] manifold prayers,[‡] guard of the mouth,* purity of body and holiness of heart;[†] each one according to his work. And let us also rest on the seventh day, and celebrate the Sunday of the Holy Resurrection, carrying out carefully and with every diligence the holy *synaxes* and rendering homages to the Father of the universe who has had mercy upon us. He sent to us *the great Shepherd of the sheep** that were scattered, to gather us back into his holy fold.[3†]

*Gn 2:2; Heb 4:4.

That we may labor at God's works

*Cf. 2 Th 3:12.
[†]Cf. Pr 31:13, 16, 31.
[‡]Cf. 1 Th 5:17.
*Cf. Ps 39(38):1; 141(140):3.
[†]Cf. 1 Co 7:34; Ps 24(23):4.

*Heb 13:20.
[†]Cf. Ez 34:5; Jn 10:14.

And give our-
selves to *ascesis*

3. Let us not lose heart at all during these holy days, but let the one who gives himself to fasting with joy, silence, wisdom, and great tranquility, who keeps himself pure from a variety of foods, who keeps from idle pleasures, who practises genuflections and incessant prayers, who is given to lack of sleep and frequent watches, in short, let everyone watch over his steadfastness, so that what is written in Acts will happen to us, *Some on planks, some on the gear of the ship, and thus all came safe to the shore.*

Ac 27:44.

And to humility
*Cf. Jr 4:28.

Mt 26:64;
Ac 7:55.

Mt 27:29.

Cf. Jr 10:9.
Mt 27:35.

Is 53:5;
1 P 2:24.

Mt 27:34.

Cf. Jn 19:5.

4. May heaven and earth mourn* during these six days of the Passover. Indeed, when he *who sits at the right hand of his Father in heaven* stands benevolent, let the king lay down in mourning the diadem he wears and his royal crown; for a crown of thorns strewn with darts was prepared for the head of the King of peace.[4] Let the wealthy lay down their varicolored robes, their violet and purple clothing, for the Lord was stripped of his garments, which were up for lots by the soldiers. Let those who eat, drink, and make merry in this world remain quiet during these days of suffering, for the Lord of life was in the midst of those *who tormented him because of our sins.* Let those who practise *ascesis* labor all the more in their way of life, even to abstaining from drinking water, which the dogs enjoy; for he asked for a bit of water while he was hanging on the cross and he *was given vinegar mixed with gall.*[5] Let wealthy women lay down their ornaments during these days of sorrow and great mourning; for the King of glory, in a shameful garment, stood . . .

*The rest
is missing*

Notes to the Second Instruction of Pachomius

(Pach. Instr. 2)

Pach. Instr. 2 [1] About the title 'archimandrite', see above Pach. Instr. 1: title, n. 1. The 'six days of the Passover' are what we now call the Holy Week. They ended with the celebration of Easter Vigil, called 'the closing of the Passover', which led to 'the Day of the Resurrection'.

[2] The expression used here (*čok ebol*) to express the completion of God's work of creation after the six days is the same that is used to express the closing (or 'completion') of the six days of the Passover.

[3] The image of the holy fold of the great Shepherd is not uncommon in pachomian documents. Ez 34:2-5 is quoted in full in Hors. Test. 8.

[4] In Paral. 18 Pachomius having asked God to send him his mercy, has a vision of Jesus with a crown of thorns and an angel tells him: 'Since you have asked God to send you his mercy, behold, this is his mercy . . .'.

[5] This text is quoted also in Hors. Instr. 5.

the letters of saint pachomius

(pach. letter)

Letter One (Greek)

LETTER OF OUR FATHER PACHOMIUS TO THE
HOLY MAN CORNELIOS, WHO WAS FATHER OF
THE MONASTERY OF THMOUŠONS; IN IT HE
SPEAKS A LANGUAGE GIVEN TO BOTH OF THEM
BY AN ANGEL, AND THE SOUND OF WHICH WE
HAVE HEARD WITHOUT BEING ABLE TO UNDER-
STAND THE MEANING.[1]

Text: Quecke,
pp. 99-100

1. The God of wisdom, the unhesitating God,
the irreproachable God, has given rest to your
spirit. You must also give rest to your spirit, so
that Zion may rejoice in the days of her nativity.

2. Do the work of the ι, which was called o in
the old days.

Place δ also before your eyes, so that it might
be good for your soul.[2]

ρ has stretched out his hand to reach you;[3] this
is ι, which is the sepulcher, your resting place.[4]

Sing to the ω, lest the ω sing to you.[5] Let the
shameless age rejoice with you so that you do not
rejoice with the shameless age.[6]

Remember the η. Do not forget the new moons,
which are the days of the poverty of your resting
place.

Take with you the ι, which is from them, as λ

was not in the η. Because of that they have been fed without rags.

3. Return to the new moons, which is ξ from the ο. *The leaders of the tribes have prepared the wagons of the tabernacle.* With thanksgiving *they gave also the offerings of the tabernacle* with joy. And you, as a wise man, know the hair of your head on the journey,[7] so that grace may come on the ε, which are the days of your childhood.[8] Is not τ a new moon? η is the Passover. In all this do not forget the ς, which is called   .[9] This one is in communion with the ρ. He has given him his portion so that he may be made wealthy in it.

Nb 7:2-3.

4. The characters of the letter which are written are δ and ι.

Greet the head, the feet, the hands, the eyes and all the rest of your spirit, which is α.

Letter Two (Greek)

Text: Quecke, p. 100

LETTER OF OUR FATHER PACHOMIUS TO THE FATHER OF THE MONASTERY, SOUROUS, WHO ALSO RECEIVED THE GRACE OF THE ANGELIC LANGUAGE ALONG WITH PACHOMIUS AND CORNELIOS.[1]

1. Remember that I wrote to you ο in the letter because of the τ,[2] for it is written. Remember also and write η because of the ς, for it is written.

2. Is not ξ ο? υ is κ. In all these things, remember and write π and ι, so that the α be well written in the grace of those who are above.

3. Is not μ ο? κ is τ. Open your mouth and wash your face,[3] so that your eyes see and you read the characters well.

4. Watch yourself so as not to write δ over φ, lest your days grow old and your waters diminish. Remember and write θ and ρ, so that the ρ be well written.

Letter Three (Greek)

LETTER OF OUR FATHER PACHOMIUS TO COR-NELIOS, THE FATHER OF THE MONASTERY CALLED THMOUŠONS.[1]

Text: Quecke, pp.100-107

1. *Honor God and you will be strong.* Remember the groanings of the saints ϛφ.

Pr 7:1.

2. Let the house be according to its years. Let it be well-arranged according to the custom of the saints, not in temporal foods or in looking at the *likeness of anything in heaven or on earth.*

Ex 20:4; Dt 5:8.

Have ω, in order to be able to come before God *in the day of visitation* safe from the reproach made to Martha.

1 P 2:12.
Lk 10:41.

Prepare the house according to its limits.

3. Keep θ, lest you receive the reproach made to the one to whom it was said, *Give me the account of your stewardship;* or the reproach made to the one *eating and drinking with drunkards,* because he did not *give himself to digging* or *to giving food at the proper time.*[2] Because of that, the same was done to him, because he forgot the law of his God and *did not visit the sick.*[3] Therefore he became *tossed about,*[4] without bread, like the *pretentious** and the *arrogant†* who *did not build the house‡* ε. O man, know their conscience; the battle of the Lord is in their hands, and they have been charged with dominating their own flesh, in order to be able to avoid the reproach of

Lk 16:2.
Mt 24:49.
Lk 16:3.
Mt 24:45.

Mt 25:43.
Is 57:20.
*Si 10:27.
†Pr 21:24.
‡1 Ch 17:6.

*Dn 13:50-62.
†Jr 49:8.
‡Is 16:6;
Jr 48:29.
*Gn 21:10-16.
†Col 3:2.
Qo 10:10.

Pr 23:12.

Ez 11:5-6.

Daniel,* the ruin of Esau,† the hardness of
Moab,‡ the dismissal of Ishmael* and the deception of a full belly, because *their thoughts were
on the things that are on the earth.*†5

4. *The great wealth of man is wisdom.* O man,
apply your heart to discipline, do not *multiply
the dead in your insolence* and your negligence,
because of the deception of your heart. O man,
do not look at visible things. *The hired man is not

*Jn 10:12
†Lm 5:17-18.
‡Dt 33:29.
*Eph 6:14;
Ws 5:18;
Is 59:17.
Lk 12:33.

*Is 11:8.
†Eph 5:18;
Cf. Si 19:2;
Pr 23:31.
‡Cf. Gn 9:21.

the shepherd.*6* *The foxes dwell in the dark
places.*† Hold *the sword of your triumph.*‡ Know
*the breastplate of righteousness** and do not despise the dwelling place of wisdom. *Make for yourself purses that will not wear out,* so that you will
be able to *put your hand into the viper's lair.** *Do
not drug yourself with strong wine,*†7 from which
comes beggary and people walking naked.‡

*Cf. Lv 15:19-30.
†Pr 15:19.
‡Pr 10:4.
Qo 10:18.

Lm 5:13.

5. Remember that, concerning the menstru-
ating woman, a commandment was given to expel her* because her *ways are strewn with thorns.*†
Poverty humbles man‡ and *the house groans in
the idleness of the hands.* Do not *collapse under
blows of sticks*8 τρ. The foolishness of the belly is
harder than all these.9 The deception of the eyes
is the defection of the wise. The dismissal of the
wise is the desire of the flesh for the flesh, shedding blood over blood.

1 Co 3:9.

2 Co 9:3.

6. All you *fellow workers with God,* do not *lose
the object of your boasting.* Before all, know that
you are ω. God, in whom you are running, will
agree with you, so that you may not become like
those who rejoice in any word whatever, lest the
thought of your intelligence be turned into fool-

Cf. 1 Co 1:20.

ishness. A drunken man does not help another
drunken man. The one who has got lost does not

guide the one who is lost.[10] And if he guides him, *a curse on him, because he has led a blind man astray on the road.*[*][11] The *wisdom of the saints*[†] is to know the will of God, as people with whom God fights. They say, 'God is in us'. At the end their joy *was turned into mourning,*[12] because they did not know the mystery of God and did not find the way of the saints so as to work along it. Therefore, *they have been flogged and they did not feel pain; they have been beaten up and they did not have knowledge* in all these things.

7. O man of God, *return to the high place,* which is the *knowledge of wisdom.* It is written indeed, *You shall not covet* and again, *You shall not get drunk.* Covetousness is not one thing, and drunkenness is not one thing. *The sinner boasts of* the works of his hands. It is said also to others, *What house did you build me?,* because for forty years they had been listening to the voice of God without offering him sacrifices; because it was not for his sake that they had fasted seventy years;[*] because *their heart was after their abominations;*[†] because you did not pause for the one who said, *Pause and know that I am God,*[13] and up to now they have not paused.

8. You are asked, O man, *Why do you love vanity?*[14] and why has your *heart become stubborn? Cain also tilled the soil in order to bring a sacrifice to God*[*] and then he *built a town*[†] but he *did not* do all these things *according to the knowledge* which is pleasing to God.[15] Noah and all his house *were piloted on a boat,*[*][16] *Abraham was a very rich man.*[†] Isaac left his blessing to Jacob.[‡] Jacob knew whom he should love,[*][17] and he wrote a law in his blessings.[†] Joseph helped his own

*Dt 27:18.
†Pr 9:10.

2 S 19:3;
Jm 4:9.

Jr 5:3.
Pr 23:35.
Ps 7:7.
Qo 7:12.
Ex 20:17.
Eph 5:18;
Cf. Pr 23:31;
  Si 19:2.
Ps 9:23.
Is 66:1.

Am 5:25;
Ac 7:42.
*Zc 7:5.
†Ez 33:31.

Ps 46(45):10.

Ps 4:3.
Ex 7:13.
*Gn 4:2-3.
†Gn 4:17.

Cf. Rm 10:2.

*Ws 10:4.
†Gn 13:2.
‡Gn 27.
*Gn 37:3.
†Gn 49:2-27.

*Gn 45:5; 50:20.
†Gn 39:7-10.
‡Gn 50:24.
*Ws 6:17.
†Ws 10:8.
race* because he hated sin.† He disclosed to them that *God would visit them,*‡ and he likewise revealed to them *the care for discipline** and *the memorial of his wisdom.*† After that arose Moses who broke the deceit of life and despised wealth in order to show us the place of wealth and the dwelling place of wisdom. Therefore Joshua was his minister because he knew the power of discipline, and Nb 14:6. Caleb joined him.[18] The stupid men did not know Is 5:20. these things. Therefore *they called light darkness.* And He gave them directives by which they should walk. In all this they did not find their own heart[19] and did not return to walk by his directives. Therefore each one attended to his own works and not to God's works.[20]

9. O man, how long will you not hear the voice of him who tells you, *Pause and know that I am* Ps 46(45):10. *God?*[21] But they did not pause; instead each one *Jr 3:17; 9:13;
 Si 5:2.
†Mt 25:43.
‡Ez 18:31. *followed his own soul.** They *did not visit the sick.*† Why are you dying?‡[22] Do not go into the trap. These are the reminders given to the believers, that by walking in them and striving in the commandments they will do the works worthy of eternal life.

Mt 6:26. 10. *The birds of heaven do not sow or reap.* God has allowed them to take of everything and to eat freely. Like an unjust and wicked man who looks unjustly at other people's things, they eat what does not belong to them. It has been written to us to be attentive to them ourselves, in order to Pr 1:6;
Si 3:29(31). understand all the parables,[23] to have knowledge, and not ourselves to become thieves also, but to walk instead in the way of the just of the early times who were pleasing to God. For they reproached Adam for eating what he was given

by Eve. Before he ate, everything was brought to him so that he would *give them their names* and separate them into species. After he had eaten, *he was expelled from paradise, he tilled the soil* and he begot Cain and Abel. They grew and worked, each as he had chosen. Abel's work pleased God more than Cain's, because he made offerings to God from his choicest goods while Cain gave God the cheap things. They have become a sign for the whole mankind: whoever offers God his choicest goods is likened to Abel's works while the one who brings cheap things is likened to the works of Cain or to the one who laughed at his father and went *to tell his two brothers*,[24] or again to the one who decided to build a tower in the plain of Sennaar, forgetting the one who had *piloted him on the boat* and had saved him from the water of the flood and blessed his fathers. Now he said, fleeing, 'Come, let us *dress stones and cut syca-mores and cedars,* and let us build a tower for ourselves', forgetting about the tower of Calno and how God had divided their language because they wanted to build the tower in order to abandon the Orient and to forget the law of God that he had given into their hearts. Now be sober and understand the punishment of the tower, for they shall not reach heaven. *Neither shall one stone be left standing on another* in the temple over which they disputed with Christ whether it would be pulled down. For *this generation will not pass away* before this happens to it.

11. Now is the time to act for the Lord, because our salvation is in a time of affliction.* If *those who love his salvation*† can *know his steps*‡ and *say constantly: God is great;** and if they can

Gn 3:6.
Gn 2:20.

Gn 3:23.
Gn 4:1-2.

Gn 4:4-5.

Gn 9:22.

Ws 10:4.

Is 9:9.
Is 10:9.

Jr 23:27;
1 M 1:49.

Cf. Gn 11:2-9.
Lk 19:44.

Mk 13:30.

*Cf. Jr 37:9;
33:2.
†Ps 70(69):5.
‡Ps 77(76):19.
*Ps 70(69):5.

Ps 71(70):14.

say, *My hope shall be in you always,* will they believe only in time of joy and not believe in time of
affliction?[25] It is written indeed, *What came out*

Nb 32:24;
Dt 23:24.

of your mouth, do diligently, and again, *If you
have made a prayer to the Lord, do not delay to
render* [what you have promised], *lest the Lord*

Dt 23:22.

claim it from you and it be for you a sin.[26] If you

Ps 71(70):10.

say, *My hope shall be in you always,* may you be
found confident in time of affliction, in which is
salvation.

12. Remember also that it was written for

Pr 6:3.

you,[27] *Do not be faint-hearted, observe my coun-*

Pr 3:21-22.

*sel and my thought that your soul may live. For
he who keeps the commandments is the keeper of*

Pr 19:16.

his soul.[28] You have heard others confess, *We
were covered by the shadow of death and we have
not forgotten the name of the Lord our God or*

Ps 44(43):19-20.

stretched out our hands to a foreign god. He says

Ps 18(17):5.

again, *The snares of death were before me, the
perils of hell troubled me, I found distress and*

Ps 116(114):3.

anguish; in all this our hearts have not turned

Ps 44(43):18.

away but, he says, *I invoked the name of the*

Ps 116(114):4.

Lord. Remember another noble-hearted man
who said, *I will not fear the thousands of people*

Ps 3:6.

surrounding me, because he confided in the Lord.

13. My son, do not tarry, *rouse up your friend*

Pr 6:3.

for whom you pledged yourself,[29] knowing that

Is 47:14.

all the nations are *like chaff on the fire* or *like*

Jr 13:24.

chaff driven by the desert wind[30] or *like dust*

Jb 21:18.

driven by a gale. Remember that it was written
for you: let not your heart be afraid if you see a

Cf. Ex 15:1.

horse and horseman and a great multitude, but
remember the Lord God who gave you the

Dt 8:18.

strength to act with power, and who *wants all
men to be saved and to come to the knowledge of*

the truth.[31] If you listened to the word of God, he said, *I fill heaven and earth,*[32] you shall not fear but say, our *God is both in heaven above and on earth.* Then it shall not be said of you also, *Man of little faith, why did you doubt?* and you shall answer, *If the Lord had not been with us when men rose against us, they would have swallowed us alive.* If *they have often harried you since your youth*[33] did you not also choose *to bear the yoke from your youth?*[34] For I know that you did not *turn your back away from the burden, in the same manner as your hands did not slave in bas-ketmaking,* because you love the *circumcision not performed by human hand,* realized in you for the salvation of your soul. Dangerous is the new wine!

1 Tm 2:4.
Jr 23:24.

Jos 2:11.
Mt 14:31.

Ps 124(123):2-3.
Ps 129(128):2-3.
Lm 3:27.

Ps 81(80):6.
Col 2:11.
2 Co 7:10.

Letter Four (Latin)

LETTER OF OUR FATHER PACHOMIUS TO SOUROUS, FATHER OF THE MONASTERY OF PHNOUM[1] AND JOHN, A HOUSEMASTER OF THE SAME MONASTERY.

Text: Boon,
pp. 86-89

1. We were at your place but because we were in too much of a hurry, we could not have a spiri-tual talk with you; therefore we talk to you now in a letter.

2. Strive with all your strength to follow the custom of the monastery and to do what is pre-scribed. Thus you will not prepare yourself for the punishment of the age to come, nor will you be kept in the bonds of sins, to be condemned and presented to God because of your own negligence as well as the negligence of the brothers who are

with you and co-operate with you, [and who] know that we have transmitted to them very faithfully what we were given by God.

3. Remember also the ministry and the labor of the saints, you and your friends who have learned God's will with you, so that they may also become co-heirs of the same promise and have from God the immortal faith which was created by the spirit of the prophets and strengthened by the apostles who suffered straits and persecutions for it. They believed indeed in his promises and therefore they prepared for themselves a good-smelling fragrance.[2]

Cf. 2 Co 2:14-15.

4. Let us consider therefore those to whom God has granted power, to see if we may deserve to serve them and to cling to their doctrine, putting aside all pride and resisting with great courage the sin α, which fearlessly operates in bodies; for death has been swallowed up by victory. On the other hand, how weak we are in this age, knowing that the Church is to stand and to be led toward what is good, as I have already told you. You know that *the axe does not boast without the man who uses it to cut* and that the Scriptures teach us that we have a *warrant of the death* that we must consume in order to save our soul. We should not fear ruin in the place of our pilgrimage; but we must fight to be able to have peace with those who keep the commandments of God. η. *What will be your gain if you win the whole world*[3] and have enmity with God? We must then understand what we are told, knowing that *the world, with all it craves for, is coming to an end.* Be vigilant and mind how you walk.

1 Co 15:54.

Is 10:15.
2 Co 1:9.

Mt 16:26;
Mk 8:36;
Lk 9:25.
1 Jn 2:17.

5. We know that death occurs in those who are

instructed. Therefore understand the times in which error and seduction are found. Consider the hours as well as the moments and the periods of months according to which man's life flows away; by their number we know how much time each man has lived and has been able to collect his fruits, to fill his granaries with them and prepare for sowing future harvests. Then, at harvest time, he will find the fruit of his zealous tilling, he will possess what is necessary before God and men once he has vanquished death, and he will not, when this world is done, celebrate the solemnities in old garments. The towns are destroyed and full of strangers, but the pious men have come to a wise decision. Water has run in the desert, the   Is 48:21. beasts and the birds have rejoiced. The wise and continent man will not anoint himself with the ointment that has been ruined by dying flies and   Cf. Qo 10:11(13)? has been made up for the sons of the field. We must therefore be vigilant and very carefully prepare the future banquets so we shall not be abashed when the time of rest comes, and shall not be found subject to servitude, but shall be instead *a new batch of bread,* knowing that the   1 Co 5:7. beauty of the field is with us.   Ps 50(49):11.

6. The divine word says elsewhere, *Do I eat the flesh of bulls or drink goat's blood?* Therefore,   Ps 50(49):13. *Let us not be tossed about by every wind of doctrine,*[4] because the time is coming when the saints   Eph 4:14. shall receive the kingdom. *Zion stretches out her hands; no one is there to comfort her.* The young   Lm 1:17. men are *impaired with sticks,* they will scatter the   Lm 5:13. water for their journey. *For lack of food the antlion perishes. He who is the thief's accomplice*   Jb 4:11. *hates his own soul.*[5] Avoid profane and new doc-   Pr 29:24.

*Cf. 2 Tm 2:16.
†Cf. Ex 12:48;
   Lv 19:34;
   Ez 47:22.
‡Ps 78(77):47.
*Pr 14:35.

Pr 25:16.

Sg 2:11.
Cf. Ph 4:7.

trines.* Let the stranger be like the native-born among you.† *He kills their vines with hail and their sycamore trees with frost.‡ A clever minister enjoys the king's favor.* Eat to your satisfaction what honey you may find, but not to excess or you will bring it up again.* Remember the judgement, mercy and faith: the judgement, by which regions are made habitable; mercy, by which God is glorified; faith, which is the foundation of the living and the dead, that through them we may possess hope. Struggle and strive, you and the brothers who are with you. I have written to you with images and parables so that you would search them with wisdom, following the footsteps of the saints, and that instructed in the words of God you will not fall under his judgement. Let the winter of the present age not prevent us from walking, but let us accomplish God's justice always and unceasingly, remembering His own testimony till *winter is past and the rain is over and gone.* May God be our helper in the peace which is without measure. May that peace be in all of you till the evening time is over. I wrote you all these things so that, laboring now, you may have rest in the future.

Letter Five (Latin)

LETTER OF OUR FATHER PACHOMIUS TO ALL
THE MONASTERIES CALLING ALL THE BROTH-
ERS TO ASSEMBLE IN THE GREAT MONASTERY
CALLED PHBOW IN THE DAYS OF THE PASS-
OVER AND TO SHARE ALL TOGETHER IN THE
SAME CELEBRATION.

Text: Boon,
pp. 89-92

1. You must suffer the care [that we take] to
assemble Your Prudence, so that your door may
be open before your departure from this world.
When the poor eats, he does so according to the
measure of his poverty. I told you to know the
hours and the moments of your childhood and
not to be worried about the house which is prepared [to be] your game.

Cf. Gn 27:1-26.

2. When you come to us, take care to make the
bed of the sick and not to be short of bread, and
also, if possible, to find a pillow or a head-cush-
ion, so that those who are weak may rest. This is
in order to fulfil the warning left to us in writing,
*Anyone who does not look after his own relations,
especially if they are living with him, is worse
than an unbeliever. Fennel is beaten with a stick
and cummin is eaten with bread.* If you hold the
hair of your head[1] *and find the ointment running
down your beard to the collar of your robes*[2] you
will be able *to accomplish all that has been written to you.*

1 Tm 5:8.

Is 28:27-28
(LXX).

Ps 133(132):2.

Lk 21:22.

3. We read in another place, *Let not your eyes
stop weeping; for there is a reward for your actions.** Let tears therefore run from your eyes;†
let them flow day and night, unceasingly.‡[3]

*Jr 4:11.
†Cf. Lm 1:16.
‡Jr 14:17;
Lm 2:18.

4. I want you to be like those who did not know

Cf. Jon 4:11.

Ps 64(63):4.

*Mt 6:6.
†Eph 4:14.

Cf. Heb 2:1.

Gn 7:23.

Gn 9:22-25.

Pr 14:21.
*Ex 21:17;
Lv 20:9;
Mk7:10.
†Gn 25:33-34.
Heb 12:16.

Gn 27:5-17.

Gn 27:15.

their right hand from their left.⁴ Be vigilant and bend your bows, for *your enemies have bent their bows—a bitter thing.* Remember that the saints open their door to anyone who passes by. We have the precept *to enter our room and to shut the door*⁵ lest *we be tossed about by every wind.*†⁶

5. We must then be more attentive not to be carried away in the time of kindness, but rather to imitate those times that were before the flood. Each one of the just was pleasing to God, along with his whole house and his children, and no sin was found in them. Later on, however, iniquity increased and the whole earth gave itself to vices of the flesh. They offended God, and at the time of their condemnation, when the flood covered the earth, only Noah with his house and his children was saved. While the world was perishing, he held the helm of justice and he was not vanquished by any storm of sins. But the one who laughed at him and declared his nudity to his brothers was cursed along with his descendants. Then was accomplished what was written, *He who dishonors the just man sins,* and, *A curse be upon him who curses father and mother,*⁷ like Esau, who despised his parents.† Thus it was written of him, *Let no one be a fornicator and impious like Esau.*

6. It was through Rebekah's cunning that Esau received neither the blessing nor the first-born's garment. Because he had offended his parents, they paid him back, and provoked his pride to emulate the good action by dressing Jacob in his clothes. Indeed he did not deserve to use the clothes of those whom in his pride and hardness he had neglected. Therefore they did

not divide their heritage among their sons, but
they gave everything to Jacob who dwelt in the
house with innocence and was subject to their orders. Solomon also says about Esau, *A disobedient son goes to ruin.* Moses says likewise, *Curse be
upon him who curses father and mother.* Solomon says again, *Nothing good for the deceitful
son!†* He lost the blessings therefore, and was deprived of his father's heritage.

7. What shall I say of Adam who, at the beginning of mankind, gave the first example of disobedience and contempt? To him was given power
over all the beasts of the earth, just as everything
is to be given twofold to the firstborn. But after
he held God's order in contempt he did not only
lose his power but was cast out of the place he had
received for his dwelling—just as the fornicator
is cast out of the Church and will be deprived of
his glory. Everything he endured, those who hold
God's commands in contempt will suffer, and
walking with pride they will experience the word
of Scripture, *He spoke, and the earth swallowed
them.*[8]

8. Let us imitate the example of the righteous
man who watched over his house with wisdom
and was saved by his humility while the giants'
pride was perishing. It is not surprising that he,
out of all humankind, was saved with his children
and their wives, for even beasts and birds escaped
death and were saved through obedience. Noah
sent a dove out of the ark and, complying with
the will of the one who sent it, it went and returned, thus condemning contemptuous men by
its obedience; for a bird listened to a righteous
man while men did not listen to God. All the

Gn 27:37.
Pr 13:1.
*Ex 21:17;
Lv 20:9;
Mk 7:10.
†Pr 15:15.
Gn 27:37-40.

Gn 2-3.

Nb 16:32;
Dt 11:6;
Ps 106(105):17.

Gn 8:8-11.

Gn 8:20.

beasts and all the living beings were saved through obedience then; and because they were such, [Noah] offered some of them as victims to God.[9]

9. This narrative teaches us that the saints are offered in sacrifice to God,[10] and if they obey His command, they are saved from the snares of the devil and enjoy God's good things; *not according to righteous actions of their own, but according to His own mercy,* by which we all have access to Him.[11]

Tt 3:5.

10. Having knowledge of the things to come, let us be united with one another in love that we may be able to avoid God's imminent judgement. *Do not drive anyone to anger,*[12] for fear he may die and you be left bound. His sadness would be communicated to your soul and God would pour out his anger on you, because you have poured your own wrath on your brother. Let us not forget God's commandments lest it be said of us, *They have turned their backs to me, not their faces; but when trouble comes they say 'Get up! Save us!'* He will Himself answer, 'I will blame their enjoyment and I will not let them reach the Passover to which they are called.'

Cf. 1 Th 3:12.

Eph 6:4.

Jr 2:27.

11. Let us toil, *carrying each other's burden,*[13] as Christ *carried our diseases in his body*[14] without flinching. If Christ is our master, then let us imitate him and bear his injuries, lest in the age to come we be separated from our brothers who suffered afflictions. Such was also the fate of others because they wanted to give themselves not to virtues but rather to vices.

Ga 6:2.

Is 53:4;
Mt 8:17.

12. God is our judge and our witness. *From heaven he looks down*[15] at everything and in the day of visitation *He will reward each one as his*

Ps 14(13):2;
Ps 33(32):13.

works deserve.[16] All his saints will follow him; we
ought to listen to their precepts.

I have spoken to you through my weakness.

Mt 16:27;
Rm 2:6.

Letter Six (Latin)

LETTER OF OUR FATHER PACHOMIUS TO SOU-
ROUS, THE FATHER OF THE MONASTERY CALLED
PHNOUM, AND JOHN, ONE OF THE HOUSEMAS-
TERS OF THE SAME MONASTERY.

Text: Boon,
pp. 92-95

1. I want you to understand the characters
that you wrote to me and that I wrote to you in
answer, and how important it is to know all the
elements of the spiritual alphabet.

Write ν above η and θ; write ζ above χ, μ, λ
and ι, when you have finished reading these characters.

2. I wrote to you so that you might understand
the mysteries of the characters.

Do not write ν above χ, θ and ηι; but rather
write ζ above χ, and ν above η and θ.

3. As soon as I received the characters you
wrote, I wrote back and to mysterious [words] I
also answered with sacred [words].

I noticed indeed that the characters of your letter were η and θ; therefore I also understood the
meaning and the words in the same manner, so I
could be even with your understanding, lest you
suffer some loss from us.

4. Therefore I wrote to you ςφθμ, lest perhaps
some one might say that my name is not written
ςφθμ.

And do not say: we can write χη, for you said
indeed that it is written this way.

5. Now, therefore, ϲφθμλουυουυλιλ.

Behold, I wrote to you also χ, complete and perfect all around.

6. You write χ and φ, so that you can write ϲ and μ. Behold θ is written before them.

Let it be enough for you to take care of κ and τ, in case you are to go forth.

7. We have written to you ηι because of your labor, so that you might show every solicitude before you depart.

We have indeed the same care as you have, and we did not write κ and τ.

8. I wrote to you μ. Therefore, when you see κ and τ written, write ζ in answer; when you see ϲ and φ, write ν; when you see η and θ, write μ; when you see λιλ write χ; when you see υουυ, write χ.

Therefore, now, do not write κρ in these days, because we found δ written. As for us, we wrote ϲφ.

9. Take care of α. This is indeed what is written in these days; and be attentive to ⳓ and ⳙ, which are Egyptian characters called *bei* and *thei*.[1]

We found ⳣ and ⳙ written, which are Egyptian characters called *hore* and *thei*. Therefore take care of ηι and write α, because I gave it to you for ηι: write also ϲ, because it is written τ and δ so that you be able to come to us.

10. Be careful not to forget to write ψ above κ, because it is written first, and ρ is written before it; and lest you say that θ is written and a part of χ. Therefore the whole thing is written β, lest you say that γ is written.

In every letter that I wrote to you there is something about your sitting and rising and about the shade of the exterior wall, which is outside the wall.

11. The smell of your wisdom has reached us and has compelled us to write you these things.

As for you, as wise men, understand what I wrote to you and prove yourselves to be such as my word has described.

Letter Seven (Greek and Latin)

LETTER OF OUR FATHER PACHOMIUS TO ALL THE MONASTERIES CONVOKING ALL THE FATHERS OF THE MONASTERIES AND THE HOUSEMASTERS TO ASSEMBLE IN THE MONASTERY CALLED PHBOW ON THE TWENTIETH DAY OF THE MONTH CALLED *Mesore* BY THE EGYPTIANS IN ORDER TO ACCOMPLISH PROPERLY THE REMISSION OF ALL THE SINS AND WORKS.[1]

Text: Boon, p. 95

1. The time is coming near for us to assemble together, according to the custom of the remission, following the early prescriptions[2] to convene together in order to carry out the remission and pardon. Let then everyone pardon his brother according to the commandment of God and in conformity with the laws which were written for us by God. Let everyone *totally open his heart* to his brother. Let the brothers share their judgements with one another. Let their souls be cleansed in sanctification and the fear of God. Let there not be any enmity in their hearts. Let them rather know how to act in truth with one another, for it is a commandment of the law of God *to seek peace*[3] and to walk in it before God and men, act-

Text: Quecke, p. 107

Rm 14:5; Cf. 1 Jn 3:19.

Ps 34(33):14.

1 Tm 2:2.

Ga 5:13.

Text: Boon,
     pp. 95-96

ing in truth in everything toward every man. Let them *live in peace*[4] in everything, *serving* God and *each other*[5] and not [serving] their various desires, the deceit of their eyes,[6] the deceptions of a turgid science, and the vices of the flesh. From these things arise divisions, contempt for God's law, contention, and evil thoughts which, boiling on the fire of anger, like waters overflow and foam out into bodily pleasures.

2. Therefore the law of God has been written so that the law and the rights of the bodies may be abolished and that those who walk after their desires may be ashamed and return to God at the last, and that, holding temporal things in contempt, they may seek eternal ones. So will they be prepared to receive the heritage of the saints who held the present life in contempt in order to receive the life of the age to come. In place of malice, they hoped for goodness; in place of disorder and dissension, peace and harmony; in place of carnal adoption, the service of God; so that vanquishing the incentives of the flesh they might seek the things that are pleasing to God's will.

3. It is written, *If you forgive men their sins,* *your heavenly Father will forgive you yours.* Again, *Let each one forgive his brothers from his heart.*[7] Also, *Grant pardon, and you will be pardoned.**[8] Then, *Do good to those who hate you.*†

Mt 6:14.

Cf. Mt 18:35.

*Lk 6:37.
†Lk 6:27.

Rm 12:21.

Cf. Lk 18:3.
Rm 12:17;
1 P 3:9.
*Rm 12:17.
†Rm 12:19.
‡Eph 4:32.
*Ga 6:10.

And elsewhere, *Do not be conquered by evil, but rather conquer evil with good.*[9] And this, *Do not say: avenge me on my enemies.* Elsewhere, *Never repaying evil with evil.* Again, *Doing good before all men.** And this, *Not avenging yourselves, beloved.*† And this also, *Be generous to one another,*‡ *doing good to all.** And again, *Love your*

enemies,[10] *do good to those who hate you, pray*   Text: Quecke,
*for those who persecute you.**[11]   p. 108
     4. Consider, therefore, by how many witnesses   *Lk 6:27-28;
the faithful man is compelled to avoid sin, if he   Mt 5:44.
wishes to listen to the law of God, incline his ear
to His commands, open his eyes to them and direct his heart so as to keep their observance before his eyes. There are many who wish to observe
these commands and who seek God with tears,
groaning day and night, but because of the deceit
of their eyes and the intemperance of their flesh
they died in their groaning and affliction of heart.
They were unable, indeed, to control their own
flesh and the desires of their hearts. They desired
God's law but, carried away to vanities, they were
unable to walk in it. They chose rather to walk in
other wicked things. Therefore, they groaned,
according to the word of the prophet. *The unjust*
shall be tossed about until each one faints on his   Is 57:20.
own road and each one dies in affliction, while
the just [will be] in happiness and joy.

Letter Eight (Coptic)

LETTER OF OUR FATHER PACHOMIUS TO THE   Text: Quecke,
BROTHERS WHO WERE IN THE DESERT FOR   p. 112
SHEARING THE GOATS, THE HAIR OF WHICH
THEY USE TO WEAVE HAIR-SHIRTS.[1]

     1. God seeks those who love him, as he *found*
Israel like a cluster of grapes in the desert, and as
a first fruit that has early grown ripe on a fig tree.   Ho 9:10.
     2. So, truly, Jacob, that is Israel, who had been
lost in the desert like the cluster of grapes, was
found in Mesopotamia. And Joseph, whom God

had known before his brothers, in order to give
him a kingdom at the end of his afflictions in the
desert, was found like a first fruit that has early

Gn 41:40. grown ripe on a fig tree.[2]

3. Consider [Joseph], who was such a man as
Gn 39:10. to vanquish the sin that fought against him. In
order to keep his soul pure for God, so as to be-
1 Co 6:19. come a *temple of the Spirit* and to earn the glory
of adoring God, he did not follow the desire of his
eyes and the satisfaction of the belly.

4. Now, then, consider that God does not forget any of those who fear him. He acts with righteousness, as [he did] when he ended [Joseph's]
afflictions. God did not forget him.

5. Let us then also draw courage from these
things, knowing that God is with us in the desert
as he was with Joseph in the desert. Let us then
put them in our hearts as a memorial; and, like
Joseph himself, let us keep our flesh and our souls
pure in the desert, so that God will remember us
and be with us forever.

Letter Nine A (Coptic and Latin)

Text: Quecke,
p. 117; Boon,
pp. 97-98
WORDS OF OUR FATHER PACHOMIUS THROUGH
CHARACTERS, IN A HIDDEN LANGUAGE, ABOUT
WHAT IS GOING TO HAPPEN.[1]

αω: The generations have effervesced with evil,
      which is δ;

βψ: The fruit has been accomplished on the
Cf. Heb 13:15. lips,[2] which is τ;

ιχ: God caused me to forget the poverty in my
      house, from the beginning of the moun-
      tains to their summit, which is ρ;

δφ: For the repose of the widow and the glory of
      the poor, which is ο;
ευ: The mountains have heard the joy of the
      earth, which is ξ;
ζτ: The earth has been hidden without price,
      which is ν;
ης: They cried on account of my eyes till eve-
      ning, which is ι;
θρ: Do you think they will look on the earth?
      which is η;
ιπ: They drank hidden in joy,
      which is ι;
κο: The spoils of the earth were taken without
      blood, which is η;
λξ: Unfathomed depths were made in the sor-
      row of the heart, which is ξ;
μν; Those who were hidden fled without fear,
      which is ο.

Letter Nine B (Coptic and Latin)[1]

αω: *Who knows if God will not change his mind*
      and relent: τ;

βψ: *Let heaven be glad*
      and earth rejoice: θ;

γχ: *Dan is waiting*
      for God's salvation: ο;

δφ: *Something good can come*
      from Nazareth: βι;[2]

ευ: *Blessed be God, for he provides food*
      for those who fear him: μκ;

ζτ: *The fruit of my mouth is*
      sweet on my lips: ι;

Text: Quecke,
p. 118; Boon,
p. 98
Jon 3:9.

Ps 96(95):11.

Gn 49:18.

Jn 1:46.

Ps 111(110):5.

Cf. Sg 2:3;
    Heb 13:15.

Lk 1:53.   ης: *The hungry he has filled with good things,*
                        which is η;[3]
                    θρ: *I shall not die, but I shall live*
Ps 118(117):17.   *and recite the deeds of the Lord:* π;
                    π: *Anyone who enters through me*
Jn 10:9.   *will be safe:* ι;
                    κο: *For the Lord's judgement with*
Mi 6:2.   *his people* Damascus . . . : ο;[4]
                    λξ: *For God takes pity on Israel and he consoles*
Is 49:13.   *the humiliated among his people:* μ;
                    μν: *Cold water is good to a thirsty soul*
Pr 25:25.   *and so is a good news from afar:* θρ.[5]

Letter Ten (Coptic)

Text: Quecke,   WORDS PRONOUNCED BY OUR FATHER PA-
pp. 113-114   CHOMIUS, THROUGH IMAGES TEACHING THE
                 BROTHERS OF THE MONASTERY OF THMOUŠONS
                 ABOUT THE THINGS THAT WERE TO COME.
                     BY THESE WORDS SPOKEN IN THE SPIRIT THE
                 BROTHERS WERE INFORMED OF WHAT THE SU-
                 PERIORS OF THE MONASTERIES WERE GOING TO
                 DO AND TO SUFFER.[1]

                     1. The stewards[2] have committed a crime in
                 their basket. So they had the sword of their de-
                 struction under their breast, which is the garden,[3]
                 and, at the doors of hell[4] they pursued the abun-
                 dance of the earth, or the goods that God has
                 given to men. They said, 'Come, *let us examine*
Lm 3:40.   *our paths*[5] and see if we find some leaven and
                 throw it in the dough which does not rise and does
                 not increase but perishes through hunger.'[6] *They*
Ps 57(56):6.   *have prepared a snare for their feet,* a bow for
                 their hands, and an axe for their shoulders.

2. They came to a man who had a saw in his hand. He said, 'Are you going to cut some wood?' They answered, 'No, but we want to examine our ways to see if we find some leaven and throw it in the dough which does not rise and does not increase, but perishes through hunger.' The man called his friends. *They skinned their feet and the tips of their hands*, that is their fingers, which fell to the ground. *The young raven* came and collected them. They built a nest. The hinds brought forth in their places.[7] With these, the earth became inhabited.

Jg 1:6.
Ps 147(146):9.

.

Letter Eleven A (Coptic)

WORDS OF OUR FATHER PACHOMIUS IN A HIDDEN LANGUAGE ABOUT WHAT IS GOING TO HAPPEN.[1]

Text: Quecke, pp. 115–116

Truthful in everything is God, who says: φ;   Rm 3:4.
All the torrents go into the sea κ;[2]   Qo 1:7.
*The Lord looks down from heaven** α;   *Ps 14(13):2;
There is no longer any wisdom in† Thaiman υτ;   Ps 33(32):13. †Jr 30:1.
The Lord takes pleasure in those who fear him ϛφθμλ;   Ps 147(146):11.
Wake up, God! Why are you asleep? τ;   Ps 44(43):24.
The eyes of the wise are in their heads.[3]   Qo 2:14.
The patience of the poor is a pledge ηθαμ;
For the righteous men it is a joy to execute judgement χϛ;   Pr 21:15.
A wise son is his father's joy ρυ;[4]   Pr 10:1; 15:20.
Grief of the senseless man is the one who lacks discipline ζ;
Take his garment! For he has become contemptuous ψρ;   Pr 27:13.

Ibid.	Indeed, he insults the others ϛπ;
	There will be a precious treasure in the wise
Pr 21:20.	man's mouth κμ;
	How long will you look at the contemptuous man
Hab 1:13.	and keep silent? τμλ;
Ps 119(118):123.	My eyes are worn out looking for your salvation ϛο;
Si 3:29(31);	The heart of the wise man will reflect on parables
Pr 1:6.	γ.[5]

Block of Characters

(From the Chester-Beatty Fragment of the Coptic Letters of Pachomius)

δ	η	ι	ν	ξ	ο	ρ	τ
η	ι	ν	ξ	ο	ρ	τ	δ
ι	ν	ξ	ο	ρ	τ	δ	η
ν	ξ	ο	ρ	τ	δ	η	ι
ξ	ο	ρ	τ	δ	η	ι	ν
ο	ρ	τ	δ	η	ι	ν	ξ
ρ	τ	δ	η	ι	ν	ξ	ο
τ	δ	η	ι	ν	ξ	ο	ρ

Letter Eleven B (Coptic)[1]

Text: P. Bodmer
XXXIX

Since we have heard that Zion has clothed
herself with her first glory[2], therefore ω
was not made white in the characters νγ.

Do not write ζ . . .[3]

Rather write λολ.

I know that you will write λιλ by yourself.

In all these things remember the *Alpha*.

Take care to write ι, to announce that it belongs
to him.

For so far it has been written like these, while ε
was written in ωχ.[4]

It is however written in ξ.[5]

τ is also written.

Kappa is also enlarged again.

Acquire for yourself the necessary *Thêta*.

Count on ρ . . .; write λ and χ.

Place δ before your eyes that it may be good for
your soul.[6]

Remember ς, that it returned on the first of the
months, which ξ is from ο.

Remember and write ζ because of ς, for it is written.

It is not me who says it to you, but I am confident
that you have heard [it] before this day.

ρ also has stretched out his hand.

It has reached us in these days.[7]

You have washed your face while our heart grieved
for ς, which is two hundred, because it (he?)
has promised not to forget the first of the
month.

About λ also, that you have written in [χ?], another did it[8] before us saying to them:

Mt 10:16.   *I am sending you like sheep among wolves.* We
                   have heard again about ε in ω that *two are grind-*
Mt 24:41.   *ing at the same mill; one is taken, one left.*

Notes to the Letters of Pachomius

Notes to the First Letter
(Pach. Letter 1)

Pach. Letter 1   [1] This title exists only in Jerome's Latin translation.
          [2] This identical sentence is found in Letter 11b, where it is extant in Coptic.
          [3] This sentence is also found in Letter 9b, although in a slightly different form. It is extant in Coptic.
          [4] The Greek text shows that we should read *sepulchrum* (MS M) in the Latin edition (Boon, p. 97, 14) rather than *pulchrum* (MSS EWX).
          [5] This sentence is quoted literally by Schenoute. Here is the context: 'A good, wise and truly pious father has said in a letter, with his characters: "Sing to the ω! do not let the ω sing to you!" As for me I think that he said this: "Sing to the world . . . . Do not let the world sing to you . . .!"' Cf. H. Quecke, 'Ein Pachomiuszitat bei Schenute . . . '; *Idem, Die Briefe Pachoms. Griechischer Text,* pp. 48 and 111.
          [6] This sentence is quoted by Horsiesios in an Instruction (Hors. Instr. 1: 2), where he simply changes the second person plural of the verbs into the first person plural. Note that, as in Schenoute's quotation, the two parallel members of the sentence are simply juxtaposed in Coptic, while they are subordinated in the Greek and Latin translations. See H. Quecke, *Die Briefe Pachoms. Griechischer Text,* pp. 46–47.
          [7] 'the hair of your head': we find this expression again in Letter 5: 2 and in Hors. Test. 6.
          [8] In the Latin text (Boon, p. 78, 4–5), the question mark after 'Quae sunt dies innocentiae tuae' should be suppressed.
          [9] The character that is used here is not a known character of the Coptic alphabet. It is possible that the Greek scribe was not too conversant with the Coptic alphabet. The Latin text (Boon, 78, 6) has *simma* (MS M) or C (MSS WX), omitted by MS E. See H. Quecke, *Die Briefe Pachoms. Grieschischer Text,* pp. 78–79.

Notes to the Second Letter
(Pach. Letter 2)

Pach. Letter 2   [1] Sourous (*Syrus* in Jerome's Latin translation) was one of the first three disciples, along with Pšentaesi and Pšoi (See SBo 23), and he became the superior of the monastery of Phnoum (see SBo 58). He died of the plague in 346, shortly before Pachomius' death (see SBo 119; G¹ 114). In the introduction to his *Pachomiana latina* Jerome mistakenly stated that Sourous was still alive and 110 years old in 404. He confuses him with another Sourous, perhaps 'Sourous the Younger' who replaced Theodore as father of the monastery of Tabennesi (see SBo 78).
          The title of this letter is found only in Latin. In our Greek manuscript, Letter 1 and Letter 2 form one continuous text.

²The Greek text shows that in the Latin edition (Boon 78, 15) we should read: '... *tibi U in epistula proper T scriptum est. Et recordare* ...' with MS M instead of: '... *tibi U; in epistula T scriptum est. Recordare* ...'.
³In the Latin edition (Boon, 79, 1) read *laba* (= *lava*) with MS E (cf. νίψον in the Greek text) instead of *leva* with MS M.

Notes to the Third Letter
(Pach. Letter 3)

Pach. Letter 3   ¹This title is found only in Latin.
²We find the same combination of Mt. 24:45 and 49 in Hors. Test. 14. The phrase "τὴν τροφὴν ἐν καιρῷ αὐτῆς" (*in tempore suo*) is a translation from the Sahidic New Testament; the pronoun αὐτῆς is absent from the text in the Greek New Testament. See H. Quecke, *Die, Briefe Pachoms. Griechischer Text*, p. 94, n. 4.
³This text is quoted again below, ¶9.
⁴Is 57:20 is quoted again in Letter 7: 4.
⁵Col 3:2 is quoted also in G¹ 55, SBo 70 (= G¹ 78) and Hors. Letter 4: 3.
⁶Jn 10:12 is quoted also in Hors. Test. 17.
⁷The same text is quoted again below, ¶7, where drunkenness is linked with covetousness. We find the same allusion to Eph 5:18 in Inst. 18.
⁸Lm 5:13 is quoted again in Letter 4: 6.
⁹This sentence is quoted literally in a Coptic fragment that L.-T. Lefort published under the name of Horsiesios, but must very probably be attributed to Pachomius himself. See below, Pach. Fragm. 5: 2.
¹⁰In the Latin edition, read: '*non potest uiam monstrare*' with MSS WX (cf. οὐκ ὀδηγεῖ τὸν πλανώμενον), instead of: '*quomodo erranti monstrabit uiam*' with MSS MEB.
¹¹We find the same quotation from Dt 27:18 in Hors Test. 24 where it is also preceded by an admonition about drunkenness.
¹²Jm 4:9 is quoted also in Am. letter 23.
¹³Ps 46(45):10 is quoted again below, ¶9, and in Hors. Test. 33.
¹⁴In the Latin edition (Boon, 81, 22) read: '*quare diligitis*' with MS M (cf. ἀγαπᾶτε) instead of: '*quare diligis*' with MSS EBWX.
¹⁵More is said about Cain below, ¶10.
¹⁶About Noah, see below, ¶10.
¹⁷More about Jacob (and Esau) in Letter 5: 6. Hors. Test 52 also speaks of Jacob's special love for Joseph.
¹⁸We find the same mention of the Old Testament witnesses (Abraham, Isaac, Jacob, Moses, Joshua and Caleb) in Paral. 41.
¹⁹This beautiful description of conversion as the finding of one's heart should be compared to the manner in which Palamon understood monastic formation as leading someone to come to know himself (see SBo 10, n. 2).
²⁰In Pach. Instr. 1: 2ff we have also the example of a long list of saints of the Old Testament.
²¹This text is quoted above, ¶7, and also in Hors. Test. 33.
²²Hors. Test. 33 also uses Ez 18:31 in connection with Ps 46(45):10, as Pachomius does here.
²³The same quotation occurs at the end of Letter 11a.
²⁴The same incident is mentioned in Letter 5: 5.
²⁵In the Latin edition (Boon, 84, 9) we should read '*difidit*', with MS M (cf. οὐ πιστεύουσιν) instead of '*deficit*', with MSS BWX.

[26] In the Latin edition (Boon, 84, 12) we should read '*sit tibi peccatum*', with MS B (cf. ἔσται σοι ἁμαρτία), instead of '*sit tibi in peccatum*', with MSS MEWX.

[27] In the Latin edition (Boon, 84, 15) we should read '*quod scriptum est*', with MS M (cf. ἐγράφη) instead of '*quod scriptum sit*', with MSS EBWX.

[28] Pr 19:16 is quoted also in Hors. Letter 1: 4.

[29] Pr 6:3 is quoted also in Pach. Instr. 1: 6 and in Hors. Test. 9.

[30] Jr 13:24 is also quoted by the bishop to the sinful brother in Draguet Fragm. 2: 9.

[31] The faith in the universality of God's designs of salvation is expressed with the same quotation in G[1] 132.

[32] The same notion of God's omnipresence and the same quotation occur in Pach. Instr. 1: 25 and Theod. Instr. 3: 34.

[33] In the Latin edition (Boon, 85, 14) we should read '*ab adolescentia tua*', with MS M (cf. ἐκ νεότητός σου), instead of '*ab adolescentia*', with MSS EBWX.

[34] Lm 3:27 is quoted also in Am. Letter 3 and Hors. Test. 52.

Notes to the Fourth Letter
(Pach. Letter 4)

Pach. Letter 4   [1] Jerome write *Chnum* (some MSS have *Cenun* or *Cenum*); which is obviously a deformation of Phnoum, where Sourous (whom Jerome calls Syrus) was superior.

[2] Horsiesios likewise exhorts the monks: 'Let us also hasten . . . to fill our vats of wine with the fragrance of Christ.' (Hors. Instr. 3: 3).

[3] The same text is used by Horsiesios in a call to penance: Hors. Instr. 1: 4.

[4] This text is quoted again in Pach. Letter 5: 4 and in Hors. Test. 53.

[5] The same quotation is found in Hors. Letter 4: 4.

Notes to the Fifth Letter
(Pach. Letter 5)

Pach. Letter 5   [1] 'The hair of your head': used above, in Pach. Letter 1: 3 and in Hors. Test. 6. In fact Hors. Test 6 quotes not only this expression, but the last few lines of this parapragh.

[2] Ps 133(132) is also quoted in Hors. Test. 6.

[3] Lm 2:18 is quoted also in Hors. Test. 48.

[4] Elsewhere this text is used by Pachomius to express the lack of experience of a neophyte. See G[1] 40 ('the community has many neophytes who do not know what a monk is, and boys *who cannot tell their right hand from their left*' and Paral. 1 where, after Theodore's first instruction, Pachomius says to those who have left the assembly: 'I . . . was listening to him with all my soul as one *who does not know his right hand from his left*.'

[5] This is an unusual interpretation of Mt 6:6. The text is quoted with its normal meaning in Pach. Instr. 1: 8.

[6] Same quotation used in Pach. Letter 4: 6 and in Hors. 53.

[7] Same quotation below, ¶6.

[8] Same quotation in Inst. 18. There is another reference to Dathan and Abiram in Paral. 3.

[9] In S[1] 25 Pachomius is said to have followed that example of Noah offering victims from his flock to God who smelled their fragrance.

[10]See note 9.

[11]Theodore also speaks of the Holy Spirit dwelling in us 'through mercy and not because of our works' (Theod. Instr. 3: 36). Consciousness of the importance of God's mercy and grace permeates all the pachomian literature.

[12]Same quotation is Hors. Test. 15.

[13]Same quotation in Am. Letter 3 and Hors. Test. 11.

[14]This text is surprisingly applied to s. Paul in Hors. Test. 13.

[15]Same quotation below, in Letter 11a.

[16]This theme of the reward according to each one's works, with reference to Rm 2:6-7 is frequent. See SBo 27 (= G[1] 32); Inst. 18; Pach. Fragm. 2: 3; Hors. Test. 27, 33.

Note to the Sixth Letter
(Pach. Letter 6)

Pach. Letter 6 [1]'which are Egyptian characters ... ' is obviously an explanatory clause of Jerome. The same thing happens again in the next sentence.

Notes to the Seventh Letter
(Pach. Letter 7)

Pach. Letter 7 [1]This title is found only in the Latin translation. Only part of the Greek text is extant. The first section of our text is translated from Greek; we follow the Latin version for the rest. Concerning the general meeting of all the monks of the *Koinonia* at Phbow in the month of *Mesore*, at the end of the year, see SBo 71, n. 2.

[2]These 'early prescriptions' must be either the Old Testament prescriptions concerning the Jubilee, or the New Testament precepts about the mutual forgiveness of sins. About the same custom Theodore writes: 'Therefore let us also now put into practice the commandments of our Father, as well as his precepts and his ordinances which he drew for us from the tradition of the saints' (Theod. Letter 2: 3).

[3]Ps 34(33): 12-15 is quoted in Hors. Instr. 1: 1.

[4]1 Tm 2:2 is quoted also in SBo 101.

[5]Ga 5:13 is quoted also in SBo 105 and 107; Hors. Letter 3: 1 and Hors. Test. 26.

[6]At this point we begin to translate from the Latin version, about 23 lines being missing from the Greek manuscript.

[7]This passage is quoted again by Pachomius in Pach. Instr. 1: 38.

[8]This text is quoted also in Pach. Instr. 1: 38 and Draguet Fragm. 1: 5.

[9]This text is applied to Pachomius in G[1] 42.

[10]We return to the Greek text.

[11]This passage is quoted also in Draguet Fragm. 1: 5 in another series of texts about pardon; also in Pach. Instr. 1: 38.

Notes to the Eighth Letter
(Pach. Letter 8)

Pach. Letter 8 [1]This title is found only in the Latin translation.

[2]The patriarch Joseph is often given as example to the brothers; see Pach. Instr. 1: 5, n. 1.

Notes to the Ninth Letter, A
(Pach. Letter 9A)

Pach. Letter 9A   [1]This title is proper to the Latin translation. We have a very fragmentary Coptic text of this letter. We will translate from the Latin, taking the Coptic text into account as much as possible. The Coptic fragments can help us particularly in re-establishing the correct division of the text into verses.

[2]The same text is quoted in Letter 9b.

Notes to the Ninth Letter, B
(Pach. Letter 9B)

Pach. Letter 9B   [1]Letters 9A and 9B are two distinct documents in Coptic; but they form a continuous text in Latin, and therefore there is no title for 9B in Jerome's translation. Our translation is based on the Coptic text, although the Coptic manuscript is very fragmentary.

[2]Note how Pachomius transforms the interrogative sentence of Jn 1:46 into an affirmation.

[3]The Latin version has a different biblical quotation here: *'Dominus dat mihi linguam disciplinae'* (cf. Is 50, 4).

[4]In the Coptic manuscript there were a few words — now illegible — between *Damascus* and the character 'o'. In any case, *Damascus* does not belong to the quotation from Mi 6:2. The Latin version has: *'Quia iudicium Dauid ad populum ejus Damascus'*.

[5]Here the Latin text has a short series of ten characters which certainly correspond somehow to the block of characters found after Letter 11A in the Coptic papyrus fragment of the Chester Beatty Library. The short series of characters that are found between Letters 2 and 3 in Greek is probably similar.

Notes to the Tenth Letter
(Pach. Letter 10)

Pach. Letter 10   [1]This title is proper to the Latin translation. At the end of it we find a long series of fifty characters, like those at the end of the preceding letter.

[2]The Coptic text has *oikonomos* (= οἱ οἰκονόμοι). Jerome correctly understood: 'the superiors of the monasteries' (*monasteriorum principes*).

[3]In the Latin edition (Boon, 99, 12) we should read '*hortus*', with MS M (originally) (cf. ὁ κῆπος) instead of 'ortus', with MSS EWX.

[4]This sentence is quoted by Schenoute. See H. Quecke, *Die Briefe Pachoms. Griechischer Text*, pp. 49-52 and 114.

[5]The same quotation from Lm 3: 40 is found in Theod. Instr. 3: 38 and in Hors. Test. 4 and 49.

[6]This sentence is also quoted by Schenoute. See H. Quecke, *Die Briefe Pachoms. Griechischer Text*, pp. 49-52 and 114.

[7]In the Latin edition (Boon, 100, 3), we should read '*cerui*', with all the MSS (cf. οἱ ἔλαφοι), instead of '*corui*' (Boon's correction).

Notes to the Eleventh Letter, A
(Pach. Letter 11A)

Pach. Letter 11A   [1]This title, like all the other ones, is proper to the Latin translation.

[2]In the Latin edition (Boon, 100, 9), we should read 'uadunt' with MS M (cf. πορεύονται, and Coptic *eumooŝ*),instead of 'uadent', with MSS EWX.

[3]A Coptic character would be expected at the end of this line. Actually the Greek text (H. Quecke, *Die Briefe Pachoms. Griechischer Text*, p. 109, 40) ends the line with a δ. It is missing in the Latin.

[4]We find the same quotation in Hors. Letter 2.

[5]The symetric block of characters that follows remains very enigmatic. See H. Quecke, *Die Briefe Pachoms. Griechischer Text*, pp. 24-26. A. de Vogüé has given a few more observations about the disposition of the characters, in his review of H. Quecke's publication; see *Rivista degli Studi Orientali*, vol VI, pp. 316-321.

Notes to the Eleventh Letter, B
(Pach. Letter 11B)

Pach. Letter 11B   [1]This letter has no title in Latin, as it forms a continuous text with Letter 11A. We translate from the Coptic text of the MS P. Bodmer XXXIX, the few lacunae of which can be complemented in some cases with fragments of the Chester Beatty MS published by H. Quecke in *Die Briefe Pachoms. Griechischer Text*, pp. 112-113. We have used a photocopy of the Bodmer folio, and a transcription Quecke made of it and which he has graciously permitted us to consult.

[2]Jerome understood just the opposite: *Vidimus quod Sion spoliauerit se gloriam, quam habuit ab initio.*

[3]A few letters are missing in Coptic. Jerome has: *Inter litteras NY non scribatis Z;* but there is no place for more than a few letters in the lacuna of the Coptic manuscript.

[4]Jerome understood *hn ôch* (= in ωχ) as εινωχ.

[5]The pronoun at the beginning of the sentence is masculine in Coptic. It is not clear to whom/what it refers.

[6]See the same sentence in Letter 1: 2, where we have it in Greek.

[7]This sentence also is found in Letter 1: 2.

[8]The pronoun 'it' refers to λ; but in Coptic we have a masculine pronoun.

fRagments from saint pachomius

(pach. fRagm.)

I

Text: CSCO 159
pp. 26-30

1. . . . of the flesh, in order to harvest fruit in their pure hearts and in their excellent words.

2. The second operation of the devil is this: he leaves the man with whom he is battling when he sees him inhabited by the Holy Spirit[1] and blazing like a flame, just as a serpent or a scorpion could not sting blazing iron without rendering it even more glowing. But when he sees him somewhat idle or completely negligent, he prowls around him and hides until he sees him asleep; then he leaps out at him at once and deceives him.

Cf. 1 Co 3:16.

Cf. 1 P 5:8.

Apa Pachomius [the archimandrite]

II

Again from the same.

1. Flee these men who follow their whims. Who will be able to help you? For no man can be of any use to his neighbor in such times. But hasten to acquire mourning and silence which will be for you a guide to the fear of God. Shut your ears against the abomination which most of those who bear our habit now take as a law, I mean to say, slander.

85

Ps 101(100):5.

2. You, too, say with the prophet, *I have re-jected the man who furtively slanders his neigh-bor.*[2] For he also slanders who deliberately listens to slanderous talk; the condemnation is the same, except that he will see a place he should not see. Let him therefore go to the place where he should

Cf. Ex 21:16.

go and avoid the curse of the legislator.

3. Let your words be measured and counted

*Cf. Pr 17:27;
Si 21:25(28).
†Cf. Mt 12:36.

by yourself,* knowing that you shall render an account to God of what comes out of your mouth,†

Cf. 1 Co 10:23.

including a pleasantry or even a word that does not edify. Be on your guard, monk, do not lose your wealth along with your *ascesis.* And do not become a stranger to such promises. Whatever you think and whatever you love, establish it firmly in the Lord. And keep in mind your depar-ture from the body to go to God *who will reward*

Mt 16:27;
Pr 24:12;
Rm 2:6.

each one according to his works.[3]

Apa Pachomius, the archimandrite

III

Again from the same.[4]

1. An elder has recounted this: A brother wanted to become a monk and his mother pre-vented him. He kept to his own mind and de-clared, 'I want to save my soul'. She kept impe-ding him, yet could not make him yield. Finally, she let him go, and he left. He went and became a monk, but walked negligently and spent his life unworthily.[5]

2. His mother died, and after a while he fell gravely ill and had a dream. He was carried off to the judgement and found his mother with those

who were being judged. Upon seeing him, his mother was dismayed and said to him, 'How is it, my son, that you, too, are here to be judged? Where are the words you said to me, "I wish to save my soul"?' He blushed at these words put to him by his mother; then he himself went to the punishment reserved for him.[6]

3. When he awoke from his dream, and when his fever had left him somewhat, he thought to himself, 'If my mother has given me this reproof, what will I do when I am led to the tribunal of *the righteous judge* who has no favorites†*?'[7] So he labored at his salvation with great zeal and became so renowned that others were saved because of him.

*2 Tm 4:8.
†1 P 1:17.

Apa Pachomius, the archimandrite

IV

Again from the same.[4]

1. I exhort you, brother monks, who love the Lord, to allow no such thought as this to enter your minds: 'Why, the patriarchs and the prophets also participated in the married life and were pleasing to God!' No, have no such thought, but let each one think for himself. Look in what a place and what a smoky prison were confined the prevaricating angels, *in a great darkness.* If you can rise from this great darkness where they are confined, you are responsible! Indeed, it is impossible that he who has vowed himself to God should turn back again to worldly toils and the many sorrows of those in the world.[8] As regards

Jude 6; 2 P 2:4.

Cf. 2 Tm 2:4.
Cf. 1 Co 7:28.

secular life, once someone has begotten children and is afflicted by poverty, it would not be just to go away and leave them on the pretext of monastic life.

2. I think, brothers, that together we have tasted teachings filled with the fear of the Lord. He who puts them into practice will live from them and will receive a blessing from Jesus.

Cf. Ps 24(23):5.

Text: CSCO 159
p. 80

V

1. ... the Lord.[9] It is said again in the Minor Prophets, *I will draw them to me by the bonds of my love.* Paul also has said, *We are affiliated with Christ.* Therefore, my brothers, rejoice, be prepared and *hold to the confession of hope* with firm pride until the end.

Hos 11:4.
Heb 3:14.
Heb 10:23.
Heb 6:11.

2. As for the man whose conscience will prick him anew, the first form of temperance will be the mastery of his belly, for the belly's passion is the worst of all;[10] the belly's passion brings pleasures and idle deceit. When intemperance occurs and finds such things in a man, he becomes like a well that has been filled in, a spring gone dry, a river run empty; he becomes like a crumbled palace, an orchard already picked whose fence has fallen down. The last sentence of death for the soul is the soul's unbelief.

3. You, therefore, the beloved of the Word, the Son of the Living God, be as hairs growing on the body of Christ, covered with beautiful feathers in the Church of the Most High, walking in the truth, bound to righteousness, so you may inherit the dwellings of peace. The Lord God of hosts is Himself the God who will pasture you

eternally in the joy of his grace and the content-
ment of his peace, until the end of all the ages
which do not grow old. Amen.

Notes to the Fragments of Pachomius

(Pach. Fragm.)

Pach. Fragm. [1] 1 Co 3:16-17 is quoted often; see Theod. Instr. 3: 41; Hors. Letter 3: 2 (1 Co 3:17-18); Hors. Test. 19. There is an allusion to the same text in G¹ 135.

[2] This text is quoted also in Hors. Test. 43.

[3] This theme of the reward according to each one's work, with reference to Rm 2:6-7 is frequent; see Pach. Letter 5: 12, n. 2.

[4] 'Apa Pachomius [the archimandrite]', at the beginning of fragment II is in fact a signature to fragment I, and should be at the bottom of fragment I. 'Again from the same' is the beginning of fragment II.

[5] This anecdote is found in various collections of *apophthegmata*, where it is anonymous. See the introduction.

[6] The conclusion of the story is very different in the fragment published by Zoega (see the Introduction). Here the conclusion of the fragment is: 'He blushed at the words he heard and he kept silent, not having any answer to give her. By a merciful disposition of Providence he was cured of his illness. He repented interiorly because of the visitation he had been granted by God and he enclosed himself alone. Then he began to meditate about his salvation and to weep over what he had done previously in the time of his negligence. He was moved by such ardor that many advised him to give himself a little rest lest his too abundant tears make him ill. But he refused to restrain himself saying: "If I could not resist my mother's irony how will I be able to resist shame on the day of judgement, in the presence of Christ and of all his angels".' (Coptic text in *CSCO*-159, p. 29, n. 51).

[7] Horsiesios also quotes 1 P 1:17 in a similar context, in Hors. Test. 16.

[8] This text is quoted also in Hors. Test. 34.

[9] L.-T. Lefort (*Oeuvres*, *CSCO*-159, p. XXI and 80) attributed that text to Horsiesios, but with some hesitation. It must be attributed to Pachomius, along with the *verso* of the same *folio*, where we read the Prologue to the *Praecepta et Instituta*. It is important to note that nothing, not even a title, separates the two documents.

[10] This is a direct quotation from Pach. Letter 3: 5: μανία κοιλίας χαλεπωτέρα ἐστὶν τούτων πάντων. (H. Quecke, *Die Briefe Pachoms. Griechischer Text*, p. 102, 63). Jerome's translation is not so accurate: *Ventris insania peior est omnibus malis* (Boon, p. 80, 19. See H. Quecke, *ibidem*, pp. 44-66).

InstRuctions of theodore

(theod. InstR.)

Text: CSCO 159,
p. 37

Instruction One

1. . . . will not impute the sin to him. It is this
very great happiness of man that will be ours together with all the saints. True is the word of our
Lord when he said, *Happy are those who have
not seen, and yet have believed.*

Cf. Rm 4:6.

Jn 20:29.

Instruction of apa Theodore.

2. . . . reach . . . three . . . obstacle. Not
to . . . retort; and that he who has the confidence
of John, who flung himself on the Lord's breast,
imitate him in order not to. . . .

Jn 21:20.

Instruction Two

Text: CSCO 159,
pp. 37-40

ALSO FROM APA THEODORE

1. It is by a favor from God . . . that there ap-
peared upon earth the holy *Koinonia*, by which
he made known the life of the Apostles[1] to men
who desire to follow their model forever before
the Lord of all. Indeed, the Apostles *left everything and*, with all their heart, *followed* Christ;*
they *stood steadfast with him in his trials,*† and
shared with him in the death of the cross;‡ after
which they deserved *to be seated on the twelve*

*Mt 19:27;
Lk 22:28.
†Lk 22:28.
‡Cf. 1 P 4:13.

91

thrones of glory and to judge the twelve tribes of
Lk 22:30.   *Israel....*

*13 lines are
mutilated*

2. My beloved, let us manifest a faith that is
honest according to God, and let us keep his commandments....

*About 20 lines
are missing*

3. ... that we do not forsake the law and the
commandments of our fathers; that we walk in
1 Tm 1:10;   their presence in a *sound doctrine*; that we incul-
2 Tm 4:3;   cate in the brothers the law of the *Koinonia*,
Tt 1:9; 2:1.   and ... witness to us ... a task ... let us fulfill
*About 12 lines   it ... from a novice up to a senior. Let us observe
are missing*   his commandments, from the least to the most
Cf. Ps 24(23):5;   important, so that mercy may be shown to us all.[1]
Ps 33(32):22.   Indeed, apa Pachomius, the man of God, labored
strenuously; those who are without shame blushed
before such a man.[2] Let us be mindful of the fact
that he [spent thirty-] eight years without the least
respite, day or night, according to what we have
heard.[3] Let us then practise his commandments
according to the whole law which he imposed upon us. Let us love the life of our father in order to
share with him the glory which God reserved for
him in the other world and unto eternity....

*The rest
is missing*

Text: CSCO 159,   *Instruction Three*
pp. 40-60

**God trains those   1. ... mercy ... for us in him for our sal-
whom he loves**   vation, and confidence on the day of his manifes-

tation. Truly, *those whom the Lord loves he trains,*[1] as the Scripture says, either by a tribulation coming from men, or by a reproof, as when a thoughtless word is thrust at us. And above all he causes our conscience to burn us at every moment when we do not walk as befits the dignity of the holy vocation of the habit we wear. However, he does not let us be crushed by those whom we help gratuitously according to our means.

2. Knowing therefore, my beloved, that such is the Lord's way of dealing with *those he will take to himself, chastising them,* let us be confident and let us thank him for these slight corrections which come upon us for our advantage.

Let us consider the long training by which he formed such saints as Joseph, Job, David and others of their kind, the prophets, the apostles and the martyrs; including the fathers of the *Koinonia,* Apa and our father Horsiesios. [He formed them] by hidden trials and by illnesses; he had them criticized by persons less estimable than they were, tossing at them hateful words far removed from all that is pious.

He caused serious hardships to arise among the brothers in [Apa's] time, to such a degree that so great a man as he had recourse to seculars for bread.[1] That good man with his own eyes saw his sons working little mills and licking the meal with their tongues in consequence of their great hunger. And he was vilified by the great ones among them [who said], 'You are murdering the children of men by hunger.'[2] And for long God kept him tongue-tied so he might not speak, so that he was seen by him who deigned to give his body to men and be eaten[3] because of his boundless di-

Marginal references:

1 Jn 2:28.

Heb 12:6; Pr 3:12.

Cf. 1 Tm 4:2.

Let us consider how God trained the saints
Heb 12:6; Pr 3:12.

Cf. Jn 6:52-56.

vine love. For want of bread, not once in all those days was the signal given for a meal.

3. Then, O beloved, if we have been able to admire that man, let us not be discouraged by tribulation, for what we endure today is only a small part of what those men endured. *Our salvation* [comes] *in time of tribulation*,[1] according to Scripture; and *Tribulation brings patience*.[2]

By the manner in which we have all sought to put on the acts of the habit we wear, of the name spoken over us, and of the law that we have promised before God and men faithfully to keep, we have greatly glorified the Lord who turned our hearts toward himself. Let us have confidence in this: just as he in his mercy has awakened us from the sleep of death,* so he will also in his kindness cause us *to inherit the promises*[†] he made to his saints.

Cf. Eph 3:13.

Is 33:2.

Rm 5:3.

*Cf. Ps 107
   (106):14.
†Heb 6:12.
Let us be
watchful

4. For that reason let us be watchful and let us guard the grace fallen to our lot far beyond the deserts of our works. Let us keep the law, each being a subject of edification to his neighbor and a way [for him] to enter into the joy of the kingdom of heaven. Let us therefore put our whole heart to walking in accordance with the whole law of the *Koinonia*. Let us smother the flame, detraction, complaint by the power of the Holy Spirit, that is to say by reciting the words of God night and day — as well as *all the burning arrows of the Evil One*.[1]* Let us be strong in *the shield of our faith*[†] so that when the time comes and when God visits us we may be found so far ready as to say, *I rejoiced when they said to me: let us go to the house of God.*

Cf. Rm 15:2.

Cf. 2 P 1:11.

*Eph 6:16.
†*Ibid.*

Ps 122(121):1.
Let us be firm
in the law of
the Koinonia

5. *We give thanks to God, the Father of our Lord Jesus Christ, for enabling us to forget our*

sorrows[1] and our distress in the fragrance of obedience and with the firmness of a firm faith in the
law of the holy and true *Koinonia*. That [Koino-
nia] has as its author after the Apostles Apa Pachomius,[2] the man whose God-given promises we
are ready to inherit if only we observe his commandments, *washing off every defilement of
flesh or spirit, and perfectly practising purity in
the fear of God;*[3] if in every way we are free from
giving scandal to our neighbors,[4] whether in word
or deed; if we are a fragrance[5] for those from
outside,* *that seeing our good works they may
give praise to our father in heaven,*[6]† so that
all, even those who scorn our fair conduct,‡ may
know that *we follow no trumped-up discourse or
human wisdom,* but that *the Lord is our father,†
the Lord is our chief, the Lord is our king; it is the
Lord who will give us life.*[7] Let us be glad in the
anguish of persecution and say, *In everything that
happens to us we have not forgotten you nor have
we been disloyal to your covenant, neither has our
heart turned away in retreat.*

Let us be mindful that we *have been granted the
grace not only of believing in Christ but moreover
of suffering for him.*[8] Let us reckon that all anxie-
ty, all tribulation is as nothing *through the grace
of the One who gives strength,* Christ Jesus our
Lord. Let us remember the ills and sorrows brought
on that man and on all the saints *who went dressed
in sackcloth and in the skins of goats, poor, anxious, afflicted; of whom the world was not worthy.**[9] They went with great joy,† knowing that
their salvation [comes] *in times of tribulation,‡*
and that the *sufferings of the present moment are
nothing beside the glory that will be shown to us.*[10]

Cf. 2 Co 1:3-4.

2 Co 7:1.
Cf. Rm 14:13.
Cf. 2 Co 2:15.
*Col 4:15;
 1 Th 4:12.
†Mt 5:16.
‡Cf. 1 P 3:16.

*1 Co 2:13.
†Is 64:7(8).

Is 33:22.

Ps 44(43):17-18.

Ph 1:29.
Cf. Rm 8:18.
Ph 4:13.

*Heb 11:37-38.
†Cf. Ac 5:41.
‡Is 33:2.

Rm 8:18.

Let us agree to be trained by God
*Heb 12:6; Pr 3:12.

Heb 12:11.

6. *For, he whom the Lord loves he trains; he chastises every child that he will take to himself.* * *If at present every lesson is not a pleasure but rather a pain, later it brings forth a quiet fruit of justice to those who are trained by it.* Do you not know how animals are trained, what treatment they get while being taught the exercise their master takes pleasure in?

Being then acquainted with the wholesome knowledge of Holy Scripture and the works by which God trained the saints and the fathers of the *Koinonia*, let us not lose heart but let us all say before God both inwardly and with our mouth, *May we not only be put in chains but may we even die in every place for the name of our Lord Jesus Christ.*[1] In the distress of our bodily needs and as we face the taunts of those who reproach us because of poverty and affliction, let us say, *What can separate us from the love of God? Tribulation or distress or persecution or hunger or nakedness or danger, or the sword?* and so on.[2] This is exactly the way in which the Apostle behaved, the elect of God, who told us, *Be like me as I am like Christ.*[3] So also was the way all the saints behaved and the fathers of the *Koinonia* who have nobly ended their struggle and found respite from their sufferings by *entering the place of their everlasting rest.*[4]

Ac 21:13.

Rm 8:35.

1 Co 11:1.

Cf. 2 Tm 4:7.

Cf. Heb 4:10.

Let us be steadfast in every trial

7. As for us now, least of beings and more apt for scorn than all others, we truly believe and are confident that this must also mercifully happen to us in accord with the words of Isaiah, *Do not be afraid because you are covered with shame; do not be dismayed because you are disgraced, for you will forget everlasting shame and you will no*

longer remember the disgrace of widowhood,   Is 54:4.
and in accord with all the other blessings that are
written in that book. By persevering to the end
with the fortitude of Christ, glad to be in the
midst of infirmities, insults, anxieties, persecutions, and distress for Christ, we shall indeed inherit all the blessings of the Scriptures, the breath
of God, as well as the promises that were made to
our fathers.* Not only we, *but whoever has loved†*   *Cf. Heb 6:12.
the holy life of the *Koinonia,* has endured *the dis-*   †Cf. 2 Tm 4:8.
grace that was Christ's and put up with sufferings   Heb 11:26.
without wavering; as the Apostle says, *Whoever*
wills to live in devotion to Christ Jesus will likewise
be persecuted.[1]   2 Tm 3:12.

8. *For that reason let us give encouragement*   **Let us encourage**
to each other with these words and let us edify ev- **each other in**
eryone, not merely by word but by good deeds   **all humility**
and the absence of scandal, while renewing our-   1 Th 5:11; 4:18.
selves in *the fruits of the Holy Spirit* so that we   Ga 5:22.
may *appear in the world like those shining lights.*   Ph 2:15.
So all who see us will know that we are the *seed*
that God has blessed,[1] as they see our faith, our   Is 61:9.
knowledge, our gravity in all things, our humili-
ty, and our speech seasoned with salt in the   Cf. Col 4:6.
knowledge of the Scriptures and the love of God.
[Let us] *render to each what is his due: tribute to*
him who has a right to tribute, tax to whom it be-
longs, respect to whom respect is due, honor to
whom honor should go, as the Apostle says, [Let   Rm 13:7.
us be] without human concern or love of vain glory or hypocrisy, but as if it were a matter of an
order from God; being watchful and greatly fear-
ing to be lovers of honors.

For if we become lovers of honors in this age we
oblige God to produce the record of the debt that

Cf. Col 2:14.

Cf. 2 Co 5:3.

Is 26:11(LXX);
Heb 10:27.
stands against us, and the shame of our intimate acts and thoughts at Christ's tribunal before the angels and all the saints, when we shall be naked[2] and shall not have the means of flying elsewhere than toward *the flame that consumes the foes,* nor shall we have the means of covering our shame in any way. On the other hand, if at every moment we place before ourselves our weaknesses and our evil thoughts, if we are sorry for them in this age, we shall escape everlasting shame, the flame and unfailing reproach; we will rejoice in the blessing of our fruits and in the Gospel beati-tudes, *Happy those who now are afflicted, for they shall be comforted,* and so on.[3] For that rea-son, beloved, let us look on *the insults offered to Christ as greater riches than all the pleasure* this world holds with its honors and its eases; that pleasure is but shortlived, like mist or a fugitive shadow.*

Mt 5:5.

Heb 11:26.

*Cf. Jm 4:14;
Ps 144(143):4.

The joy of
approaching the
Lord with a
pure heart
9. Who indeed does not know how sweet puri-ty is and how confident before God and man when one comes near the holy altar, the Lord's body and blood? Shall anyone seek to deny or shall he utterly desire a condemnable impurity if he thinks of the Resurrection Day when the Lord *will transfigure our lowly body into the likeness of his glorious body?* Or again, who is there who has tasted of the simplicity of a pure heart, who has flung himself on the Lord's bosom[1] in the joy of a heart free from faults and uncleanness, and yet will seek out the shades of secret thoughts and the darkening of the face, dulling himself by wicked thoughts and gloating over them? Shall he get drunk with the sleep of death, liking those thoughts because he neglected quickly to cry out

Ph 3:21.

Jn 21:20.

Cf. Lm 4:8.

Cf. Ps 13(12):3.

to God in his heart, *Save me, for the waters are surging in on my soul, I am sinking in the slime beneath me and I cannot help it.*

Ps 69(68):1-2.

10. Therefore, my beloved, who with the sole force of your own will love *the disgrace of the Cross,* let us great and small, be sober and watchful, knowing that *it is a dreadful thing to fall into the hands of the living God.*[1] Let us remember that the sufferings of a bodily illness drive from our mind all things that pertain to this age and that we long for death to be set free from pain. Then, [just think] what the place must be like *where there is grinding of teeth,* unquenchable flame, and where the worm slumbers not![2] Aware besides of the fear that one feels at the Lord's judgement seat, let us strip off the old self, with its works and its thoughts and put on the new self with its behavior,[3] so that with all the saints we may inherit the joy of the kingdom of heaven.

Let us be sober and watchful

Ga 5:11.

Heb 10:31.

Mt 8:12.

Cf. Is 66:24;
Mk 9:44.

Cf. Rm 14:10;
2 Co 5:10.

Col 3:9-10.

11. If we obey a single voice and if we wish that man to have the satisfaction of forgetting his sorrows and his tribulations, let each of us demonstrate the exceedingly wise choice he has made by listening to him who has organized us, without grumbling or any evil design or . . . but let us not permit ourselves to neglect our affairs. Let us not be content to say: 'It is just a question of obedience; if it goes wrong, no matter to us; if it goes right, no matter to us either.'[1] Surely we know that such a thought grows out of the stump of pride and of wickedness. That is the way it was with Onan who, knowing that his seed would not be to his advantage, *spilt it on the ground.* That is also the way someone behaves who, knowing that no congratulations will be his if the matter

Let us listen to Pachomius' recommendations

About 8 words are missing

Gn 38:9.

succeeds, hides it quietly, not caring for it to be known because it does not concern him. Let us take for a model the kindness of the heathen Jethro[2] who suggested the organization of a throng of sixty myriads and brought satisfaction to all the people and to Moses, who walked at the head of the people.

Cf. Ex 18:14-26.

Let us fulfil our tasks with great dilligence

12. Knowing, then, that we toil neither for someone nor for something, but that it is God who has provided us with a place to work, that we may realize that which is to our advantage[1] —whether we are the superior of the community or the one in charge of the service or someone holding any office or even a little one who has been ordered to perform some work or other—let each of us attend to it seven times over with all diligence and with all courageous activity night and day. It is indeed a test[2] that is now established among us so we may show what we are. Let no one perchance say, 'I told him once or twice what he must do and he did not listen; for that reason I will keep still'.

Let us avoid grumbling

13. We must know this: when the Lord put us to the test at the time we freely chose to become sons, we were not indolent in caring for his concerns—indeed, we are sons. Let us not grumble within ourselves while we obey, after he who commands us has refuted our explanations. No, let us not grumble, let us not be disobedient, let us bear no grudge; if we get rough treatment while performing some work, the Lord will grant us perfect tranquility, he will prepare for us in secret our inheritance as sons, he will oblige him who commands us to give us rest once again. If he caused both the fiery flame and the waters to give

rest to those who deserved it, why then will not he cause a man to give his neighbor rest?

Ps 66(65):12.

14. If we are sent to work at one of the brothers' occupations, let us toil away at the work to which we have been sent, even if we are struck, insulted, imprisoned, even if we come back to the monastery spattered with blood from the blows. If we look for compensation for what we have been subjected to, either some solace or some words of praise from human lips — 'You toiled valiantly, we thank you for enduring these great tribulations for us' — such a man makes it plain that he does not really know the Lord. For if he knew him he would know that by being congratulated on his toils by human lips he has deprived himself of the joy that comes from the voice of the Lord who says, *You who have stood by me in my trials, you shall have from me a kingdom like the one my Father has confered on me so that you may eat and drink with me at my table in my kingdom.*[1] Know then, that as you have now dealt with the one who is in your midst to try you — was it me? — so you will deal with him. Certainly the things of God at times divide us in body but not in heart.

Let us accomplish our task even when struck or insulted

Lk 22:29-30.

15. As for the brothers who are sick, let us not be tormented on their behalf, and let them not be discouraged. The merciful God knows what is advantageous for each one of us and he dispenses remedies as he likes, fashioning men for himself that they may inherit the riches of the Saviour's kingdom. Let no one among us say, 'no doubt it is because he is a very wicked man that these tribulations have fallen on him!' He who will say that to himself does not perhaps yet deserve remedy

To be compassionate for the sick

himself. And let no one rejoice to have made another greatly suffer, or be glad that another has fallen sick. That is a great wickedness of the enemy. Truly deserving of pity is the man who finds a place in his heart for that thought. Let us then have a compassionate heart for one another, for the Saviour has said, *Be compassionate, for your father is compassionate.*[1]

Lk 6:36.

About a relative in the community

16. When anyone whose brother is in the monastery comes to the gatehouse desiring to become a monk, he shall spend a month at the gatehouse.[1] His brother shall not go out to him except once a week. But he shall practise the commandment while the little one is on trial, and he shall keep his heart quite distant from him since he is his kinsman, meanwhile keeping watch over his soul, lest after some days it fall into the snare of sadness.[2] And he will be careful as well not to give scandal in the vocation of the *Koinonia*, by an affection according to the flesh but consider instead the Saviour's words, *Who is my mother? Who are my brothers? The one who does the will of my father who is in heaven, he is my brother, my sister and my mother*; He shall consider also the blessing that Moses spoke over Levi, *The one who says to his father and his mother, 'I have not seen them,' and to his brothers that he does not know them, and who has abandoned his children, he has kept your word and has held to your covenant.* Thus behaved the fathers of the *Koinonia*, Apa and Apa Horsiesios.

Mt 12:48.50.

Dt 33:9.

The instruction of novices

17. According to the love of the One who gave him the vocation, the porter shall look after [the novice] with all the salt required. He will acquaint him with the laws of eternal life. He has

renounced his parents, his brothers, his people according to the flesh and the pleasures of this world;[1] therefore, if his father comes and asks those in charge to bring him in, they shall inform him that [the novice's] reply and even the encounter with him has already been made, unless the one who commands those in charge [decides otherwise].[2] In such a case, the one in charge shall declare to [the one who commands], the brother will declare to him, and the novice will declare to his father: 'There is neither affection according to the flesh nor authority according to the flesh in our vocation, but we are all brothers, in accordance with the Saviour's saying, *You are all brothers.*'

Mt 23:8.

18. We are saying this and we are insisting on it in the name of our Lord Jesus Christ in order that we may be steadfast and strong against the storms and squalls of the enemy's wickedness, for we have learned that the Saviour defeats that enemy's devices and destroys the deceitful snares he sets for men. He grants us repentance after our failings, he offers us solace when we consider certain saints who, like us, as such things happen, fell into human failings, and whom God restored to their high rank for the sake of the fear they had of him — such great men as David and Peter and those who are like them. As for sinners, in his kindness he wipes out at once the multitude of their faults by the fear they have for him; such were the publican,[1] she who bathed his feet with her tears, and also those who are like them.

About repentance

Lk 18:13-14.
Lk 7:44.

19. So then, my beloved, we are confident that, thanks to the surpassing love of God for us, the tempests that now rage against us will not be

Temptations are only for a time

longlived, I mean either the storms arising from the passion of fleshly desires or from some other cause. He will give us the means of acquiring that rest of the flesh which we will find no longer at the moment of our anguish. If the occasion is harsh words from those who govern us, does it not occur to us that in making ourselves servants for Christ[1] we are going to feel great confidence in his presence and pardon for our sins when he comes in his glory? If the occasion is a stubborn illness and a prognosis trying our patience — for as yet we see nothing happen that we expect nor do we get any relief from what is attacking us secretly or openly — do we not remember that God the Father even allowed the devil to tempt our Saviour,[2] and that it is written about him, *He is a man wounded all over and knowing how to bear infirmities?*

We know for certain therefore that *the person whom God loves he trains*; and we give heed to the Apostle's words, *We are sunk in tribulation in every way but we are not distressed*;[3] and, *Quarrels outside, fears inside*, and, *I was given a thorn in my flesh, Satan's angel, to beat me*; and, *I dearly love God's law according to my inner self but in my members I see another law that does battle against what is in my heart and makes me captive to the law of sin which is in my members. What a wretched man I am*; and, *The evil which I do not wish, I do.* Though according to the justice that is in the law he is faultless, in what way is he without reproach? By being *Christ's messenger*.[4] Now what he has experienced and written about the failings of those of our kind who had no faith, he did to the end that we should not weary

Cf. 1 Co 7:22.

Cf. Col 3:4.

Cf. Mt 4:1-11.

Is 53:3.

Heb 12:6;
Pr 3:12.

2 Co 4:8.

2 Co 7:5.

2 Co 12:7.

Rm 7:22-24.

Rm 7:19.

Cf. Ph 3:6.

2 Co 5:20.

and that we should not give ourselves up to those
who would devour us, when we answer and say,
'We have been cast away, and we shall no longer
try to be of any use to God.' This is not what the
Scriptures, the breath of God, tell us.

20. Now, we see that some among us, both
great and small, feel a certain resentment after
having promised God to walk by his law, after
having renounced all they had for this vocation,[1]
each according to his strength under the urging
of the Holy Spirit, after making it plain to all who
see them [that] 'We are sons of the holy vocation
of the *Koinonia*',[2] after announcing to others,
'There is no obstacle on the path we have taken',
after instructing others who wish to become
monks, 'Come stay with us, share with us in the
holy commandments God gave to Apa'.[3] Well,
after all that they have tried to turn back, giving
scandal to those who had come to them and to
those who through them had come near God.
They want to put God's gift to scorn and they become unmindful of the fear of him; as it is written, *It is a dreadful thing to fall into the hands of
the living God.*[4] They turn their wisdom into fol-
ly, without reflecting that *our existence is like a
mist that appears for a little while.* They find ex-
cuses for fleshly thoughts and passions; for when
we set about satisfying our desires and when we
resist God's grace, who knows if we shall live or if
we shall avoid some grievous illness? At all events,
we bring it about that what is thrown up in our
heart is excluded from the glory of the cross in accordance with the Gospel of God.

21. That is therefore why we cannot hold back
but we have spoken in this way so that the warn-

Cf. 1 P 5:8.

Some of us
nourish
resentment

Heb 10:31.

Jm 4:14.

Cf. Gal 6:14.

A warning for
all of us

ing from God's side should be for all of us in
general. Should there be anyone who feels resentment in his heart against another man, we declare before God and at the same time in your
midst that we will act in accord with the law Apa
established, from a small commandment to a
great one.[1]

**If our superiors
give scandal**

22. If it is our superiors who give us scandal,
then let us not obey them, and let us not trample
underfoot[1] any rule established by our fathers.
Only let each of us, great or small,[2] be ready to
present a defence to God. He who shall judge the

Ps 9:5.

universe with justice through his only Son Jesus
Christ, will give us his sentence. For we have
promised [to fulfil] God's law, and till now we
have not done so. On the contrary we have each
been negligent in regard of the other, even to the
point of being resentful and of not edifying his

*Cf. Rm 14:19;
    1 Th 5:11.
†Cf. Mt 5:22.

neighbors according to God's commandments.*
Let us recall the Gospel oath† so as not to hate
but rather to love a man who will make known a
transgression.

**God has given
us some
appeasement**
*Cf. 2 Co 1:3.

23. *Let us give thanks to God, the father of
our Lord Jesus Christ,** for having made us also
worthy to receive from him some little joy amid
the overflow of our afflictions. For appeasement
comes to our dejected hearts, thanks to the depth
of our humility and the steadfastness of our faith.

Cf. Rm 14:12;
    1 P 4:5.

We pray earnestly and with tears that God may
grant pity and pardon to all of us, that he may
not reckon up our account; that on the contrary

Cf. Ps 51(50):9.
Cf. Rm 6:4;
    Eph 4:23-24.

he may pay no attention to the sins of any of us;
but that renewal may come to us through his
help, that he may purify us of the evil appetites of
the soul and of the body, that he may make us too

worthy to say, *He has stripped off my sackcloth and wrapped me in gladness.* [1] May he cause each of us to go back to the beginnings of his vocation, that is, to the expectation of the promises God made to our father Apa, to him whose commandments we have promised [to observe], walking truly in fulfilment of the law, that is to say, *being all of one heart,* [2] *toiling for one another, practising brotherly love, compassion and humility,* according to the apostle Peter's words; following one voice alone, and with the conviction of faith putting his words into practice. We know indeed that by listening we become *servants for Jesus' sake,* concerning whom we have heard the Father's voice declare in the Gospels, *This is my well-beloved son; he enjoys my favors. Listen to him.*

Ps 30(29):11.

Ac 4:32.
1 P 3:8.

2 Co 4:5.

Mt 17:5;
Lk 9:35.

24. Knowing then, my beloved, that we have made such a promise before the Lord our God, and that he will ask each of us for an accounting of his promise, of a great one proportionate to his high rank, of a little one proportionate to his lowly position, let us not be negligent nor forgetful of our salvation. On the contrary let us renew ourselves through Christ Jesus who grants us strength. Let us each give his heart to the other, carrying the Cross of Christ; let us truly be his followers, [1] in conformity with what we promised him of our own free will and without constraint.

Let us be mindful of our promise

Cf. Eph 4:23.

Cf. Mt 10:38;
Lk 9:23; 14:27.

25. We rejoice that all those who keep their affliction to themselves did not spread it abroad through the tongue's fire which *infects the whole body* and shows forth the evil of pride growing in a man's heart. Let us rejoice still more over those who attune their hearts to the hearts of each of

Let us keep our affliction to ourselves

Jm 3:6.

them, steering clear of this age's glory which consists in admiring ourselves in what we do, before the appreciation of men, as hardworking or good managers, under pretext of a bootless candor. On the contrary let us keep watch on ourselves lest we hear the reproachful voice of the Lord saying, *They have already had their reward*; and again, as Paul says, *You bring God into contempt by disobeying the law.* As for us, therefore, let us rejoice, we who have been ready with all our hearts to be followers of God, having grasped the power of the word spoken by the Saviour, *The one who humbles himself like this little child is greatest in the kingdom of heaven.*

Mt 6:2.

Rm 2:23.

Mt 18:4.

26. We see as well the fervor of the love of each of us by the calm speech, the manner in which each justifies his neighbor more than himself.

Our love for our neighbor

God's love for men brings it about that salvation and fervor come to us in proportion to the haste each of us makes to be renewed in *the fruits of the Spirit*, to awaken from the slumber of negligence, to be cleansed of the filth of indifference and of the sluggishness of worldly thoughts, and in proportion to the heat of the flame of our continuous recitation night and day. Then the *enemies** grow weak, they who set snares for us[†] to throw us off the way of eternal life,[‡] the way recommended to Apa, the father of the *Koinonia*, by the God of Abraham, Isaac, and Jacob. Through the power of God we begin to bring shame on the wicked forces who are saying in secret, *God has deserted them; let us run and seize them, for there is no one to rescue them.*

Ga 5:22.

*Cf. Ph 1:28.
[†]Cf. Eph 6:11.
[‡]Cf. Ps 16(15):11.

Ps 71(70):11.

The custody of our lips

27. Would that we could make known to those who do not know its sweetness the custody of our

soul, which is *the custody of our lips* when there is
nothing profitable to say, in order to be a cause of
edification for one another and a wholesome example to the novices who have come to us in answer to the Lord's call. We have surrounded ourselves with a saving rampart which is love for
God's law and for the vocation of the *Koinonia*,
so as to walk on this earth after the manner of
heavenly inhabitants and of the life of the august
angels, *so that all those who see our good works
may give glory to God* and may know that we are
disciples of Christ, so as to love one another without hypocrisy.

28. We see all that, we struggle in it, we renew
ourselves, and we glorify the merciful God, for *he
does not deal with us according to our sins nor
punish us according to our iniquities.*[1] On the
contrary, he has *in the multitude of his mercy
changed our mourning into joy, he has stripped
off our sackcloth and wrapped us in gladness.*[2]
It is the pledge of every good thing he promised to
our fathers of the *Koinonia* which he has placed
in us beforehand, that we might not be cast away
from the holy vocation of rebirth. [Of this pledge],
he made us fasten the roots and the stocks, but we
have covered its young shoots by our negligences
and our own whims.

29. And he, the Lord of the universe, Jesus
Christ, Lord of all, would not so forsake us as to
allow to gloat over us those who set up ambushes
for Adam's progeny. On the contrary, he has in
his kindness made a secret call, *Arise, wake up
from the sleep of death*[1] and from the rottenness
of wicked thoughts. And to his angels, mighty
forces which carry out what he says, he has given

Pr 13:3.
Cf. 2 Tm 2:14.
Cf. Rm 14:19.

Mt 5:16.

God's mercy for us

Ps 103(102):10.
Cf. Ps 51(50):3.

Ps 30(29):11.

He is calling us to life

Cf. Ps 25(24):2.

Eph 5:14;
Cf. Eph 2:5.
Cf. Ps 103(102):20.

orders to set us free from the shackles of our sins. It was thus that of old he called to Lazarus who was dead and putrid, *Arise, come out; and the dead man arose and came out, his feet and hands bound with bands and his head wrapped in a shroud. The Lord gave the order: Unbind him,*

Jn 11:43-44.

let him go. Would that we might keep his commandments to the very end and that we might be

Jn 12:2.

found seated at dinner with him, like [Lazarus], in the joy of the kingdom of heaven!

Let us strengthen our brothers
Cf. Rm 5:2; 8:19.

30. Let us pray that when the glory of the sons of God shall be manifested, no accusation may be leveled against any of us, and that none of us may be cut off from the joy of the promises [made to] our fathers, for turning back because of thoughts coming from him who shoots his wicked arrows

Cf. Eph 6:16.

into our hearts.[1]

Cf. Col 1:23.

As for us who rely on faith, as we were taught by our fathers since we were entrusted to them by

Cf. Lk 22:32.

the Lord, it is our duty to strengthen the brothers

\

who have loved the regulations of the *Koinonia* with all their heart. Night and day, if it can be done without scandal, let us not fail to encourage them with the wholesome teachings of our fathers and with holy knowledge. Let us fear greatly lest for negligence a soul which could have been saved be brought to destruction.[2] Let us also keep in mind *the Good Shepherd laying down his life for*

Cf. Jn 10:11.

his sheep.[3] Even if we should happen to be ill-treated by someone greater than ourselves or by those who have been monks before us, let us not turn back to avoid striking the stranger who scoffed

Cf. 1 S 17:10.

at the multitude of Israel. Let us control ourselves in the face of insults as did the mighty David. Let us refuse Saul's sword and his human clothing, lest we trip over it; but in the face of wickedness let us take hold on youth and let us, in the name of the Lord of Hosts, strike that which embitters and upsets the brothers, with the courage of faith and with humility. Let us reply without wrath.[1] Let us strip the mask off those who spout words that bring harm and disaster to souls. Let us also batter the ramparts of the crowds with gentleness. Let us chasten the wicked thoughts of our hearts, even keeping silence and having before our mind's eye the struggle of those who have finished their battle with distinction.

Thus it is that Paul, who endured in his body the sufferings of Christ, has taught each and everyone of us how to live: *They were tried by taunts and blows, and as well by chains and prisons; they were stoned, they were sawn in two,* and so on. Of himself he says, *I am content to be in the midst of infirmities, insults, destitution, persecutions, distress for Christ.* For, the last end of every saint and of every father of the *Koinonia* has shown us all clearly that they were *Christ's messengers.*

31. Therefore, let none of us be fainthearted and say, 'Elsewhere away goes a true quietness', for is it not true that quietness of thoughts proceeds from a sound faith? Indeed, who will ever be able to incline man's heart toward an excellent action and a thought that belongs to heaven, except Him who brings men his Christ? Or what faithful man will ever be able to say, 'It is Paul, or Apollos, or Cephas who is saving me'? Or has anyone failed to hear the Lord saying to his chosen disciples, *If you loved me you would rejoice in my going to my father, for my father is*

Cf. 1 S 17:39.

Cf. 1 S 17:43, 49.

Cf. 2 Co 1:5;
Col 1:24.

Heb 11:36-37.

2 Co 12:10.

2 Co 5:20.

Let us not be
fainthearted

Cf. 1 Co 3:4.

Jn 14:28.
Jn 16:7.

Cf. Ga 6:3.
1 P 5:9.

2 Tm 2:19;
Cf. Nb 16:5,26.

*Mt 9:17;
Lk 5:37.

Rm 8:29.

Let us not be afraid of men's reproaches
Cf. 1 Tm 2:6.

Mt 28:20.

Mt 5:11.
Jn 15:20.

Jn 15:18.

Let us put our trust in God

1 Co 3:5.

greater than I; and again, *If I go away, the Comforter will come to you.* We are saying this without trying to compare our worthless words with those that carry so much weight, and we by no means reckon ourselves now to be something. But let us be *strong in faith*, and let us make firm by our obedience the law's interior rampart. This is the way *the Lord knows his own*, and has entrusted them to the grace of his Holy Spirit. *No one puts new wine into old wineskins.* * *Those indeed whom he knows he has predestined them to share in the likeness of the image of his son.*

32. Then we know that no [mere] man has given us such a gift, but that it is indeed the Lord who has given himself up to save all men, and that it is he who has said, *I am with you always, even to the end of time.*[1] Therefore let us not be at all fainthearted, neither let us be afraid of men's reproaches. Let us not lose heart if they insult us, for the Lord has just encouraged us, *Happy are you when people abuse you, when they cast over you all kinds of wicked and lying words about you on my account; rejoice and be glad, for your reward will be great in heaven.*[2] And again, *If they persecuted me, they will persecute you.* And yet again, *If the world hates you, know that it hated me before you.*[3]

33. We know then for certain that his Spirit will dwell in us and will give us power. Let us therefore not become discouraged, neither let us think that any human image will provide us with consolation and advancement. In fact, we have just heard Paul say, *What is a Paul, what is an Apollos*, what is a Cephas? We have learned as well, *Even if a woman exists who can forget the*

fruits of her womb and not take pity on them,
even so will I not forget you, Jerusalem, says the
Lord. Now, Jerusalem is every soul that has be-   Is 49:15.
come the dwelling place of the Spirit of God. We   Cf. Eph 2:22.
have also heard the great prophet Elijah com-
plaining against Israel, and God did not act according to Elijah's thoughtlessness. Jonah God re-   Rm 11:2-4.
proached, for God had not acted in accord with
Jonah's disgust over his people's wickedness. [He   Jon 4.
reproached] also the disciples who said, *Let fire*
come down from heaven and burn up those who
did not welcome you. Let us, therefore, learn   Lk 9:54.
from this that all flesh is earth and ashes, as we
are assured by Abraham, friend of God; only   Gn 18:27.
God's bounty endures. Therefore let us lean upon
the Lord; he will grant his bounty to the men who
will become his dwelling-place.

34. When we *exchange the glory of imperish-*   **Let us not look**
able God for the images of perishable men, truly   **for human glory**
we affirm that if the weaknesses of each and every   Rm 1:23.
person, which are known to God, were revealed,
we should be hard put indeed to answer each
other. It is for that reason that we urge you not to
think of one another as different from what we
see, although in point of fact the full reality of
our weakness is not mutually apparent. Indeed,
God conceals us from one another in time of
weakness, while at the time of glory—which is
God's glory—he clothes us with it. Now, therefore, who but He alone can know the measure of
God's kindness? Let us therefore acknowledge
our weakness and praise God to whom glory is
due and say, even we, *If we climb into heaven,*
you are there; go down to the depths of hell, you
are there with me; if I take the wings of the morn-

ing, and if I abide at the seas' horizon, truly your

Ps 139(138):8-10. *hand is there.* For we have just heard him say, *I*
Jr 23:24. *fill heaven, I fill earth.*[1] And again, *I will dwell there, I will walk there, I will be their God, and*
2 Co 6:16, 18;
Lv 26:11-12. *they shall be my people, says the Lord, the Almighty.*

Let us be imitators of Pachomius

35. So then, having understood the exact meaning of all this according to the true knowledge of the Scriptures, the breath of God, let us be imitators of Apa Pachomius' life. Let us acquire his confidence in this age and the next.

Cf. Ps 25(24):2. Let us put our trust in the Lord, for he it is who comforts us and encourages us. He it is who always gives us strength, *to him* [it is] *and to the Word of his grace* [that] *we have given ourselves over.* [He it is] *who has power to build us up and*
Ac 20:32. *to give us an heritage among all the saints.*[1]

Let us choose the vocation of the *Koinonia*

36. Let us choose the part of the vocation of the holy *Koinonia* and mutual love with everyone, seeing the attitude of the Fathers of the *Koinonia* the great desire that shone in all their hearts for the love of the *Koinonia*, and the love which had previously been rooted in them. [That love] has now by Christ's grace come to light after we ourselves had shrouded it with the veil of our negligence, while through our lack of fear we had quenched the warmth of the Holy Spirit who dwells within us through mercy and not because
Cf. Tt 3:5. of our works.[1]

Let us repent, be watchful, and give thanks
Cf. Ps 35(34):19.

37. God, who is merciful, has not forgotten us to the point that the wicked one might rejoice at our loss. On the contrary, in his love he wakens us from the sleep of death, and in his mercy he goes on prodding us day by day, saying to our hearts, *Wake up, you who sleep, rise from the dead, and*

Christ will shine on you. Knowing the great grace   Eph 5:14.
we have inherited—for *he has not dealt with us
according to our sins, and he has not punished us
according to our iniquities*—let us repent, let us   Ps 103(102):10.
be watchful and let us give thanks to Him saying,
*Blessed be you, Lord, for having taken me as
your own, and not having gladdened my enemies
in my regard*; and let us repeat Jeremiah's words,   Ps 30(29):2.
*At the end of my captivity I repented, then I
sighed over the day of my shame.* For we know,   Jr 31:19.
and Isaiah has taught us, that *If we return and if
we groan we shall be saved and we shall know
where we stand in times of trust in what are but
vain things* and in wicked thoughts that are not   Is 30:15.
from God.

38. *Let us search our ways and examine our*   **Let us seek
footprints; let us return to the Lord our God; let   **God**
*us lift up our hearts on our hands before God who
is in heaven.*[1] And when our heart is minded to go   Lm 3:40-41.
away from the Lord, let us turn back and seek
him out ten times over. The Holy Spirit has taught
us indeed in the Scriptures, the breath of God, to
seek him out with our whole heart, saying to us
through Isaiah, *Seek God, and if you find him,
call to him while he is still near you. Let the wicked man abandon his way and the lawless man
give up his designs; let him return to the Lord
who will take pity on him; for he will grant you
full pardon of your sins.*   Is 55:6-7.

39. Knowing what God's mercy is, therefore,   **Let us not
and his forgiveness, we must not spoil days and   be negligent**
days on end, we must not be negligent through
lack of fear, becoming slack and quenching the
fire of the Holy Spirit and the love of the law of
freedom which he has called forth in us, on the

excuse of lacking the means of bodily subsistence. By this our Creator teaches us for our soul's salvation, as it is written, *Our salvation is in time of distress*; and, *We are sunk in tribulations in every way but we are not distressed*; and, *Tribulation brings patience. Through steadfastness therefore*, says the Lord, *you will win your souls.*

40. Because of this, let us not allow what is according to the flesh to persecute what is according to the spirit;* neither let us, using the body as pretext, quench the lamp that has been lit in us. We must therefore not contradict to the point of thinking or of speaking contrary to the faith in the Holy Scriptures. But *those whom he loves, God chastises*; he afflicts and puts them to the test in every thing to see *whether they will keep his commandments or not.* Yet, what God is looking for in us are *the fruits of the Holy Spirit*; we must not be negligent concerning them, for it is about them that we shall be questioned.

41. Let us keep it in mind to stir up one another, so that we may bring forth all our fruits into things pleasing to God. Let us be aware that God is concerned with us, to the end that we may work at that which is needful to the body and that we may become a pure temple for God.[1] Now then, my brothers, consider that none of us should be faced with exclusion at the time of the joyful confidence, on the day of the manifestation of the Lord's glory. *A little while, indeed and truly, the one who is coming will have come; he will not delay; my righteous one will live by faith.* It must not be that because of faintheartedness or of some whirlwind there should be any lack in our perfect free choice of the vocation of the holy

---

Is 32:2.

2 Co 4:8.

Rm 5:3.

Lk 21:19.

Let us cultivate the fruits of the Holy Spirit
*Cf. Ga 4:29.

Cf. Ps 18(17):28.

Heb 12:6;
Pr 3:12.

Dt 8:2.

Ga 5:22.

Let us encourage one another
Col 1:10.

Cf. 1 P 5:7.

Cf. 1 Co 3:16-17.

Cf. 1 P 4:13.

Heb 10:37-38.

Koinonia, by the grace granted to us by God, not according to our works, but in consequence of a gift. . . .

Eph 2:8-9.

18 pages of the manuscript are missing

42. . . . so as not to let him speak words to his neighbor with calm and with grace seasoned with the salt of the Scriptures, to the point that the heart of the speaker is still farther away because of the flame of his faintheartedness, which is mingled with the haughtiness of him he is addressing.[1] In this latter they call forth indifference and discouragement toward the gifts of the divine grace that has touched him. It was however through that man that the Lord called him and that the Saviour persuaded him to scorn all this age's desires and to follow Him in the form of the humility and of the love for Him he sees in us. This is therefore why we give our lives for one another, and [we also bring forth] the other *fruits of the Holy Spirit* which he has brought into being in us through *ascesis* in all things including the desires of the flesh. After we have involved ourselves in all these desires, then, by negligence in our attitude and by our speech full of mercy in a perfect love, we appear different from one another; and this causes indifference and disaster in those whom the Lord has edified through us.

43. For this reason we must avoid scandalizing one another within the vocation to which we are called, lest we be in danger not only by reason of our own sins and negligences, but also by reason of other men the Lord has edified, for having in any way given scandal to them ⟨and to⟩ those who are outside the vocation of the holy *Koinonia*.

To give our lives for one another

Cf. Col 4:6.

Mt 19:21.

Cf. 1 Jn 3:16.
Ga 5:22.

Cf. 1 Jn 4:18.

Let us not scandalize one another

Cf. Eph 4:21.

Cf. 1 Co 3:1-2.

Cf. Is 54:13;
  Jn 6:45.

Ps 26(25):2.
Ps 139(138):24.

Cf. 1 Th 2:7.

Let us then pay heed to what we hear in the Holy Scriptures; let us know the teaching of Christ the true Doctor; and let us receive with joy the doctrine which flows from his goodness. For during the time we were little ones he fed us with the food of little ones;[1] and when we began to grow up in the rebirth, he wanted to nourish us with the food of truth. In his great love for us he neither put us to the test nor overburdened us, but he wanted to make it known that we are God's pupils and that we are sons of those who ask him, *Test me, Lord, put me to the test, cleanse with fire my loins and my heart, see whether there exists in me a pernicious path.*

44. Truly, we shall be most grateful in our diligence in knowing his mercy. From the time we were little ones, that is, when we were not yet fit to wage the war of the cross, he has warmed us up. . . .[1]

22 pages are missing

45. . . . of the saints, which our father Apa did and taught to the brothers according to their rules. Those who obeyed him reproduced that man's behavior in the end of times.

46. Now hear a case of this kind in our father Jonas of Thmoušons, a man whom Apa regarded as of great fame, a man who was worthy of high regard for his ascetical practices and his courage. . . .

11 lines are missing

... to those who urged him on while being his inferiors on every count. That was precisely why the enemy gained nothing from him, and why the son of iniquity did not outwit him at the time of the disorder that arose when the powerful men rose up against Apa Horsiesios, the Lord's anointed.

Cf. Ps 89(88):22.

47. My beloved, since we have deserved to be called to share in the formers' inheritance, let us make our own their behavior that we may be found to be sons of our fathers . . . .

The rest is missing

Notes to the Instructions of Theodore

Notes to the Second Instruction
(Theod. Instr. 2)

Theod. Instr. 2: 1   [1]In another Instruction, Theodore speaks of the holy and true *Koinonia* that has as its author after the apostles Apa Pachomius (Theod. Instr. 3: 5). In a prayer to God, in SBo 108, Pachomius also attributes to God the institution of the *Koinonia*: 'Lord . . . who have assembled this holy place, namely this holy *Koinonia* which was established from the beginning by our fathers, those holy apostles whom you have chosen and loved . . .'.

Theod. Instr. 2: 3   [1]Theodore makes an allusion to the same text in SBo 198.
     [2]For the rest of this paragraph the Coptic text is very mutilated. We translate it as it has been reconstructed by Lefort in his edition. But the reconstruction is conjectural in many points.
     [3]The figure of thirty-eight which is a restoration of the Coptic text by Lefort (*CSCO*-159, p. 39, n. 13 and *CSCO*-160, p. 39, n. 12), corresponds closely enough to the chronology given by the author of the Coptic Life which gives thirty-nine years for the length of Pachomius' life as a monk. But it is very difficult to accept that figure as accurate. See SBo 123, n. 4.

Notes to the Third Instruction
(Theod. Instr. 3)

Theod. Instr. 3: 1   [1]This quotation will be repeated throughout this Instruction as a leitmotiv; see ¶¶2, 6, 19, and 40.

Theod. Instr. 3: 2   [1]See SBo 39; G[1] 39.
     [2]Cf. SBo 65 (= G[1] 70) where an old man, seeing Pachomius going down with some of the brothers into a well to clean it, said: 'Is this old man taking the children of men down into that well in order to kill them?'.
     [3]Cf. Pach. Instr. 1: 42 where the following reproach comes from Christ's lips: 'Did I not bless you with my body and blood as food of life?'.

Theod. Instr. 3: 3   ¹The same text is quoted again below, ¶5, and also in Hors. Test. 42.
   ²This quotation also recurs below, ¶39.

Theod. Instr. 3: 4   ¹Note that the two members of Eph 6:16 quoted in this ¶ are given in inverted order. Eph 6:16-17 is quoted also in Hors. Test. 19, and there is a clear allusion to it in SBo 14 and here below, ¶30.

Theod. Instr. 3: 5   ¹2 Co 1:3-4 is used again below, ¶23, where the second part of the text is paraphrased. 2 Co 1:5 is quoted in ¶30.
   ²On the connection of the *Koinonia* with the apostles, see above, Theod. Instr. 2: 1, n. 1; on the role of Pachomius as founder of the *Koinonia*, see Theod. Letter 1: 2, n. 4.
   ³The same text is quoted in Am. Letter 3, and we find an allusion to it in G¹ 49.
   ⁴We find the same preoccupation with not scandalizing the brothers in Pach. Instr. 1: 40.
   ⁵Cf. Hors. Instr. 1: 2, where Horsiesios says that 'the life of our holy father is an angelic life perfuming the whole world'; and the author of S¹ 25 quotes in reference to Pachomius 2 Co 2:15: 'We are the fragrance of the Christ of God'.
   ⁶The same quotation occurs below, ¶27.
   ⁷This text is quoted also in Hors. Test. 43 where, as well as in the present ¶, the beginning of the verse in Is 33:22 ('The Lord is our judge') is replaced by the 'The Lord is our father', which is from Is 64:8. It is quoted also in SBo 101, where it starts with the 'The Lord is our God'.
   ⁸We read the same recommendation with the same quotation in Hors. Test. 5. Ph 1:29 is quoted also in Am. Letter 34.
   ⁹Heb 11:37-38 is quoted often. See above, Pach. Instr. 1: 13, note 3.
   ¹⁰The same quotation occurs in Hors. Test. 50.

Theod. Instr. 3: 6   ¹The same quotation occurs in Pach. Instr. 1: 29.
   ²A similar recommendation, with the same quotation, comes in Pach. Instr. 1: 21.
   ³This text is quoted about Pachomius, in S¹ 3.
   ⁴This text is quoted in Hors. Fragm. 1: 2.

Theod. Instr. 3: 7   ¹2 Tm 3:12 is quoted in Paral. 17, in the description of the vision Pachomius had about the future of the *Koinonia*.

Theod. Instr. 3: 8   ¹The same quotation occurs in Hors. Test. 48.
   ²Cf. Pach. Instr. 1: 33: 'In the world you went about praised as one of the elect and when you arrive in the valley of Josaphat, place of judgement, you are found naked'. Cf. also *ibidem*, ¶38.
   ³The same quotation occurs in Hors. Test. 41.

Theod. Instr. 3: 9   ¹See a similar allusion to Saint John in Theod. Instr. 1: 2.

Theod. Instr. 3:10   ¹The same quotation occurs in ¶20, in G¹ 132 (in an Instruction by Theodore) and in Hors. Test. 10.
   ²The same biblical reminiscence is found in SBo 107 and G¹ 96.
   ³The theme of conversion, with reference to putting off the old self and putting on the new (Col 3:10.12), is central in pachomian spirituality. For example, in SBo 17, it is said of Pachomius that he strove to imitate Palamon

'in every work that *he put on himself*'; in G[1] 65 Theodore is said to have refused to treat his own brother Paphnouti as a brother according to the flesh, because 'he had already *put off the old man*'. Cf. also Pach. Instr. 1: 30.

Theod. Instr. 3:11 [1]Cf. Hors. Test. 9: 'Let him do what he wishes, it does not concern me.'
[2]In the Coptic text *Jethro* is spelled *Iothor*.

Theod. Instr. 3:12 [1]With Lefort (*CSCO*-159, p. 45, n. 70; *CSCO*-160, p. 46, n. 76) we read *nobre* instead of *nobe*.
[2]*Dokimasia*: see *Didachè*, c. 16,5: τότε ἥξει ἡ κτίσις τῶν ἀνθρώπων εἰς τὴν πύρωσιν τῆς δοκιμασίας.

Theod. Instr. 3:14 [1]Lk 22:30 is quoted in Theod. Instr. 2: 1.

Theod. Instr. 3:15 [1]The same quotation comes in SBo 142.

Theod. Instr. 3:16 [1]Cf. Pr. 49.
[2]Compare this with the manner in which Theodore received his brother (SBo 38; G[1] 65) and also with the manner in which Pachomius received his sister (SBo 27; G[1] 32).

Theod. Instr. 3:17 [1]Cf. Pr. 49 and S[10] 2.
[2]Cf. Pr. 53.

Theod. Instr. 3:18 [1]The mercy of God toward the Publican is also mentioned in Paral. 10 and in Hors. Reg. 12.

Theod. Instr. 3:19 [1]Cf. Hors. Test. 19 where all the brothers are said to be 'subject to a free servitude (*liberae seruituti*). See also Hors. Letter 3: 1.
[2]Pachomius also refers to the Lord's temptations in Pach. Instr. 1: 56.
[3]Text quoted again below, ¶39 and in Inst. 18.
[4]Text quoted again below, ¶30 about the saints and the fathers of the *Koinonia*.

Theod. Instr. 3:20 [1]'. . . having renounced all they had for this vocation'; on the place of renunciation in pachomian spirituality, see Pach. Instr. 1: 41, n. 1.
[2]Cf. below, ¶27 and Hors. Test. 23: 'We shall, therefore, love one another and show that we are truly the servants of our Lord Jesus Christ and sons of Pachomius, and disciples of the *Koinonia*'.
[3]'. . . the holy commandments God gave to Apa'; cf. Hors. Test. 28: 'If these are the commandments of God, which he handed down to us through our Father'; *ibidem*, ¶46: 'Let us not abandon the law of God, which our father received from Him and handed down to us'.
[4]See above, ¶10, n. 1.

Theod. Instr. 3:21 [1]Cf. above, Theod. Instr. 2: 3: 'let us observe his commandments, from the least to the more important'.

Theod. Instr. 3:22 [1]With Lefort we correct *hôn* into *hôm*, although it does not give a meaning entirely consistent with the rest of the ¶. But it is still more difficult to find an acceptable meaning for *hôn*.

²Cf. Hors. Test. 23: 'Brothers, let us be equal from the least to the greatest'.

Theod. Instr. 3:23   ¹The same quotation occurs in Am. Letter 28, in Hors. Test. 42, and below, ¶28.
²Ac 4:32 if fully quoted in S¹ 11 as the model for the way of life of the *Koinonia.* See also SBo 194; Hors. Reg. 51 and Hors. Test. 50.

Theod. Instr. 3:24   ¹On the importance of the theme of carrying the cross in pachomian spirituality, see Pach. Instr. 1: 19, n. 1.

Theod. Instr. 3:28   ¹The same quotation occurs again below, ¶37.
²This text is quoted also in Am. Letter 28 and Hors. Test. 42.

Theod. Instr. 3:29   ¹This text is again applied to the resurrection from the death of sin, below, ¶37 and in Pach. Instr. 1: 6. See also G¹ 62.

Theod. Instr. 3:30   ¹See above, ¶4, n. 1.
²Cf. Hors. Test. 14: 'Let no one perish through your fault.' See also the description of Pachomius' care for the brothers, in S¹ 25: 'He also fashioned, as well as he could, each soul individually and he strove hard so that if anyone did turn away from him, no one else would be better able to bring him back to the work of God. He acted in this way lest he lose someone he could not save while another person could . . .'.
³Hors. Test. 17 also gives the Good Shepherd as an example to the superiors; and G¹ 54 describes Pachomius as the servant of the Good Shepherd visiting the monastery day and night.

Theod. Instr. 3:32   ¹Mt. 28:20 is quoted, with various interpretations and applications, in SBo 189, G¹ 135 and twice in Paral 18.
²Mt 5:11 is quoted also in SBo 186 (= G¹ 142), and there is an allusion to it in Pach. Instr. 1: 23.
³The same quotation occurs in Hors. Test. 41.

Theod. Instr. 3:34   ¹Note the same notion of the omnipresence of God, and the same quotation in Pach. Letter 3: 13 and Pach. Instr. 1: 25.

Theod. Instr. 3:35   ¹The same quotation occurs in Hors. Test. 56.

Theod. Instr. 3:36   ¹Pach. Letter 5: 9 speaks likewise of the reward that the saints receive 'not according to righteous actions of their own, but according to His own mercy.'

Theod. Instr. 3:38   ¹The same text is quoted entirely in Hors. Test. 49 and partially in Pach. Letter 10: 1; Hors. Reg. 11; Hors. Test. 4. See also Pach. Instr. 1: 26.

Theod. Instr. 3:41   ¹1 Co 3:16-17 is often quoted; see Pach. Fragm. 1: 2, n. 1.

Theod. Instr. 3:42   ¹Because of the defective beginning of the text, the meaning of this whole ¶ remains obscure.

Theod. Instr. 3:43   ¹1 Co 3:1-2 is quoted in S¹ 11 where Pachomius is described as establishing step by step a form of common life.

Theod. Instr. 3:44   ¹This text of Saint Paul is applied to Pachomius in the account of his death (SBo 118). See also SBo 58.

letter of our father theodore to all the monasteries about the passover

(theod. letter 1)

Text: Boon,
pp. 105-106

1. Close at hand is the solemnity of the Unleavened Bread, when it is time to celebrate the Passover, about which Moses gave this precept to the people coming out of Egypt: *You shall eat it very quickly.* The righteous king Josiah also celebrated the Passover with great care in his days, and the account of his zeal has come down to us. The Apostle also has this to say about it: *Christ, our Passover, has been sacrificed.* In Him *therefore let us celebrate the feast,* as we have been commanded.

The Passover is at hand

Ex 12:11.

2 Ch 35:1-19.

1 Co 5:7.

2. *Put a girdle around your waist and the sandals of the Gospel on your feet, having your staves in your hands with your lamps lit,*[1] so that we may be able to eat the Passover hastily. Let us go *up to Jerusalem**[2] *six days before the Passover,*† and let us sanctify ourselves in order to celebrate the holy day in holiness, *in purity and truth, having got rid of evil and wickedness.*[3] This is the commandment we have received from the Apostle and from our Father who founded the life of the *Koinonia.*[4]

Let us go up to Jerusalem
Ex 12:11;
Lk 12:35;
Eph 6:15.

*Jn 11:55.
†Jn 12:1.

1 Co 5:8.

3. Let us all assemble together in peace, in compliance with rules which should not be for-

Let us all assemble

123

saken. Let no one of us desire to stay in his monastery if this has not been decided by the superiors. Likewise let no one come to join the assembly except by order of the superiors.

Exhortation to the superiors

4. As for us who are seen to be the masters of the brothers and to teach them their rules of life, let us not allow them to stay home without serious necessity, lest the assembly of the Passover be forsaken by our fault and we be found guilty of depriving the precepts of our Father of any value. Let us rather consider his writings as the norm of truth, and glorify God *who made his families like flocks, at the sight of which the righteous rejoice and all wickedness must harden its heart.*[5]

Ps 107(106): 41-42.

Exhortation to all the brothers

5. Let us, the elders of the sons of Israel, with our seconds, all come to the Passover and let no one be found remaining behind without fulfilling the rules of our Father. Likewise, let the stewards of the monasteries, the housemasters and all the classes of brothers, let all the members come into one body to build the temple of God. Let us assemble in peace and harmony, and so fulfill the aim of the saints and the rules of our Father.

The catechumens

6. As for the catechumens[6] in the monasteries who are expecting the awesome remission of sins and the grace of the spiritual mystery, let them be taught by you that they must weep and lament their past sins and prepare themselves for the sanctification of their souls and bodies, so that they may bear the reception of the Lord Saviour's blood and body, the very thought of which is awesome.[7]

Our Father's precepts

7. You know very well the other things you have to do to prepare yourselves at the proper

time, and it is not necessary to remind you of them by letter. Our Father has ordered them.

8. We and all the brothers who are with us wholeheartedly greet you with all the brothers who are in your monasteries.

Greetings

LETTER OF THEODORE

II

(Theod. Letter 2)

1. The time has come[1] for *Judah to celebrate his feasts and carry out his vows,*[2] that *the Lord's portion may be with his people Jacob, his share of inheritance [with]*[3] *Israel,*[4] *so that he may suffice for them in a time of burning thirst in the desert.* He said indeed, *Behold, those who serve me shall eat, but you, you will be hungry; behold, those who serve me shall drink, but you, you will be thirsty; behold, those who serve me shall rejoice, but you, you will be covered with shame; behold, those who serve me will exult with gladness, but you, you will cry out in the sadness of your heart and you will howl in the anguish of your spirit.*[5] We know then that at any time[6] he must make a whip of cords and chase all those who sell in the temple.[7]

2. Thus we acknowledge that God will not forget the race of Judah with whom he once concluded his covenant, as it is written, *If heaven rises up higher, says the Lord, and if the firmament lowers itself to the level of the earth, I will not reject the race of Israel for all that they have done before me.*[8] After this they too will say, *If the Lord turns back our captivity, we will be like persons consoled. Then our mouth will fill itself with joy and our tongue with gladness;* as it is also written, *The springs of water will not disappear from*

Na 2:1(1:15).

Dt 32:9-10.

Is 65:13-14.

Cf. Jn 2:15.

Jr 31:37(38:35).

Ps 126(125):1-2.

127

Jr 18:14.

Mt 24:35;
Mk 13:31;
Lk 21:33.
Ps 62(61):12.

the rock, nor the snow from Lebanon, and the
water will not withdraw itself, driven violently by
the wind. And again, *Heaven and earth will pass
away, but my words will not pass away.* Let us reflect on this and scrutinize it three times; *Power
belongs to God, and his is the mercy.*

3. Therefore let us now also put into practice
the commandments of our Father, as well as his
precepts and his ordinances, which he drew for us
from the tradition of the saints.[9] Let us, as he
commanded us, take care of the remission[10]
which acting as a mystery causes forgiveness, pur-
ification, and a healthy conscience. So let us
make an effort in this way to gather in a single
place according to the custom of all the established [rules],[11] and to come to a single place at
Phbow on the first of Mesore,[12] so that we begin
in this way to spend[13] in . . . that which is pre-
scribed to us, after you have finished till the first
of Mesore in all things, either the buying or the
selling. In order to begin . . . the first of Mesore
for the new year.[14]

4. And so, make some effort, that no negligence take place; fulfil all your customs in the
usual manner. But let us take care of this great
word from Moses: *Be watchful, do not allow a
hidden word to come to your heart, that is to say,
an evil word, so that you may say: the year of remission is near.*[15] If therefore, it is not said to us
also, *Do not prevent your hand from giving to
your poor brother or to the needy,*[16] we will in return be told, *May your buying and your selling
. . . just before God and men.*[17] Then, when it
will be asked of us, we can swear without fear, so
that we may not incur judgement on the day of the

Dt 15:9.

Dt 15:7.

visitation because of buying and selling. Rather
may the declaration you proffer be sincere in
your conscience before God; it is the seal of sin-
lessness. Then our Father in the other age will be
able to witness for us, 'This is how I have commanded them'. For it is written, *He is our mediator*[18] *before God, so that we may be saved from all
sins*[19] . . . by the truth . . . we and our seed . . . for   Cf. 1 Jn 2:1-2.
ever.[20]

Notes to the Letters of Theodore

Notes to the First Letter
(Theod. Letter 1)

Theod. Letter 1   [1]This is a very interesting combination of texts: the mention of
the girdle around the waist, the sandals and the staff comes from Ex 12:11, but
the mention of the lamps comes from the parallel text of Lk 12:35. Moreover,
the sandals mentioned in Ex 12:11 become here the 'sandals of the Gospel'
(*calciamentis euangelicis*) under the influence of Eph 6:15. Lk 12:35-37 is
quoted twice by Horsiesios: see Hors. Test 19 (Lk 12:35-37) and Hors. Letter
3: 1 (Lk 12:35-36).
   [2]Horsiesios uses this text in the same manner in Hors. Letter 4: 2.
   [3]This text also is used by Horsiesios in Hors. Letter 4: 3. Horsiesios may have
had this Letter of Theodore in front of him, since he writes (Hors. Letter 4: 5):
'let us remember our father Theodore . . . who wrote to us some [. . .]'.
   [4]*Pater noster a quo coenobiorum uita fundata est* is very similar to Hors.
Test. 12: *Pater noster qui prius instituit coenobia*. In both cases we translate
the plural *coenobia* by the singular *Koinonia*, since there is little doubt that
the Coptic original had *Koinonia*. In the Greek of G[1] τὸ κοινόβιον corresponds always to the *Koinonia* of the parallel Coptic texts, and means either
the whole pachomian congregation (see Halkin, pp. 11,21; 23,17; 25,9; 36,19;
54,11; 66,36; 74,1; 78,13; 81,4) or its way of life (see Halkin, pp. 15,15; 17,2;
77,32; 78,28). It never means a *coenobium* or local monastery. The word is absent from Am. Letter. In Paral. it is used as in G[1] (see Halkin, pp. 126,20;
132,10) except for one instance where it is used in the plural, and with the
meaning 'the *Koinonia*' (Halkin, p. 141,21), as in the *Pachomiana latina*. The
plural *coenobia*, in Jerome's translation, here and in Hors. Test. 12, must be
considered a stylistic variant. Theodore himself uses the singular in a very
similar passage that has been preserved in Coptic: ' . . . the holy and true
Koinonia that has for its author . . . Apa Pachomius' (Theod. Instr. 3: 5).
   [5]Ps 107(106):41-42 is quoted three times by Horsiesios: Hors. Letter 1: 3; 4:
5; and Hors. Test. 13.
   [6]There were a number of catechumens in the pachomian monasteries. Each
year those who had been 'catechized' received baptism during the Easter
celebration, for which all the brothers of all the monasteries assembled at
Phbow.

[7]The same attitude of 'holy fear' in the presence of the Eucharist is expressed in Hors. Reg. 14: 'About the mystery of our salvation: When we are summoned to it, let us prepare in great fear'. On that attitude in early christian spirituality, see J. Quasten, 'Mysterium tremendum. Eucharistische Frömmigkeits-auffassung des vierten Jahrhunderts', in *Vom christlichen Mysterium* (Düsseldorf, 1951) 66-75.

Notes to the Second Letter
(Theod. Letter 2)

Theod. Letter 2   [1]This beginning repeats the beginning of Pachomius' seventh letter, which is also a letter of convocation to the general assembly of all the brothers at the end of the year, in the month of *Mesore*. About that meeting, see SBo 71, n. 2 and 3.

[2]Na 2:1(1:15) is quoted also by Horsiesios in a letter which may also be a convocation to the general assembly of the month of *Mesore*; see Hors. Letter 3: 2.

[3]We follow Quecke's translation: '... damit der Teil des Herrn mit seinem Volke ...' (H. Quecke, 'Ein Brief von einem Nachfolger Pachoms', p. 432). De Vogüé's translation is also possible: '... la portion de son héritage Israël'. The exact meaning of the Coptic sentence remains uncertain, because of the absence of a conjunction before 'his share'. See H. Quecke, *loc. cit.*, p. 429.

[4]Dt 32:9 is quoted also in Hors. Test. 48.

[5]The same text is quoted in a slightly abbreviated form in Hors. Test. 22, where Horsiesios threatens damnation to those who violate the rules of renunciation of personal material possessions.

[6]The expression *ša ouoeiš nim* could also be translated by 'till a certain time' or 'at a certain time'. There is in this Letter a particular use of the preposition *ša*. Its normal meaning, which is 'till' does not seem satisfactory here. H. Quecke ('Ein Brief von...', p. 428, with note 6) suggests that the meaning could be 'at'. See also H. Quecke, 'Eine Handvoll pachomianischer Texte', pp. 223-224.

[7]Jn 2:15 is also quoted by Horsiesios in an appeal to personal poverty; see Hors. Test. 28.

[8]Hors. Test. 37 uses this text to give the brothers confidence in God's mercy.

[9]Pach. Letter 7: 1 also refers to 'custom' and to 'the early prescriptions'.

[10]According to the few mentions of it found in the Lives (see SBo 71, notes 2 and 3; SBo 144, note 3), the general assembly of the month of *Mesore* had a purely administrative character. In *La liturgie*, pp. 366-370, we therefore understood the Coptic word *ouêt* in the material sense of rendering accounts, and we considered the mention of remission of sins that we find in Jer. Pref. 8 and Pr. 27 as well as in the title of Pach. Letter 7, as Jerome's additions. But the use of *ouêt* in the present context obliges us to admit that—at least at some period in the evolution of pachomian practices—a form of forgiveness of sins was an important part of the assembly of *Mesore*. Further in this letter, the word *ouêt* appears in a quotation of Dt 15:9, where it corresponds to the Greek ἄφεσις (= Latin *remissio*). See H. Quecke, 'Eine Handvoll', pp. 224-225; A. de Vogüé, 'Epîtres inédites d'Horsièse et de Théodore', p. 256, n. 14.

[11] A word is missing in Coptic. 'Rules' seems the obvious restoration.

[12] The first of *Mesore* corresponds to the 25th of July on our calendar. The literal translation would be 'Till the first of *Mesore*'.

[13] The translation 'to spend' is conjectural, because of the *lacuna*. We could also translate 'to sow'. See H. Quecke, 'Ein Brief von einem Nachfolger Pachoms', p. 430.

[14] The meaning of this sentence will be less obscure if we remember that *Mesore* was the last month of the year by the Egyptian calendar. According to the customs of Egyptian administration, there were at the end of the year general meetings, rendering of accounts, appointments to offices, etc. (See F. Ruppert, *Das pachomianische Mönchtum*, pp. 323-325). Therefore in this also Pachomius adopts the customs of his culture and his time.

[15] The initial conjunction (*esče*) which we have translated 'if' could also mean 'as if' or 'indeed'. See H. Quecke, 'Ein Brief', p. 429.

[16] There is a clear allusion to this same text in Hors. Test. 23.

[17] An unidentified quotation.

[18] Pachomius is called 'mediator' also in Hors. Test. 30. The word is applied to Christ in 1 Tm 2:5; Heb 9:15 and 12:24; and to Moses in Ga 3:19-20. On Pachomius' role as mediator, see F. Ruppert, *Das pachomianische Mönchtum*, pp. 188-201, and H. Bacht, *Das Vermächtnis des Ursprungs, Excursus II*, pp. 213-224.

[19] In SBo 208 Horsiesios quotes the same text, applying it to Theodore who has just died, saying: 'he will be an ambassador for us in the presence of God and of our father Pachomius.'

[20] 'for ever' or 'till the end'.

fRAGMENTS fROM THEODORE

(theod. fRAGM.)

Text: CSCO 159
pp. 60-62

1. . . . to wish your souls to be pure and so to be masters of yourselves as not to speak evil of anyone, that your efforts be sound before God, for the Lord knows that this is an abomination before God; thus, he quickly withdraws from man the effort of his mouth.[1]

Speak evil of no one

Cf. Jm 4:11.

Cf. Ps 101(100):5.

2. Truly, if a man guards his mouth* and acquires humility, the angels will be his friends here below; his soul will be a perfume poured-out; the angels will carry his remembrance before God day and night, whether he is a monk or a secular. Besides, many a man in the world is watchful on this point. As for me, I know many who have acquired a great humility and have watched themselves not to speak evil of anyone; on the contrary, they underestimate themselves constantly and praise the others, saying, 'It is within the power of God that we should find a little place in heaven'.

Guard one's mouth with humility
*Cf. Qo 5:1;
Jm 1:26.

Apa Theodore, the archimandrite.

133

From the same

Be aware of God's gifts

3. Yes, truly, if a man knew of every good thing that is hidden from him, he would not utter so much as two words until evening, but he would make himself blind, deaf, and dumb for God. Listen again to this wise observation: When a wise man, one who really fears God, sees a blind man, or a lame or dumb man, or one possessed by a demon, will his heart not react, at least if he is a sensible man? 'Who am I, that God should have left me my body in a good state of health? Could these men not have produced many things?'

Love your neighbor and hold your tongue
*Lv 19:18;
Mt 19:19
*Lv 19:18;
Mt 19:19.
†Jm 1:26;
Cf. 1 P 3:10.
‡Cf. Nb 10:33.

4. The precept *Love your neighbor as yourself**[2] surpasses all the commandments, and we owe it to the Lord to fulfill it. Truly, these two commandments, *Love your neighbor as yourself** and *Hold your tongue*† will march with honor at the head of your people,‡ until [your people] reach the kingdom of God, monks as well as seculars.

Example of a loving, humble brother

5. As for me, I know someone in the community who has never said an evil word against anyone; on the contrary, he loves every one as [he does] his own body. Whenever a thought is even imposed upon his mind by men, he says, 'God weighs all things; it is he who will sunder my soul from my body at any time'. Now, therefore, man must quietly at every moment place the lamp of

Cf. Mt 5:15.
The rest is missing

his soul upon the lamp-stand. . . .

Notes to the Fragments from Theodore

[1] For lack of its beginning, this ¶ is as obscure in Coptic as it is in our translation.
[2] We find the same quotation in SBo 48 (= G¹ 53); G¹ 38 and Paral. 39.

InstRuctions of hoRsiesios

(hoRs. InstR.)

Instruction One

INSTRUCTION OF OUR HOLY FATHER APA
HORSIESIOS, PRONOUNCED AT THE HOUR OF
MORNING, ON SATURDAY. IN THE PEACE OF
GOD. AMEN.

1. God invites us by [the mouth of] the holy
psalmist, David, *Come, my sons, listen to me; I
will instruct you in the fear of the Lord.* Let us
also, my brothers, fix our attention on God's love
for us; let us hasten to love him, *not by word of
mouth merely, but in word and deed.* It is said
clearly, *He who wishes to love life and see beautiful days, let him keep his tongue and lips from
evil, in order to avoid deceitful conversations; let
him stand far from evil and practise what is right;
let him seek peace and pursue it, for the eyes of
the Lord are turned toward the righteous, and his
ears are inclined to their prayers.*
2. Of what life is he speaking, my beloved?
What are the beautiful days, if not the life that
will endure eternally in heaven and the days of rejoicing in the rest to come; *As are the days of the
tree of life, so will be the days of the people,* according to the voice of the great Isaiah. *Surely
there is still a seventh-day rest for God's people;
for he who has entered into his place of repose
has, he too, rested from his labors, just as God*

Text: CSCO 159,
pp. 66-70

Ps 34(33):11.

1 Jn 3:18.

Ps 34(33):12-15.

Is 65:22.

135

Heb 4:9-11.

Cf. 2 Co 2:14-15.

Cf. 1 Co 7:29.

Cf. Ps 27(26):13.

A section is
missing here

Jr 8:23(9:1).

A few words
are missing

rested from His.[1] *Let us also, brothers, hasten to enter into this place of rest.* With good deeds, let us wage every battle, and let us not allow the demon to make us strangers to the kingdom of God by deeds that are incompatible with the honor of Christianity and especially those in no way conformable to our holy habit. Indeed, the life of our holy fathers is an angelic life, perfuming the whole world.[2] We must therefore allow no pleasure now to revile our holy habit. This brief period of time must not make us strangers to the age to come; a pleasure quickly-spent must not make us strangers to the great blessings of the Lord in the land of the living. On the contrary, 'let the shameless age rejoice with us, [and] let us not rejoice with the shameless age',[3] according to the injunction of our holy Father, apa Pachomius, who says, indeed....

3. ... throwing them in the hole of the abyss,[4] each one being thrown to the punishment he has deserved according to his evil deeds, while the righteous are received in the enjoyment and comfort of good things, in the measure of each one's toil. This being so, what should we do? Let us allow a spring of tears to flow every day, day and night. Let us, too, say with the weeping Jeremiah, the great prophet, *'Who will give some water to my head, and a spring of tears to my eyes? I would weep for my sins day and night.'* Let us first of all confess our sins before this ... which is full of terror and trembling tears. Let us invoke the goodness and mercy of our God, while we are in this exile of tears and before death overtakes us. Let us realize that we are miserable and wretched.

Let us take care of our souls with all diligence, for it is of the soul that it is asked . . . the other helps us in the assistance to our body. The miserable soul is all alone when it falls into sin; no one else will offer it a hand in its punishments.

A few lines are missing

4. Now, my dear sons, let us esteem nothing as more precious than [our soul's] salvation. Let us repent our past sins while we are in the land of tears, our hands and feet free and unfettered, not yet in the tomb and a prey to worms, and while the flesh, an object of concern, is not dissolved and reduced to dust. Well, shall we say on that day that it is riches which have deceived us? The judge will say to us, 'Have you not heard him who cries out in the Gospel, *If a man gains the whole world and brings harm to his soul, what shall he offer in exchange for his soul?*'[5] If we say that it is the enemy that has deceived us, he will answer by saying to us, 'Did Eve of old gain anything for having said, *It is the serpent that deceived me*'? Now, my dear sons, let us watch, with all attentiveness, over our little soul; no doubt it will be saved and will find a bit of rest. . . .

Mt 16:26;
Mk 8:36;
Lk 9:25.

Gn 3:13.

A section is missing

5. . . . the doctrine? Where are purity and humility? Where are peace and meekness? Where are sweetness and love? Where are my father's teaching and my mother's instructions? Where are these and the others, to put them as a crown on myself? Where are the faithful, the righteous and all the saints? Let them come and spit in my face, because I have not followed their teachings. Where are the prophets and apostles? Let them come and cover me with shame, because I have disobeyed their words of life, till I am upon the

Pr 1:8.

Pr 1:9

Cf. Dt 25:9.

Cf. Pr 17:11.
Cf. Ps 55(54):4.

final day and given over to the pitiless powers and
to death's terror. Oh, that there were repentance,
now! Oh, that I may do penance even to the point
of shedding my blood!

6. Where is my body, this body that God has
afforded me as a field to cultivate, where I might
Cf. 1 Co 3:9. work, and become rich? I have destroyed it, rendered it sterile. I have heaped up in myself iniquities and sins for which I shall be delivered up to
punishments. Woe to me, for I have been taken
as a thief, chained down as a murderer, and I am
now delivered to tribulations, sorrow and punishment in hunger and thirst!

7. I assure you, whoever lives, man or woman,
great or small, rich or poor, if we are negligent
and fail to repent, we shall suffer all the torments
mentioned above and we shall suffer even greater
ones than these. We shall weep miserably and no
one will listen to us. Therefore, let us continue to
implore our Lord and God, Jesus Christ, day and
night, while we are in this place of exile and deceit, crying out and saying, Have mercy on us,
our Lord! Forgive us, our God, all the misdeeds
into which we have fallen in the past! Grant us
correction for the future, teach us a way that is
pleasing to you, grant we may accomplish the desire of your heart! We shall find mercy before you
when we present ourselves to you. For yours is all
pity, mercy and glory, which belong to the Father
and Holy Spirit from the beginning unto eternity.
Amen.

Instruction Two

SECOND DISCOURSE, FOR THE MORNING OF
THE SAINTS, ON SATURDAY. IN THE PEACE OF
GOD. AMEN.

Text: CSCO 159,
pp. 70

God said to the faithful Abraham, *Do my will
before me, be without sin, and I will make a covenant with you.*[1] They have fulfilled this word,
they have followed the example of the saints, and
God has made a covenant with them.

Gn 17:1-2.

As for us, my brothers, if we accomplish God's
will, if we follow the example of our blessed fathers, if we are without sin, God will watch over
us.

. . . keep the foundation of the faith of all the
saints.

*2 pages are
missing*

Cf. Heb 11:4.

Instruction Three

THIRD DISCOURSE OF APA HORSIESIOS, WHICH
HE GAVE ON SUNDAY MORNING.

Text: CSCO 159,
p. 70-71

1. The Holy Spirit said in an exhortation, *My
son, honor God by your genuine efforts, give him
the first-fruits of your righteousness, so that your
granaries may be filled with wheat and your vats
with wine.*

Pr 3:9-10.

2. In what sense does he refer to granaries and
vats? No doubt he speaks of the granaries and
vats of the soul, those that the farmers of righteousness fill with spiritual wine through their efforts and sweat, accepted as the price of the fruits
of piety. The holy Apostle will indeed persuade us
of such an economy, *You are God's building,*

1 Co 3:9.

God's farm. For us, too, it is a matter of pride to take care of the vineyard of our soul, according to the good pleasure of God, not planting in it di-

Cf. Dt 22:9.

verse plants, that is to say, not allowing evil to be mixed with the good that is in us. Rather, inasmuch as we are part of the true vine, Christ Jesus our Lord, we have God the Father as our farmer, according to the voice of our Saviour who declares, *I am the true vine, and my Father is the*

Jn 15:1.

farmer. And again, *Solomon has a vineyard in a*

Sg 8:11.

place called Baal-hamon.[1]

3. Let us also hasten to fill our granaries with wheat worthy of heaven, and to fill our vats of

Cf. Jl 2:24;
2 Co 2:15.

wine with the fragrance of Christ,[2] thanks to the teachings of our blessed and righteous father, Apa Pachomius, of all our other holy fathers, and of those who are still with us today. Indeed, they are springs of the water of life watering their green

*Cf. Qo 2:6.
A few words
are missing

plantation,* that is to say, we . . . spiritual, watering the vineyard of our souls with thoughts that are worthy of heaven and sayings that exhale their sweetness. For, *they leap on the mountains, they*

Sg 2:8.

trample in the valleys, that is, the apostles and the prophets. And to us also it is said, *My brother,*

Sg 8:14.

run; do as the gazelle and the young stag which are on the perfumed mountains.

4. Happy are we also to have a share in the grace of our holy fathers, according to the holy voice of Baruch, *Blessed are we, Israel, for what*

Ba 4:4.

is pleasing to God has been revealed to us.[3] And again, *Happy are you, Israel! What other nation*

Dt 33:29.

can compare with you and is saved by the Lord? As for us, my brothers, let us abide by the teach-

Cf. Pr 6:20.

ing of our fathers. Let us not forsake it, let us keep it all our lives. Let us follow the fragrance of

their love and of their holy manner of life[4] in
Christ, so that we too may walk with great joy by
the grace of the Holy Spirit, saying, 'May we be
received in the place that was made for us!'

Instruction Four

FOURTH DISCOURSE. SUNDAY MORNING. THE
BROTHERS SHALL BE SEATED, IN ORDER TO BE
ATTENTIVE TO THE WORD. IN PEACE. AMEN.

1. The Spirit of God says in his goodness, *Do
not desist doing good to anyone who is in want,
as long as your hand has the means of doing so.
Do not say, 'go and come back; tomorrow I will
give you something.'* By these words the Holy
Spirit actually teaches us not to put things off
from day to day, but to do to our soul all the
good that is possible, so as to adorn it with every
virtue worthy of heaven, so as to clothe it with
brilliant vestments according to this agreeable
voice, *Let your clothes be brilliant at all times;
let your head not lack in oil.* We must adorn it
with ornaments as a bride, put on it a diadem as
for a bridegroom, and we too, say, by the voice
of the prophets, while we exult with holy Isaiah,
*May my soul exult in the Lord, for he has clothed
me in a garment of salvation*[1] *and a cloak of joy;*[2]
*he has adorned me with ornaments like those of
a bride and has put on me a diadem as on a
bridegroom.*
2. As for us, my brothers, it is a great happiness to inherit the blessing of our fathers. Now,
then, there exist two types of want: the one of the
body; the other of the soul. If it is a lack of piety

Text: CSCO 159,
pp. 72-73

Pr 3:27-28.

Qo 9:8.

Is 61:10.

Cf. 1P 3:9.

to neglect those who are in want of corporal things and not to give them what is necessary to their body, it is much worse if we neglect him whose soul is in need. For nourishment and clothing are necessities of the body, but the soul requires spiritual nourishment and a brilliant garment, that is to say, purity, the pride of the angels, which each person must provide for his soul. Indeed, the Spirit of truth did not only speak of visible want, but also of that of the soul, which must not be overlooked. On the contrary, let each person be more zealous to gather for himself spiritual nourishment and spiritual clothing. He who abides by the recommendation of the Spirit of God shall say with an exulting voice, *Our earth will give its fruit; our God, bless us; bless us, our God.* And then we shall say with confidence, *Lord, with the five talents you have given me, behold, I have earned five more.*[3] For whoever struggles will hear this sweet voice coming from the Lord, *Well done, excellent and faithful servant, since you have been faithful in a small thing, I will establish you over much; enter into your master's happiness.*[4]

Ps 67(66):6.

Mt 25:20.

Mt 25:21.23.

Text: CSCO 159
pp. 73-74

Instruction Five

THE FIFTH DISCOURSE OF OUR FATHER APA HORSIESIOS. SUNDAY EVENING.

The Spirit of God teaches us, through Solomon the wise, to build the house of our souls upon an ample and solid foundation. For this is how a rich man, when he has decided to build a beautiful home for himself, begins, by preparing all the

Cf. 2 Ch 3:3.

materials for the house — gold, silver, wood, iron and stones — in order to lay the whole foundation solidly with whole stones, and to tie the whole structure of the house together with pieces of iron. The decoration of the walls . . . of gold and silver, brilliant by. . ., so that all who see it stand in admiration of the finishing of the house. Thus said the Spirit of God, signifying to all of us that each one must build up the house of his soul with a decoration that is not earthly, but with one that is worthy of heaven; not with gold or silver, but with the blood of . . . immaculate, Christ* . . . the written act levelled against us;† he who for our sake accepted smiting so that we, on our part, should *crucify the flesh with its passions and desires*; he to whom *was given wine mixed* [with gall], so that we, on our part, [should reject] the gall of sin; he who has tasted death for us all, *in order to destroy him who had power over death, that is to say, the devil,* so that sin may not reign . . . the body which Jesus drew from Adam . . . ; he who rose from the dead, so that . . . the hope of the resurrection . . . which he did not build up . . . the strength of our . . . the holy. . . .

Cf. Dt 27:6.

A few words are missing

*Cf. 1 P 1:19.
*About 15 lines are missing here
†Col 2:14.

Ga 5:24.
Mt 27:34.
Heb 2:9.

Heb 2:14.

Cf. Rm 6:4.

The rest is missing

Instruction Six

Text: CSCO 159, pp. 74, 22-75,30

The beginning is missing

1. '. . . in your heart.[1] If the sun, the moon and the stars which illumine the whole earth were made by the word of your mouth, then who will be able to think about you, who are the creator, how you exist, how you are in reality? Or what mouth will be able to bless you as you are blessed?'

2. When you have thought about all those marvels and about the great things which he has created by his word[2] and, on the other hand, about your littleness—for he created you while you did not exist, he the Almighty and Eternal, that you might be and if he had not made you, then even your remembrance would not exist—after that, never fail unceasingly to bless him, saying, 'May you be blessed, Lord, who fashioned me from earth when I did not exist'. Say this until the godless thought that the demon will have thrust into your heart has completely vanished from it; and you will bless the Lord in this way, promptly and joyously. Do not be afflicted whenever these impure thoughts cross your mind; then the devil, who tries you, will quit and say, 'I importune him with these evil thoughts in order to punish, him, and behold, he progresses still more, blessing God instead of cursing him.' This is the way in which the adversary has been overcome at all times and in everything by all the saints who have blessed the Lord who drew them from nothingness into existence.

3. As to perseverance in prayer, especially at night, act according to your strength. We are not unmindful of what is written about the Lord, *He spent the night in vigil, praying to God.* Moreover, when you pray, if you wish not to be negligent or distracted by many thoughts, then, when your hands are outstretched, do not hasten to drop them to your side,[3] for through fatigue and pain these thoughts will come to an end and you will be as if you saw the Lord to whom you are praying, as it is written of Moses, *He held himself firm, as though he could see the Invisible One.*

Ps 33(32):6.

Dt 32:6.

Lk 6:12.

Heb 11:27.

4. Also, when you pray, accuse yourself frequently, saying, 'Lord, blessed God, why have I lived all this time in ignorance of you? From childhood, I have not known that it is you who *fashioned me in my mother's womb,* that it is you who have nourished me in every way, and that my life-breath was in your hands without my knowing it.' Then you will ask him straightway what his whole will is, that he may grant that you may fulfill it, *to love him with all your heart, all your strength and in every thought, and your neighbor as yourself,* according to his commandment. You will ask him also about the fruits of the Holy Spirit, that he grant us the manner of acquiring them, either bodily purity, or purity of heart, mercy, goodness. . . .

Jb 31:15.

Cf. Ps 143 (142):10.

Lk. 10:27.

Ga 5:22.

The rest is missing

Instruction Seven

Text: CSCO 159, pp. 75-79

HERE ARE THE TEACHINGS THAT OUR HOLY FATHER APA HORSIESIOS PRONOUNCED ON THE THINGS THAT WERE CAUSING HIM ANGUISH, AND ON THAT THING, THAT IS, FRIENDSHIP.[1]

1. I am drawn to speak because of the sorrow of my heart, yet I am also drawn to remain silent because of my shortcomings, which accuse me. The sentiments of my heart torment me into speaking, yet my failings stand in the way, prompting me to be silent. It is better for me to speak than to remain silent; I shall speak of the greatness of monasticism, which has been humbled.
2. O monasticism, arise and weep over your-

self; arise and weep over your respectable habit, which will be worn by those who are in a class with swine and mules! O monasticism, arise and weep over your little children who have deflowered their virginity and over your young men who, like them, have lost it. Arise and weep over your great men, one time great and glorying in your habit; but behold, they are about to die a startling death because of the beauty of the little children they have seduced! Arise and weep over those who come to us, lest they too become immeshed with those who have become a scandal to them!

3. O man, move away from those littler than yourself, and you shall escape all tribulation, all affliction, all trial, all illness, both here and beyond. All perversity, all evil, all sin, all shamelessness, all blindness are the lot of him who seeks one littler than himself. On the other hand, *every-thing true, everything fitting, everything that is righteous, every blessing, every virtue,*[2] every joy in the Spirit, all charity and every mercy, the whole will of God and Jesus, Son of God — may these be upon the head of him who moves away from the one who hankers after him.

Ph 4:8.

4. O evil friendship, detested by God and his angels! O wicked laughter, whose taste is that of gall! O cursed may you be, friendship of which I speak and which will be pursued by the wrath of God! O evil friendship, whose laughter has been the ruin not only of great ones, priests, superiors[3] of men, superiors of women, who glorified in their brilliant habit and the word of their mouth!

5. I adjure you before God, my brother, move away from evil friendship. But perhaps you will

reply and say, 'You are thereby teaching me enmity'. No, indeed; but on the contrary, be at
peace with your neighbor, because of God and
the commandment. But you peer this way and   Cf. Heb 12:14.
that anxiously, you watch until you have found
the propitious moment, then you give him what is
concealed in an inner hem of your garment, so
that God also and his Christ will pour out their
anger and their wrath on you and on him; then
there will be no means for you to go this way and
that. Truly, you fool, if there is no shame in your
friendship, why are you ashamed and afraid to
speak with him openly?

6. O evil friendship! O gall without sweetness!
O incurable illness! I mean him who loves someone littler than himself. O what a father — the one
who endures someone telling him, 'This is my
son,' and plays with his own death! I mean him
who wishes to deflower his virginity. O what a
brother — the one who does not come to the aid of
him of whom he says, 'This is my brother', when
he sees him making his way to the feet of death,
and not only does not teach him, but laughs and
rejoices at his ruin! What shall I say or what shall
I leave unsaid in regard to this pestilential love? I
mean those who yesterday were proud and were
instructing others, and who presently are stiff-
ened like sheep in this most wicked scab. Or shall
I speak of those who are not yet deformed by this
wicked scab and this itch?

7. Perhaps you think, my brothers, that the
plight of such a friendship is easy. Let him who ignores this plight realize that it is the plight of hell
with its punishments, in order not to be drawn into
evil friendships by the language of small children,

their shameless carriage, the changing aspect of their evil eyes, the lustre of their face, the clatter of their feet, their customary gluttony. On the contrary, pay no attention to their evil carriage. O brother, remember that this deceptive beauty will pass and perish in the ground; as for you, a great affliction will befall you because you have tasted that honey whose bitterness is greater than anything.

8. Let us think, my brothers of the time that is rapidly passing us by. Let us not squander it on these deceptive pleasures. Let us on the contrary recall our fathers, who were steadfast throughout their existence without yielding to these evil pleasures. Let us think, my brothers, that in any case judgement will be passed. If, on the one hand, a man dies in youth, I believe he will not escape the following reproach, 'If at such an age you have lived in these sins, what would your abominations have been had you lived a long time?' And on the other hand, if we die in old age without having renounced sin, the following reproach will be made to us, 'After such a long time you have not renounced sin!' What shame will be ours, who have not renounced sin, this pestilential and despicable affection. . . .

9. . . . know that you have gone astray in this humanity. Do not then impute your straying to him who invites you to life; do not impute your negligence to him who leads you to the light, him who awakens you from slumber; do not impute to him your negligence; to him who scolds you do not impute your own fall. Him who pulled you out of the dung hole, do not stick in the dung

Cf. Qo 7:11.

*A whole section
is missing*

Cf. Lm 3:2.

Cf. Jn 11:11.

Cf. Lm 4:5.

with yourself. By making him like yourself, you draw over him your own rotten friendship. Rather, listen to me. I will create hostility and a barrier between your friendship and his.

10. Some from the circle of your friendship go out with a made-up face; they wear a bandeau around their face; they put this black thing over their eyes under pretext of illness; they have numberless rings attached to their handkerchief, and on their belt, fringes that flap behind them, like calves frisking about in an enclosure. Often they bathe quite naked without necessity;[4] they wear soft shoes on their feet — *she went out taking pride in the desires of her soul* — they mince along in the assembly; they accost their friend with a boisterous laugh, like the noise of thorny twigs cracking under a cooking pot.[5] They build themselves alcoves; they adopt the customs of the crows and vultures out in the world, making themselves comparable to them in their food: dead meat and rotten venison. They fill their alcoves with every kind of transgression. The word of the prophet will be realized in them, *Death has climbed at your alcoves.* At times also, the word is spread that the superior will come to inspect the alcoves upon which are found Israel's abominations; they run in disorder to take them away from the alcoves and bury them in the ground or throw them elsewhere, and they invite men to enter and receive homage. Who will rejoice at this moment? Those who live a life of renunciation. Who will laugh at him? Those who will be seized with fear because of the transgressions he has committed or are discovered to be his doing. Who [will be] among those who are laughing at you? Those who

Ml 4:2(3:20).

Jr 2:24.

Cf. Qo 7:6(7).

Cf. Zp 2:14.

Cf. Ez 8:9.

Jr 9:20.

Cf. Ez 8:1-18.

Cf. Is 2:10.

keep the precepts of their fathers, who are bound together in the faith and who walk, brilliant in the confidence of Christ.

Cf. Phm 8.

11. Such, then, is the nature of your friendship. Now learn what the friendship of those from heaven is like. First of all, they attach themselves to men who control their belly, who are full of knowledge, who have learned prudence, who are perfect, who are lovable, who are eager to listen attentively, who are firm in the faith of the *Koinonia*, who *seek peace and purity*,[6] who accuse no one, who do not rejoice over anyone's fall, who do not alienate anyone's feelings towards his companions, and who do not temporize in order to avoid the trials of tribulation, but persevere in doing what is agreeable to God.

Heb 12:14.

12. And now, negligent man, return to the depths of the divinity, walk in these, cease not to walk in these; shackle yourself with the bonds of life, that your soul *may return to its repose*. Cease hating the righteous and arousing bitterness in the respectable people from whom you have been separated by these words, *There is no sinner in the assembly of the righteous*. If you learn a humble speech, you will be courteous to your brothers; if you reject the rudeness of your disobedience, those in charge of you will be pleased with you. Stop striking [your brothers with the sword of your] tongue; turn away from you the word said in Jeremiah, *Their tongue is a dart that wounds, the words of their mouth are snares*. Whenever you are negligent, you fall like leaves, because you lack direction.

Ps 116(114):7.

Ps 1:5.

Jr 9:7.
Cf. Is 64:5.

13. And now, renounce sin. Perhaps, by instructing you, we are like him who *glues clay on*

clay, or like him who awakens someone asleep at
night in deep slumber. Watch out that you be not   Si 22:9.
classed among those who. . . .   *The rest is*
                                                       missing

Notes to the Instructions of Horsiesios

Hors. Instr. 1   [1]Heb. 4:10 is partly quoted also in Theod. Instr. 3:6.
[2]Cf. S[1] 25 where Pachomius is said to offer the brothers to the Lord as sacrifices, the fragrance of which God smells; and Theod. Instr. 3: 5 where the brothers are called to be a sweet odor for those from outside.
[3]This is a direct quotation from Pachomius' first letter. Horsiesios has only changed the second person plural of the verbs into the first person plural. We must note also that in the Coptic text the two parallel members of the sentence are juxtaposed, while the Latin and Greek translations subordinate them. (See H. Quecke, *Die Briefe Pachoms. Griechischer Text*, pp. 46-47.
[4]The attribution of the next two ¶¶ to Horsiesios is doubtful. See the Introduction.
[5]Same quotation in Pach. Letter 4: 4.

Hors. Instr. 2   [1]This text is quoted in G[1] 17 as an expression of the whole law.

Hors. Instr. 3   [1]The same quotation occurs in Hors. Test. 28. The biblical image of the vine and the branches, inspired by Jn 15, is used by Horsiesios in Hors. Reg. 4, and also by Pachomius in Pach. Instr. 1: 37. The pachomian *Koinonia* is called the vineyard of the Lord by Horsiesios, who uses Is 5:7 in conjunction with Sg 8:11 in Hors. Test. 28. See also Hors. Test. 47 and SBo 104.
[2]Cf. another allusion to 2 Co 2:15 in Pach. Letter 4: 3.
[3]Ba 4:1-5 is largely used by Horsiesios. It is fully quoted in Hors. Test. 50; Ba 4:2.4-5 is quoted both in Hors. Letter 3: 2 and 4: 2; and Ba 4:4 in Hors. Instr. 3. Note that Ba 4:3 is also quoted in Paral. 39.
[4]'manner of life': ἀναστροφή; this word is used only once in G[1] (¶106, Halkin, p. 69, 27). In Coptic *politeia* is more currently used.

Hors. Instr. 4   [1]'Garment of salvation': Horsiesios quotes the same text in a slightly different version in Hors. Test. 27: '*iustitiae uestimentum*'.
[2]Is 61:10 is quoted also in Hors. Test. 48.
[3]The same verse is quoted by Pachomius in Am. Letter 14.
[4]The same text is used again by Horsiesios in the same manner in Hors. Test. 14; it is quoted about Pachomius in SBo 114.

Hors. Instr. 6   [1]Lefort published the *folio* containing the following text immediately after Instruction Five. But there was a *lacuna* of sixteen pages between the two texts, and it is highly improbable that the present *folio* belonged to the fifth Instruction. We prefer to consider it a fragment of a sixth Instruction.
[2]Same allusion in Pachomius' prayer in S[1] 16.
[3]See the description of Pachomius and his brother John praying with hands outstretched, in SBo 19 ('moving neither their feet nor their hands, which they kept stretched out lest sleep overtake them.')

Hors. Instr. 7   ¹The attribution of this text to Horsiesios is doubtful; see Introduction.

²Same quotation in S¹ 2.

³*Archègos*: This word is never used as a title for a superior in any pachomian source, if we except the three instances in the present Instruction. But the title is common in Schenoute's writings. See F. Ruppert, *Das pachomianische Mönchtum*, pp. 288-290.

⁴Cf. Pr. 92.

⁵Qo 7:6(7) is quoted also in Am. Letter 23.

⁶Heb 12:14 is quoted by Hors. in Hors. Letter 3: 4 and twice by Pachomius in Pach. Instr. 1: 36.

letters of horsiesios

(hors. letter)

Letter One

Text: CSCO 159, pp. 63-65

The beginning is missing

1. ... [*Man did not come from woman; no, woman came from*] *man; for man was not created for the sake of woman, but woman for the sake of man.* Solomon likewise said, *Many women have acquired riches, many have done admirable things,* like Judith who in her wisdom took away the head of Holofernes; and also Susanna who for God's sake killed the desire of her heart and repulsed the elders.[1] Again, Solomon said, *But you have surpassed them all.* Indeed, God gave Solomon a wisdom and understanding as abundant as the sand that lies on the seashores. Again, he said, *He who rejects an excellent woman, rejects good things.* And again, *Good things will befall the righteous.* And again, *Because of your sins he has....*

> Women of the Bible
>
> 1 Co 11:8-9.
>
> Pr 31:29(29:47).
> Jdt 13:8-10.
>
> Dn 13:1-23.
> Pr 31:29(29:47).
>
> 1 K 5:9(4:29).
>
> Pr 18:22.
> Pr 13:21.
>
> *12 lines are missing*

2. ... to the Lord, indeed, she has said this. And again, *If it is a disgrace for a woman to have her hair cut off or her head shaved, let her wear a veil,* for Solomon said, *For all those who are with her are covered.* And again, *The pious woman will be praised.* And again, *Wisdom is praised in the streets, she speaks boldly in the public squares, she*

> **The pious woman will be praised**
>
> 1 Co 11:6.
> Pr 31:21(29:39).
> Pr 31:30(29:48).

153

Pr 1:20-21.

Pr 1:7.

Pr 19:23(20).

To live accord-
ing to God's will
*Dt 29:18.

Dt 27:15-26.

*Cf. Ps 1:2;
   Ps 119(118):
   47-48.
†Dn 9:23;
 10:11,19.
‡Is 62:4.
Rm 12:2.

Cf. Is 62,4. ?

Ps 107(106):
   41-42.

To do God's
whole will

Mt 5:19.

Pr 13:33.

Qo 8:5.

Pr 19:16.

Ps 19(18):9.

Pr 6:23.

*is preached at the corners of the walls, she speaks
with confidence at the city gates.* And again, *The
fear of God is the beginning of wisdom; prudence
is a good thing for him who will practise it.* And
again, *The fear of the Lord works for life, whereas he who has no fear will dwell in places where
eternity will not visit him.*

3. Let no one say, *I shall walk according to the
desire of my heart, and purity will be mine.** The
curses which Moses pronounced against such a
man are too numerous to be quoted, but it is he
who said that his will lay in [God's] commandments.* Again, Daniel, *A man worthy to be
loved.*†² Again, *You shall be called 'My Delight',
and your land, 'The Inhabited'.*‡ Paul said also, *So
that you may know the will of God, which is good,
agreeable to him and perfect, so that you may be
for me a land that I love.* And again, *He has
made the families like flocks, so that those who
are righteous may see and rejoice and all wickedness must hold its tongue.*³

4. The Gospel says again, *The man who in-
fringes one of these lesser commandments will be
called the least in the kingdom of the heavens,
whereas the man who keeps them and teaches
them to men will be called great in the kingdom
of the heavens;* for it is said, *He who keeps the
commandment is safe; he who keeps the commandment will not know an evil word.* And
again, *He who keeps the commandment keeps his
soul;*⁴ *the commandment of the Lord is a light
that enlightens the eyes of the little ones; the good
commandment is a lamp.* Moses too said, *You
shall honor your father and your mother so that
good things may befall you, and that you may*

have a long life in the good land. And again, *He who speaks ill of his father and mother shall die.* And again, *The eye that mocks his father, and that abandons the old age of his mother shall be pecked out by the raven in the valleys and eaten by eaglets.*

5. Moses said, *You shall honor your father and your mother.* * Now, the Son of God has come and said to us, *He who comes to me without hating his father, mother, brothers, wife, children and his own soul, who does not carry his cross and come after me, cannot be my disciple.* And Paul said, *I die daily, I swear to it by the pride I take in you;* not that we may learn that man dies daily, but rather in order to show that he spoke of the Cross of the Son of God. And again, *According to the covenant I made with you at the time of your exodus from the land of Egypt, my Spirit stood among you; take courage, for once again I will shake the heaven and the earth, the sea and the dry land, and I will shake all the nations; all the treasures of the nations shall flow in and fill my house with glory. Mine is the gold, mine the silver! says the Lord, the Almighty; and I will give peace in this place, peace of soul, a saving peace to all who will assemble to work for the erection of this temple.*[5] And again, *Those who work at the temples get their food from the temple.*[6]

6. It is said again in the Gospel according to Mark, *Destroy this temple made by hands, and I will erect in this place a temple not made by hands.*[7] John also said, *Destroy this temple and I will raise it up in three days.* The ignorant Jews said to him, *It has taken forty-six years to build this temple, how could you raise it up in three*

Ex 20:12.
Ex 21:15.

Pr 30:17(24:52).
To carry Christ's Cross
*Ex 20:12.

Lk 14:26-27.
1 Co 15:31.

Hg 2:4-9.

1 Co 9:13.
Resurrection

Mk 14:58.
Jn 2:19.

Jn 2:20-21.

days? They did not realize that he was speaking to them of the temple of his own body.

May we understand what is written for each one of us; *The end of the discourse, listen to all of it; fear God, keep his commandments, for God will cause every creature to appear before him in order to judge it for every act in which it has been*

Qo 12:13-14.

forgetful, either for good or for evil.[8] I greet all of you, and pray that you may be safe in the Lord.

Text: CSCO 159
pp. 65-66

Letter Two

APA HORSIESIOS WRITES TO HIS BELOVED SON, THEODORE, WHO IS REVERED AND WORTHY OF LOVE. GREETINGS.

First of all, I greet your piety and dispositions which are perfect in every good work. Truly, when I remember your filial attitude and your fraternal love, I am filled with joy. I have said, It is my duty to write and greet your wisdom, since it

Pr 10:1; 15:20.

is written, *A wise son is his father's joy.*[1] And again, *Give the wise man an occasion and he will become wiser; teach the righteous man and he*

Pr 9:9.

will busy himself to learn even more. And again, *Great peace to those who love your name, and no*

Ps 119(118):165.

stumbling block for them.[2] For it is said, *It is God who builds up Jerusalem; he brings back Israel's exiles;*[3] *he heals all their ills, dresses all their wounds, counts all the myriad stars, and gives*

Ps 147(146):2-4.

each of them a name. And again, *When I fashioned the stars all the angels blessed me with a*

Jb 38:7.

loud voice. And again, *The stars rose from*

Jg 5:20.

heaven and fought with the Sisara. And again, *A star will appear in Jacob, and a man will arise in*

Israel; he will crush all the chieftains of Moab and all the sons of Sheth;[4] for Paul has said, *The man who acts in us is God.* And again, *It is I who sow, Apollos who waters, but God who gives the increase; thus it is not the work of him who sows or who waters, but the work of God who gives the increase.* And again, *You want to put Christ to the test, who speaks within me.* David also said, *The harbors of the river shall be the joy of the city of God; the Most High has purified his dwelling; God is within her and* [she][5] *shall not be shaken.* And again, *There is a harbor of righteousness for the sum total of the efforts of our fathers.* And again, *Draw water with pleasure at the springs of salvation.* The prophet says again, *The mountains will gush forth sweetness, the hills milk, and all the springs of Judah water; there is one spring. . . .*

Nb 24:17.
Ph 2:13.

1 Co 3:6-7.
2 Co 13:3.

Ps 46(45):4-5.

Cf. Jr 50:7(27:7).

Is 12:3.

Jl 4:18.
The rest is missing

Letter Three

1. . . . to the brothers . . . Theodore . . . toward God . . . father Theodore sick. . . . We have not known the thing that he . . . to you. . . . *Console one another . . . one another. . . . We beg you in the name of Christ to be reconciled to God.* . . . one another and may no disorder take place . . . disorder. What has happened is, in fact, not much . . . as David [said] . . . *all the earth.*[1] Now . . . father . . . nets [?] and of . . . I will give you . . . of those who stand upright. *It is difficult to find a faithful man who walks saintly in righteousness.* And, *A righteous father gives good food.*[2] Now then, *may your loins be girded, your lamps lit, and may you be like servants waiting*

A call to watchfulness

Cf. 1 Th 5:11;
2 Co 5:20.

Cf. 1 K 2:2.

Pr 20:6-7.
Pr 23:24.

Lk 12:35-36.

for their master to return from the wedding feast,[3]
as it is written in the Gospel, *In the middle of the*

Mt 25:6.

night there was a cry: the bridegroom has come![4]
Five wise virgins who were ready entered with the
bridegroom; those who were not ready were [left

*Cf. Mt 25:10-12.
†Cf. Mt 24:44;
    Lk 12:40.
‡2 Co 9:4.

behind the] door,*[5] so that we too may be ready,†
for the Apostle has [said], *Lest they come to you
and I find you not ready;*‡[6] but [let us take care]
to be ready, for David has said, *God, my heart is*

Ps 57(56):7;
    108(107):1.

*ready, my heart is ready. You were called to lib-
erty; yet let not our liberty, my brothers, become
an occasion for the flesh; but by the love of the
spirit be servants of one another,*[7] *for the whole of
the law is fulfilled in a single word, in that you*

Ga 5:13-14.
1 Co 10:24.33.

love your neighbor as yourself. For he has said, *I
do not seek my own advantage, but that of others.*[8]
For, *a slave, when called in the Lord, is a freeman of the Lord. Similarly, a freeman, when he is*

1 Co 7:22.

called, is a slave of Christ.

**Invitation to
the feast**
*Na 2:1(1:15).

2. . . . [the prophet] has said, [celebrate] *your
great feast, Judah, and* [carry out] *your vows,**[9]
for no one defiled or impure will begin to [pass]

Na 2:1(1:15);
Is 52:1; Cf.
Ac 10:4; 11:8.

through you again. And . . . that our father has
said, he who is Apa, since we know . . . covenant
with him, as Moses says in Leviticus, *My covenant
Jacob, my covenant Isaac, my covenant Abra-*

Lv 26:42.

ham. And let us remember also what our father
has ordered us not to change, but more and more
we write to you to comfort one another, for the
bones sustain the flesh, for he said, *All my bones*

Ps 35(34):10.
Pr 15:30.

will say, God, who can be your equal?[10] and
again, *The good fame rejoices the bones.* It is
written again in Baruch, *Walk in the perfume of*

Ba 4:2.

*wisdom in the face of its light. Blessed are we Is-
rael, for what is pleasing to God has been revealed*

to us. *Take courage, therefore, people of God, for he remembers Israel.*[11] And let us remember the word of the prophet, *The covenant I made at the time of your exodus from the land of Egypt. My spirit stood among you. Take courage, for once again I will shake the heaven and the earth, the sea and dry land, and I will shake all the nations; all the treasures*[12] *of the nations shall flow in and fill my house with glory. Mine is the gold, mine the silver, says the Lord, the Almighty. Since the final glory of the house will be greater than the first, says the Lord Almighty. I will give peace in this place, I will give peace of soul for salvation to whoever works, to whoever assembles to erect this temple.*[13] As the Apostle says, *Those who work at the temples get their food from the temples; those serving at the altar receive their portion from the altar.*[14] So that we may know this temple of which he has said, *Destroy this temple made by hands; I will erect in this place a temple that is not made by hands;*[15] and, *After he was raised from the dead, his disciples remembered that he was speaking of the temple of his body.*[16] *The temple of God is holy, and you are that temple; let no one be deceived.*[17] But *boiling in spirit, being servants of the Lord, zealous without hesitation, sharing with the saints in their needs, persevering in prayer, bless those who persecute you, bless and do not curse them. Rejoice with those who rejoice, weep with those who weep. Think this single thought towards one another, not looking toward haughty things, but walking with the humble.*[18]

3. And when they had crossed the Red Sea, they reached Marah[19] and could not drink the

Ba 4:4-5.

Hg 2:6-9.

1 Co 9:13.

Mk 14:58.

Jn 2:21-22.
1 Co 3:17-18.

Rm 12:11-16.

Symbolism of the wood

water of Marah, for it was bitter. But the Lord pointed out some wood to Moses; he threw it into *the water and the water became sweet,* and the people drank. Likewise others *cut wood from the bank of the Jordan and a piece of iron fell into the river, and the man of God took the piece of wood and threw it into the water, and the piece of iron floated.* Likewise David said, *Say among the nations, the Lord has reigned by the wood. Whether the wood falls to the south or to the north, where the wood falls, there it will lie.* Again, *By the blood of the wood I will be purified.*[20]

Ex 15:23-25.

2 K 6:4-6.
Ps 96(95):10.

Qo 11:3.

Confidence in God

4. Because of this, therefore, may we find [the place] of Christ in ourselves, for it has been said, *You have been stamped with the seal of the Holy Spirit of the promise,* and . . . because of the place . . . was found. . . . Because of this the Apostle has said, *Pursue peace and purity, without which no one will see God;*[21] do not, therefore, lose your confidence which possesses a great reward. Having therefore some confidence toward that which is holy, *let us therefore approach with confidence the throne of grace, in order to find mercy, when we are in need of help.*

Eph 1:13.
3 lines are missing

Heb 12:14.

Heb 10:35.
Cf. Heb 10:19.

Heb 4:16.

To comfort each other
*1 Th 5:14.

5. [We are] writing to you, therefore, my dear brothers, so that you may *comfort the weak,*[22] *if we are not near you in body, we are however with you in spirit,* and, moreover, remember the word which is written, *If you love one another, everyone will know by this that you are truly my disciples.*[23]

1 Co 5:3.

Jn 13:35.

Greetings

6. We greet you and all those who are with you; all those who are with us greet you. We pray that you may be saved in the Lord,* dear brothers. The grace of our Lord Jesus Christ keep you all. Amen.†

*Cf. 2 Co 13:7-9.
†Cf. Rm 16:24;
   Ga 6:18;
   Ph 4:23; etc.

Letter Four

1. ... *Persevering in prayer,* as it is written, *sharing with the saints in their needs, bless those who persecute you,* he said, *bless them and do not curse them. Rejoice with those who rejoice, weep with those who weep. Think a single thought one towards another, not looking toward haughty things, but walking with the humble.*[1]

Brotherly spirit

Rm 12:12-16.

2. Fulfilling also what is written, *Before the Passover a crowd went up to Jerusalem to purify themselves;*[2] let us also be in purity at our meeting, *walking in the perfume of wisdom in the face of its light,* as it is written in Baruch; and, *Blessed are we, Israel, for what is pleasing to God has been revealed to us. Take courage, therefore, people of God, for he remembers Israel;*[3] and again, Better a righteous man who has no idols; indeed, he will keep himself far from their [reproach]. . . .[4]

Going up to Jerusalem

Jn 11:55.

Ba 4:2.

Ba 4:4-5.

3. *The night is almost over, it will be [daylight] soon. Let us [therefore take off] the works of darkness and put on the armour of the light.*[5] The servant.... *Let us celebrate, not with old yeast, nor with the yeast of evil and [wickedness, but] with unleavened bread of purity and truth.*[6] ... Also, *The one who will fail to go up to celebrate the feast of the Tabernacle ...* that I have purified ... of the Lord. And again, *You ... go up to this feast; [as for myself], my time has not yet come to go up to this feast....* On the great day of the feast, Jesus [went up to] the temple and cried out, [saying,] If a man is thirsty, let him come to [me and drink. As] Scripture says, Torrents of living water shall flow from him* ... for us; and again, An ointment ... child loves you ... of ointment.*

The time of celebration is at hand
Rm 13:12.
9 lines are mutilated

1 Co 5:8.

Zc 14:18 or 19.

Jn 7:8.

*Jn 7:37-38.
7 lines are mutilated

We must not anoint. . . . Let us not think about

Cf. Col 3:2.
earthly things. . . .[7] *[Therefore,] let us not pass judgement on one another, but let us rather make up our minds not to be the cause of your brother*

Rm 14:13.
tripping [or falling. If] because of an ailment your brother suffers, you are no longer walking according to [love. By] your ailment do not kill

Rm 14:15.
someone for whom Christ died. And not . . . wise only for us, for he has said, *Woe to those who are [wise] only for themselves and intelligent before*

Is 5:21.
Pr 10:17.
themselves.[8] Likewise, *Wisdom which ignores correction deceives; whoever does not heal himself all alone in his affairs is brother to the one*

Pr 18:9.
Pr 9:7.
who ruins himself all alone. They are bitter, the corrections of the impious, but the lips of the wise

*Pr 12:8.
†Pr 12:23.
‡Pr 11:16.
heal. * *The wise man is a sensitive [throne],*† *but a woman who hates truth is a throne of derision.*‡ *Do not say to your brother, Take out the dust from [your] eye, while not seeing the plank which*

Mt 7:4-5.
Pr 4:25.
is in your own eye. Hypocrite! but, he said, *Open your eyes and look at the uprightness;* do not allow the [Evil One]. . . .

To be watchful
2 *lines are missing*
*Mt 13:27.
4. . . . let us remember . . . drunkenness. *Was it not good seed that you sowed in your [field]? Where does this darnel come from?**[9] And [again], Truly I have planted a vine completely fruitful; how is it [you have turned to bitterness,*

Jr. 2:21.
vine] foreign?[10] So that we may know that . . . David says, *He loved cursing; may it recoil on him! [He did not love] blessing; may it shun him!*

Ps 109(108): 17-18.
He wrapped curses around him like [a garment]; and as a . . . and, *It has entered into his belly like*

Ibid.
Ps 119(118):131.
water; and again, *[I have opened] my mouth and taken my breath* . . . outside of me. And. . . . And, *Do not quench the Spirit, do not treat the*

[*prophecies*] *with contempt* ... [11] the Spirit from
... but let us acquire for ourselves ... who prepared their lamps ... [12] if there comes the voice
... which was in the beginning until ... and let
us not neglect ... themselves ... being ready ...
in Canaan ... as, *The man who digs a pit for his
neighbor will fall into it; the man who throws a
stone, it will fall on him. The man who cuts wood
will be in danger from it; the man who tears down
a wall, the serpent will bite him....* [13] *The Chaldaeans lit the furnace,* but *their garments had no
smell of burning about them, and the fire did not
scorch them; but the fire came out and burned
those who lit it*; and the word was fulfilled for
them, that *he who lights evil will perish in it; he
who is the accomplice of a thief hates his own
soul;* [14] *he who shakes hands with a man guilty of
homicide will flee, but will not be in safety.*

5. Let us therefore pay attention to God's
word to Moses, *The place on which you stand is a
holy ground,** as, *The place where you are has its
foundations in purity, peace and fear*; knowing
that our Father who assembled us through God
was righteous and pleasing to God; he it was who
taught us the God we did not know. And he taught
us also to take care of one another, when we did
not know the word which is [said] for him, *If a
righteous man teaches.... If a righteous man
[dies, his] hope does not waver.* [15] Let us remember his commandments and his laws, which he established for us so that we may observe them in
their truth. And let us also remember our father
Petronios, who passed his short time with us according to the [custom?]. And let us remember
our father Theodore ... who wrote to us some ...

Marginal references: 1 Th 5:19-20. Cf. Mt 25:7. Pr 26:27. Qo 10:9. Qo 10:8. Cf. Dn 3:46. Dn 3:27(94). Dn 3:48.22. Pr 19:6. Pr 29:24. Pr 28:17. **Remember the recommendations of Pachomius and Theodore** *Ex 3:5. Cf. Ws 4:7.

that there might be fulfilled the word of Joshua
son of Nun who says, *Moses, the servant of the*
Lord has sent me;[16] as, *You have revealed your*
words that enlighten..., *the law which instructs*
the small and [the great];[17] *I rejoice in your words*
more than the one who has found a vast treasure,[18]
and again, *Your companions... many, their be-*
ginnings were powerful...;[19] and again, *Great*
peace for those who love your name; no stum-
bling block for them!...[20] It is good ... to the
Lord ... hope in God, and again, *The light has*
shone in the darkness for the upright. ... The
Lord lights up my lamp, God lights up my dark-
ness;* and, *As is his darkness, so also is his light;*†
and, *He made families like flocks, so that those*
who are righteous may see and rejoice and all
wickedness must hold its tongue. Who is the wise
man who does not observe these things and does
not know the mercies of the Lord?[21]

6. For this reason, therefore, it is fitting for
him in any case to go to his brothers and for us to
be wise and good to one another. *For hatred pro-*
vokes enmity, but the wise man quenches anger;
the impious man on the contrary makes it grow.
The man who wants to separate companions
seeks some pretext; such a man will always be
prone to quarrels.

7. Let no one say, therefore, 'I want to remain
in this place' or else say, 'I want to go into that
community'; but let us all remain in what is established and commanded.[22] May no one, therefore, stretch ... assembly which has been fixed
for us by our righteous father, so that the God of
our fathers may make us worthy also of the assembly which will take place in the age to come.[23]

Side notes (left margin):

Jos 14:7.

Cf. Ps 19(18):7-8.
Ps 119(118):162.

Ps 119(118):165.
4 lines are
mutilated
Ps 112(111):4.
2 lines are
mutilated
*Ps 18(17):28.
†Ps 139(138):12.

Ps 107(106):
41-43.
Brotherly
love

Pr 10:12.
Pr 15:18.

Pr 18:1.
Detachment

18 lines are
missing

And this will happen to us if we correct and admonish each other for our salvation, as it is written,
Better open reproaches than hidden friendship;   Pr 27:5.
and *Better are wounds from friends than kisses
from an enemy.*   Pr 27:6.

8. So may it come to pass that the love of the   Conclusion
Lord may be in us, as he said to his disciples in this
way, *By this everyone will know that you are truly
my disciples, if you love one another,*[24] so that by   Jn 13:35.
this we may know the truth of the Truth[25] we who
are free, as the Lord has promised in the Gospel.
Greetings in the Lord.

Notes to the Letters of Horsiesios

Notes to the First Letter
(Hors. Letter 1)

Hors. Letter 1   [1]The examples of Judith and Susanna are mentioned together as
well in Pach. Instr. 1: 25.
   [2]In Hors. Test. 52 we find the same quotation, but Jerome's translation is different: 'a man of desires'.
   [3]This text is quoted twice again by Horsiesios: Hors. Letter 4: 5 and Hors. Test.
13, and also once by Theodore in Theod. Letter 2: 4.
   [4]Pr 19:16 is quoted by Pachomius in Pach. Letter 3: 12.
   [5]Hg 2:4–9 is quoted again by Horsiesios, with the same omissions, in Hors. Letter
3:2. Verse 9 is quoted also by Theodore in Am. Letter 32.
   [6]In Hors. Letter 3: 2 we find also this same quotation of 1 Co 9:13 following Hg
2:4–9 and being followed by Mk 14:58.
   [7]The same quotation occurs in Hors. Letter 3:2. Horsiesios probably used his
First Letter while writing Letter Three (or *vice versa*).
   [8]This text, which is the conclusion of the Book of Qohelet, is used by Horsiesios
to end this letter and also to end his Testament (Hors. Test. 56). It is also used in
Hors. Test. 10.

Notes to the Second Letter
(Hors. Letter 2)

Hors. Letter 2   [1]The same quotation occurs in Pach. Letter 11A.
   [2]Horsiesios used this text again in Hors. Letter 4: 5.
   [3]Ps 147:2 is quoted again by Horsiesios in Hors. Test. 49.
   [4]This text is quoted again in Hors. Test. 48.
   [5]The Coptic text has: 'he shall not' (*nfnakim an*), which is obviously a mistake.

Notes to the Third Letter
(Hors. Letter 3)

Hors. Letter 3   [1]Pachomius uses this text twice (SBo 118 and 121) to express his conviction that the time for his death has come. Petronios does the same (SBo 130). Cf. also Vit. Ant. 91: 'I am going the way of my fathers, as Scripture says'.

[2]In S[1] 12 this text is applied to Pachomius' nourishing his first disciples. Here, it is undoubtedly to Pachomius and Theodore that Horsiesios applies this same text as well as the preceding one.

[3]The same text is quoted in Hors. Test. 19, where it opens the exhortation to all the brothers without any special responsibility, those who are considered as 'free servants'. See also Theod. Letter 1: 2: 'with your lamp lit'.

[4]Horsiesios makes reference more than once to the parable of the ten virgins. See Hors. Reg. 3; Hors. Letter 4: 4 and Hors. Test. 20 where it concludes an exhortation to chastity.

[5]See other references to the same parable in SBo 118 and Pach. Instr. 1: 51.

[6]In the New Testament text the second verb is in the third person plural, like the first one.

[7]Ga 5:13 is quoted in Hors. Test. 26, where 'the occasion for the flesh' seems to be the practice of entrusting an object or a deposit to a brother, something aimed at the renunciation of material possessions. See also the 'call to liberty' mentioned in Hors. Test. 47. In SBo 105 and 107 there is an interesting combination of Ga 5:13 and Eph 4:2. Furthermore, in the quotation of Ga 5:13, both here and in SBo 105, 'in works of love' (N.T.) has been replaced by 'by the love of the spirit'. See also Pach. Letter 7: 1 (mutual service).

[8]The same text is used again by Horsiesios in recommendations to the housemasters (Hors. Test. 15) and to the superiors of the monasteries (Hors. Test. 40). See also Hors. Test. 31.

[9]The same text is quoted by Theodore at the beginning of a letter summoning the brothers to the assembly of the month of *Mesore* (Theod. Letter 2: 1).

[10]This text is quoted by Theodore in SBo 155 as an example of a text which in the literal sense does not edify and must therefore be understood in the allegorical sense.

[11]This text is often quoted by Horsiesios: see Hors. Instr. 3: 4, n. 1. Note that in the present quotation verse 4:2 is different from the text of the Septuagint, which reads: διόδευσον πρὸς τὴν λάμψιν κατέναντι τοῦ φωτὸς αὐτῆς.

[12]'treasures' or 'elect'. The Coptic substantive *sotp* means '*chosen, elect* person or thing' (Crum, *A Coptic Dictionary*, p. 365B). The Hebrew *hemed-doth* has the same ambivalence. The Septuagint understood 'the chosen things' (τὰ ἐκλεκτὰ), but the Vulgate understood 'the chosen person' (*desideratus cunctis gentibus*, i.e. the Messiah).

[13]See above, Hors. Letter 1: 5, n. 1.

[14]See above, Hors. Letter 1: 5, n. 2.

[15]This text is also quoted in Hors. Letter 1: 6, where it is explicitly ascribed to Mark.

[16]Cf. Hors. Letter 1: 6 quoting Jn 2:19-21.

[17]The image of God's temple is used in Pach Letter 8: 3; Theod. Letter 1: 5; Theod. Instr. 3: 41; and Hors. Test. 19 and 28. See also G[1] 135 and Pach. Fragm. 1:2.

[18]We find the same quotation at the beginning of the next letter (Hors. Letter 4:1) but without the inversion we find here. In both cases, Rm 12:13b ('You should make hospitality your special care') is omitted.

[19]In the Sahidic text, the spelling is *Myra*. This is the first of a long series of quotations, each one containing the word 'wood' (= the Cross).

[20]Although it is introduced as a scriptural quotation, this text is not found in the Bible. But a similar text is cited in the letter of Barnabas, 12,1 as a quotation from a prophet: "Ομοίως πάλιν περὶ τοῦ σταυροῦ ὁρίζει ἐν ἄλλῳ προφήτῃ λέγοντι "Καὶ πότε ταῦτα συντελεσθήσεται; λέγει κύριος· "Οταν ξύλον κλιθῇ καὶ ὅταν ἐκ ξύλου αἷμα στάξῃ."'

[21]Same quotation in Hors. Instr. 7: 11 and in Pach. Instr. 1: 36(bis).

[22]1 Th 5:14 is used in S¹ 25 to describe Pachomius' pastoral solicitude, and in Hors. Test. 15 where it is addressed to the housemasters.

[23]Jn 13:35 is quoted again, and with the same inversion, in Hors. Test. 23 where the context is about the perfect equality that must reign among the brothers, thanks to a total renunciation. The same quotation — but with the inversion — occurs in Hors. Letter 4: 8.

Notes to the Fourth Letter
(Hors. Letter 4)

Hors. Letter 4   [1]See above, Hors. Letter 3: 2, n. 10.

[2]Theodore used the same text in a letter of convocation to the celebration of the Passover.

[3]See above, Hors. Letter 3, 2, n. 3.

[4]This text is from the apocryphal Letter of Jeremiah, v. 73. It is quoted also by Pachomius in Pach. Instr. 1: 53 (see *ibid.* n. 3).

[5]Same quotation in Hors. Test. 38 and in Jud. Prol. See also Hors. Reg. 19.

[6]The same text is used by Theodore in a convocation to the Passover (Theod. Letter 1: 2).

[7]Text quoted in SBo 70 (= G¹ 78) in a praise of Theodore. See also Pach. Letter 3: 3.

[8]This belongs to a series of curses from Is 5:8-23 which Hors. Test. 47 says the monk should try to avoid by his way of life.

[9]The image of the darnel, taken from the parable of the darnel sown in a field of good wheat (Mt 13:24-30, 36-43), is often used, e.g. in SBo 6; 106; 142 and in G¹ 38.

[10]The end of the quotation is obscure in Coptic; and the translation is approximate. See Hors. Instr. 3: 2, n. 1.

[11]Same quotation in Hors. Test. 53.

[12]See also Hors. Letter 3: 1, n. 4.

[13]Theodore, in his first instruction to the brothers as father of the *Koinonia* after Horsiesios' resignation (see SBo 141), uses this text to lament that the brothers have nullified Pachomius' rules.

[14]The same quotation occurs in Pach. Letter 4: 6.

[15]Although this text is introduced as a biblical quotation and has some similarity with Ws 4:7, it cannot be considered a direct quotation.

[16]The same image of Joshua as Moses' helper is applied to Theodore in SBo 78 and to Horsiesios in SBo 132 (= S⁵ 126).

[17]Verses 7 and 8 of Ps 19(18) are quoted (in inverted order) in Hors. Test. 5.

[18]The same quotation occurs in Hors. Test. 43.

[19]Unidentified quotation. Cf. Ps 19(18):8–9.

[20]Same quotation in Hors. Letter 2.

[21]This text is quoted also in Hors. Letter 1:3; Hors. Test 13 and Theod. Letter 2: 4

[22]The appointment of the superiors was changed at the two general assemblies of the Passover and of the month of *Mesore.* This was the practice of Pachomius (G¹ 83), of Theodore (SBo 196), and of Horsiesios (G¹ 122). Cf. Jer. Pref. 7.

[23]About the assembly of the brothers in the age to come, see Hors. Test. 3 and 50. See also A. Veilleux, *La liturgie,* pp. 377–378.

[24]See Hors. Letter 3: 5, n. 2.

[25]Cf. Hors. Test. 10: 'ueritas erudiuit ueritatem'.

fRAGMENTS fROM hORSIESIOS

(hORS. fRAGM.)

Text: CSCO 159,
pp. 81-82

. . . we were not able to go to the city to receive this reverend man, because of the dangers we had heard of.

This is why we have all heard about this name of monk, we have all taken the habit, thinking that the habit would be our recommendation to God. But when we break the laws of the habit, we are all cowards, we desert. We have been taught: O wretched man, keep purity, and you will enter into the city of God. And the foolish man says, 'I wish to enter the city, but the pleasures of impurity I cannot renounce'. So then, you are saying, 'I desire to come to God laden with matter!' The wretched man declares, 'I wish to please God, while yet being burdened with cares!'

On purity

Cf. Heb 12:22.

A. APA HORSIESIOS, ARCHIMANDRITE

B. ALSO FROM THE SAME.

It is also good that he who truly repents be on his guard against these three wiles of the devil. Indeed, at the time a man begins to repent, [the devil] instils within him the guileful thought of vowing to God a rigorous *ascesis* when he has the fear of God and has promised never to sin against

On ascesis

him. The astute one acts this way because he knows that, if someone once experiences too much weariness, or especially if he becomes ill, he will relax his *ascesis*, and will certainly lose the fear of God. Now for man to lose the fear of God or to fall back into his former sins is indeed the beginning of a false vow.

With discretion

Hence, it is better for a man, when he is about to make a covenant with God, not to specify his ascetical practices, but rather to say, 'Lord, whatever I can do, short of illness or excessive fatigue, I mean to do, knowing that it is you who will give me the strength.' And if he stalls a moment, the fear of the Lord will keep him, till he returns to the Lord, to his ascetical practices, and to a moderate corporal mortification; the fear of the Lord, which dwells in a pure heart, will increase. This fear is indeed unlimited; so that this man will receive the light to walk confidently toward the judgements of God, at the moment when he appears before the tribunal of God, and when he is judged on whatever he has done since the day when he first heard God's law.

Cf. Ps 46(45):
2(LXX).

An old man and one who is impotent, since they can[not] afflict themselves....

the Book of our father horsiesios

WHICH HE GAVE TO HIS BROTHERS AS A TESTAMENT
WHEN HE WAS ABOUT TO DIE.

(hors. test.)

1. *Hear, Israel, the commandments of life.* Listen and understand prudence. Why are you in the land of your enemies, Israel? You have grown old in an alien land.[1] *You have been defiled with the dead and accounted with those in hell. You have abandoned the fountain of wisdom. Had you walked in the way of God, perhaps you would be dwelling in peace. Learn, then*—he says— *where your prudence is, where the strength* of glory and virtue *is, where understanding, where the light of the eyes is and peace. Who has found* [wisdom's] *dwelling, and who has entered her treasure house?*

Baruch spoke this on account of those carried off into captivity to the land of Babylon, [the land] of their enemies, because they would not heed the instructions of the prophets and forgot the law God had given them through Moses. This is why God inflicted punishments and sufferings on them and laid on them the yoke of captivity, instructing them as his own, just as a father corrects his sons. He is unwilling to see them perish, once set aright, but wishes to save them through repentance.

Prologue
Baruch's lesson

Bar 3:9-15.

Cf. 2 P 3:9.

171

Paul's lesson

Rm 11:21.

1 Co 10:11;
cf. 10:6.

Beware of
forgetfulness

Cf. 2 P 3:9;
Rm 2:4; 2 P 3:15.

Cf. Rev 3:21.
Cf. 1 P 2:21.

Cf. 1 Co 5:1-13.

1 Co 5:5.
Ps 112(111):1.

*Ps 94(93):12.
†Ps 119(118):32.
‡Dt 6:2.

2. Therefore we, too, ought to remember the words of the Apostle, who said, *If God did not spare the natural branches, neither will he spare us,* who have neglected to keep his commandments. *All these things happened to them as a warning; they were written down to be a lesson for us,*[1] *upon whom the end of time has come.* They, indeed, were transferred from the city of Judah to the city of the Chaldaeans, changing places on earth. As for us, if God sees us negligent, we shall lose our city in the world to come. Forsaking joy, we shall be handed over to a captivity of punishments and shall lose the eternal happiness which our fathers and brothers[2] found through their unstinting toil.

3. May forgetfulness not overcome us therefore. Let us not look upon God's patience as ignorance. He holds back and delays so that, when we have been converted to a better state, we may not be handed over to torments. When we sin, let us not think God consents to our sins because he does not take immediate vengeance. Let us rather reflect on this: passing soon from this world, in the world to come we shall be separated from our fathers and brothers who are already in possession of the place of victory. We, too, shall possess it, if we are willing to walk in their footsteps and to attend to what the Apostle Paul did even here below, separating saints from sinners,[1] and giving the offenders *over to the destruction of the flesh,*[2] *that* [their] *spirit may be saved.*

Happy the man who fears the Lord, and he whom the Lord corrects to improve him, and *he to whom He teaches His law,** *that he may walk in his commandments*† *all the days of his life.*‡

[Blessed too] *the one who does not complain
about his sin.*   Lm 3:39.

   4. Therefore, let us *examine our paths** and   **Call to self-
ponder our own steps. *Let us return to the Lord*   scrutiny*
and stretch out our hands up toward heaven,[1]   *Lm 3:40.
that he may be our helper on *the day of judge-*   Lm 3:40-41.
ment, and that we may *not be confounded, when*   1 Jn 4:17.
we speak to our enemies at the gate, but may we   Ps 127(126):5.
rather be worthy to hear, *Open the gates! Let the
people who keeps* justice and *truth enter.* The   Is 26:2.
man who has truth at heart and possesses peace
can say, *We have put our hope in you forever,*
*Lord.** Let us remember the Lord, and may *Jeru-*   *Ps 31(30):1;
salem well up in our heart,[†] lest we forget about   Cf. Ps 52(51):9.
the man of whom this was written:[2] *Blessed is the*   [†]Jr 51:50.
*man who puts his trust in the Lord, whose hope is
in him. He will be like a fruitful tree by the water-
side, that thrusts its roots down to the moisture.
He will not be afraid when hot weather comes.
He will have leafy branches, and, in a dry spell,
he will be green, bearing unfailing fruit.*[3]
*Troublesome above all is the heart, and so is
man.*[4] *Who can understand him? I, the Lord,
search the hearts and probe the loins, to give each
man according to his ways.* [5]   Jr 17:7-10.

   5. Let us examine ourselves and not treat light-   **Study of
ly the faults we have committed. Let us study   our Father's
with an anxious heart each command of our Fa-   commands**
ther[1] and of those who have taught us. *We should
not only believe in Christ, but also suffer for his
sake,*[2] and understand the mystery of which it is   Ph 1:29.
said, *The breath of our face is Christ the Lord.*   Lm 4:20.
And elsewhere, *Your law is a lamp to my feet and
a light on my path.* And again, *The Lord's word*   Ps 119(118):105.
gave me life. And, *The law of the Lord is pure,*   Ps 119(118):50.

bringing souls to conversion; the commandment

Ps 19(18):7.
Ps 19(18):8.

of the Lord is bright, giving light to the eyes.[3]
And the Apostle says, *The law is holy and the pre-*

Rm 7:12.

cept is holy, just and good.

If we understand all these things, we shall be worthy to hear, *When the just man falls, he shall*

Ps 37(36):24.

suffer no harm, for the Lord holds his hand. And again, *The just man falls seven times and rises*

Pr 24:16.

again.

Call to
repentance
*Cf. 2 P 3:9.
Cf. Rm 13:11.

6. Now then, brothers, since *God is patient* with us and urges us *to repentance,** let us *wake up from* deep *sleep,*[1] *because our adversary, the devil, like a roaring lion, is looking for someone to devour. He must be resisted steadfastly, and* [you] *must realize that the same struggle was the*

1 P 5:8-9.

lot of our forefathers.[2] Let us not grow weary of laboring and sowing the seeds of virtue, that we

Cf. Ps 126(125):6.

may be able to harvest joy in the future. Let us hear Paul teaching, *But you who have paid heed to my doctrine, instruction, zeal, patience, perse-*

2 Tm 3:10.

cutions.... And, following the example of the saints,[3] *having Jesus to lead us and bring us to*

Heb 12:2.

perfection, let us persevere in what we have begun. Let us understand the hair of our head on the way,[4] that there may be *ointment in our*

Ps 133(132):2.

beard to *flow to the collar of the robe,* that we may be able *to fulfill the whole of what has been*

Cf. Lk 21:22.

written.[5]

Admonition to
the superiors
in general

7. Therefore, leaders of monasteries and house-masters,[1] to whom men are entrusted and with whom are found **K** or **I** or **E** or **A**, [or]—to say it in plain language—to whom individual men are committed, each along with their groups,[2] *let*

Cf. Tt 2:13.

them await the coming of the Saviour and furnish an army arrayed with arms for his inspection. Do not refresh them in their bodily needs without giving them spiritual nourishment. Or again, do not teach them spiritual things while oppressing them in their bodily needs, namely, food and clothing. But give them food for soul and body alike; and give them no opportunity for negligence. Or what is this justice of ours, that we oppress the brothers with work while we enjoy leisure? Or that we impose *on them a yoke which we are unable to bear?*

Cf. Ac 15:10.

We read in the Gospel, *With the measure you have used, it shall be measured out to you.*[3] Therefore, let us share with them both work and refreshment, and let us not consider our disciples slaves and allow their distress to be our joy, lest the Gospel utterance accuse us along with the Pharisees, *Woe to you, doctors of the law, who bind unbearable burdens and place them on men's shoulders, while you dare not touch them with so much as a finger.*

Mt 7:2; Mk 4:24; Lk 6:38.

Lk 11:46; Mt 23:4.

8. There are some who consider themselves as living by God's law,[1] and say to themselves, 'What do I have to do with other men? I seek to serve God and fulfill his commandments. What others do does not concern me.' These does Ezechiel admonish, saying, *Shepherds of Israel, do shepherds feed themselves? Do they not feed the sheep? See, you drink milk, you are clothed with wool.*[2] *You have killed the fat sheep. You have not strengthened the weak ones. The cripple you have not bound up. The stray you have not brought back. You have not looked for the lost.* You have worn out the strong with work. *You have scattered my sheep, because they had no shepherds.*[3] Therefore, *the Lord will call in judgement his elders*

On pastoral concern

Ez 34:2-5.

Is 3:14.
and his leaders. Then this will be fulfilled in us, *Your creditors are despoiling you, and those de-*
Cf. Is 3:12.
*manding restitution lead you astray.*⁴ How much more should we be hearing, *Happy are you, O land, whose king is nobly born. Your princes eat*
Qo 10:17.
*at the proper time to gain strength,*⁵ and they will not be overcome.

The same care
for all
9. Therefore, O man, do not cease to recommend and to teach the things that are holy down to the last soul entrusted to you, and to *present*
Tt 2:7.
*yourself as an example of good works.*¹ And be especially careful not to love one and hate another. Show an equal attitude to all, lest the one whom you love God hate, and the one whom you hate God love. Do not, in the name of friendship, consent to anyone who is going astray. Do not press one down and raise another up, to the loss of your
Cf. 1 Th 3:5.
own labor.

When the housemasters sit in the lower places, where our father has strictly forbidden [them] to sit,² they must take care lest any of the brothers cause an injury to a superior and the latter pass a verdict and say, 'what business have I with a contemptuous man? Let him do what he wishes, it does not concern me. I shall not warn or correct him, if he goes astray. Whether he is saved or lost does not concern me.'³

O man, you who say these things, understand that you are overcome by anger and hatred has so taken hold of your heart, that the brother is lost more through your fault than through his own sin. You ought to forgive him and receive him when he repents, that you may be able to say that passage from the Gospel, *Forgive us our debts, as*
Mt 6:12.
*we forgive those who are in debt to us.*⁴ For, if you

want God to forgive you your sins, you must forgive your brother whatever he has committed
against you, mindful of that precept, *You must
not bear hatred for your brother in your heart,*   Lv 19:17.
and of the warning of Solomon, *Rouse up your
fellow citizen for whom you have pledged your-
self.*⁵ And again, *Cease not to correct the child;*   Cf. Pr 6:3.
for if you strike him with the rod, he shall not die.   Pr 23:13.
Hear also Moses who says, *You shall reprove your
neighbor severely, lest you incur the sin in his
place;* and may the warning of Solomon not come   Lv 19:17.
again, *The man who does not warn his son to
guard himself from perditon shall be swiftly destroyed.*   Pr 24:22(LXX).

10 .Let all to whom care of the brothers has   **Responsibility of**
been committed prepare themselves for the com-   **the superiors**
ing of the Saviour and for his fearsome tribunal.¹   **before God's**
For, if rendering an account for oneself is fraught   **tribunal**
with danger and apprehension, how much more
so is undergoing torment for the sin of another
and *falling into the hands of the living God?*² We   Cf. Heb 10:31.
cannot plead ignorance, for it is written, *God will
bring every deed to judgement, in everything
which was neglected, whether good or evil.*³ And   Qo 12:14.
we read in the Apostle, *We must all be laid bare
before the tribunal of Christ, and each one shall
be rewarded for what he has done, whether good
or evil.*⁴ Isaiah, too, indicates *the appointed day*   2 Co 5:10.
*on which God shall judge the world in righteous-
ness,* saying, *Behold, the day of the Lord is com-*   Ac 17:31;
ing—a day of rage and anger, for which there is   Cf. Ps 10(9):8;
no remedy—to make the earth a desert and to   96(95):13;
wipe sinners from it.   98(97):9.
        Is 13:9.

For we know that we have to keep in mind everything written in the law, foretold us by the

Cf. Rm 15:4.

prophets, and taught us by our holy Father, and that we shall have to render an account for each of these: why we did not do it or why we did it with negligence.[5] For, He *to whom all judgement*

Cf. Jn 5:22.

was entrusted by the Father speaks, and Truth has taught the truth: *Do not imagine that I am going to accuse you before the Father. Moses in whom you hope is the one who will accuse you. If you believed Moses, you would believe me too,*

Jn 5:45-46.

since I am he of whom he was writing.

Everyone must stand before Christ's tribunal *Rm 14:10; 2 Co 5:10.

11. We learn from all this that *we must stand before the tribunal of Christ*[*1] and be judged not only for each deed but also for each thought. And, after we have rendered an account of our own life, we shall likewise render an account for those who were entrusted to us. And not only is this to be understood of the housemasters but also of the superiors of the monasteries and of each of the brothers belonging to the rank and file,[2] be-cause all must *carry each other's burdens and so*

Ga 6:2.

fulfill the law of Christ.[3] Let them hear the Apos-tle writing to Timothy, *Timothy, guard what is entrusted to you, avoiding profane novelties of speech and the profession of what is falsely called*

1 Tm 6:20.

knowledge.

God has also entrusted a deposit to us: the brothers' way of life.[4] While laboring on their behalf, we look forward to future rewards, lest

Ex 5:11.

this be said to us as well, *Let this people go*; and lest, if we forsake the traditions of our father, this be hurled at us: *Those who have my law do not know me; the shepherds have rebelled against*

Jr 2:8.

me. Then he rebukes others, saying, *I put my heritage into your hand, but you have shown it no*

Is 47:6.

mercy; you have oppressed the old with the yoke.

Not only must we hear this; we must also under-
stand it, for *whoever ignores* [this] *will be ignored.*   1 Co 14:38.
And in another place it is written, *Because you
have rejected knowledge, I too will reject you
from my priesthood.*   Ho 4:6.

12. And so, dearest brothers, you who follow   **Make Pacho-**
the life and precepts of the *Koinonia,* remain   **mius proud**
firm in your resolution once made and fulfill the   **of his sons**
work of God,[1] that our Father, who was the first
to establish the *Koinonia,*[2] may say with joy to the
Lord on our behalf, 'According to what I have
handed on to them, so they live.' The Apostle,
while still alive, said as much, *I praise you for remembering me in everything, and maintaining
my traditions just as I have handed them on to
you.*[3]   1 Co 11:2.

13. Therefore, superiors of the monasteries,   **Admonition to**
be solicitous and with justice and the fear of God   **the superiors in**
show every concern for the brothers. Do not mis-   **general**
use [your] authority arrogantly, but *offer yourself
as an example* to everyone and to the flock under   Cf. Tt 2:7.
you, like our Lord, who gave himself as an exam-   Cf. 1 P 5:3.
ple in everything,* and *made his families like*   *Cf. Jn 13:15.
flocks.†[1] Have compassion on the flock entrusted   †Ps 107(106):41.
to you, and be mindful of that statement of the
Apostle, *I have witheld nothing*[2] *that I might an-
nounce to you the whole will of God.* And again, *I*   Cf. Ac 20:20.27.
*have not ceased imploring each of you and teach-
ing you publicly.*[3] See how much love and how   Cf. Ac 20:31.20.
much mercy there was in the man of God, who
was not only *solicitous for all the churches but is*   *Cf. 2 Co 11:
weak with those who are weak*[4] and *carries the*   28-29.
sufferings of all.†   †Cf. Is 53:4.

Let us be on our guard that no one be scandalized and ruined through our negligence, and that

we do not forget the words of our Lord and Saviour, who says in the Gospel, *Father, not one of*

Jn 18:9. *those you gave me have I lost.* Let us not despise any soul, lest anyone perish through our hardness of heart. For, if anyone dies on our account, our soul will be held guilty for his. Our Father used to impress this on us continually and he used to warn us,⁵ so that this saying might not be fulfilled

Mi 7:2. in us, *Each man oppresses his neighbor.* And again, *If you are biting and devouring one another, watch out that you be not consumed by*

Ga 5:15. *one another.*

From this it is clear that *the man who preserves*

Cf. Pr 16:17. *the soul of another is guardian of his own soul.*

Admonition to
the 'seconds' of
the monasteries

14. And you also, who are the seconds of the monastery, show yourselves first in virtue. Let no one perish through your fault.¹ Do not incur the same reproach as the man *who ate and drank with drunkards and who did not give food to his fellow servants at the proper time. The Lord will come on a day he does not expect and at an hour he does not know. He will cut him off and send him to the same fate as the hypocrites, where*

Mt 24:45.49-51. *there is weeping and grinding of teeth.*² May a like sentence not befall any of you. But, *when the*

Ac 3:20. *time of consolation comes,* may we deserve to hear, *Well done, good and faithful servant; since you have been faithful in a small thing, I will put you in charge over much; enter into your master's*

Mt 25:21, 23. *happiness.*³

Admonition to
the housemasters

15. And you, the housemasters of the individual houses, *be ready to answer all who ask you for*

1 P 3:15. *an account of the faith*¹ *that is in you. Warn those who are unruly . Console the fainthearted. Support the weak. Be patient to all.*² Listen to the

1 Th 5:14.

Apostle's warning, *Fathers, do not drive your children to anger,[3] but bring them up on the discipline and admonition of the Lord.* And know that *more is required from the man who has received more, and more will be exacted from the man who has been entrusted with more.* And do not consider only *what is useful to yourself, but also what is useful to your neighbors,[4]* lest the Scripture be fulfilled in you which says, *Because each of you seeks the advantage of his own house, heaven shall withhold its dew and earth shall not yield its fruit,* for you have made your talk harsh against me. And elsewhere it is said, *Because you did not do* [it] *to one of the least of these, you did not do* [it] *to me.*

Eph 6:4.

Lk 12:48.

Cf. 1 Co 10:33.

Hg 1:9-10.
Cf. Ml 3:13.
Mt 25:45.

16. I will say it again and again and will repeat it: Take care not to love some and hate others,[1] to sustain this one and to neglect that one, lest your toil be found wasted and all your sweat be lost. Then, when you have left the body and have been freed from the turmoil of this world, you may think you have entered the harbor of tranquility only to meet with the shipwreck of injustice; and [then] *with the measure you have used, it shall be measured out to you*[*2] by him who *is no respecter of persons in judgement.*[†3] If anything mortal[‡] or shameful has been committed in the houses through the negligence of the housemasters,[4] after the offenders are punished, the housemaster will also be held guilty of the offence. Our father of holy memory used always to impress this on us.[5]

Impartiality

*Mt 7:2; Mk 4:24;
Lk 6:38.
†1 P 1:17;
Dt 10:17.
‡Cf. 1 Jn 5:16-17.

17. For this reason, let each one guard the flock committed to him with all care and solicitude. Let them imitate the shepherds of the Gos-

Pastoral care

pel who were not asleep but keeping watch when-
the angel of God came and annouced to them the

Cf. Lk 2:8-14.

coming of the Saviour. The Saviour himself says,
The good shepherd lays down his life for his sheep.[1]
But the hired man, since he is not the shepherd[2]
*and the sheep do not belong to him, leaves the
flock and runs away when he sees a wolf coming.
And the wolf snatches the flock and plunders it;
this is because he is a hired man and does not care*

Jn 10:11-13.

about the sheep. Now, about the good shepherds,
Luke writes this story, *But there were shepherds
on guard, keeping the night watches over their
flock. And the angel of the Lord came to them,
and the glory of God shone around them, and
they were very much afraid. And the angel said to
them: Do not be afraid. For, behold, I announce
to you a great joy which shall be for the whole
people. A Saviour, who is Christ the Lord, has
been born to you today in the town of David. And
this shall be for you a sign of the fact: you will
find the baby wrapped in swaddling clothes and*

Lk 2:8-12.

lying in a manger.
Surely these were not the only men at that time
who were grazing their sheep and following their
flock through the wilderness. But because they
were the only solicitous ones and because they
overcame night's natural sleep for fear of stealthy
wolves, they deserved to be the first to hear what
had happened nearby, whereas sleeping Jerusalem was unaware. For this reason, David says, *Be-*

Ps 121(120):4.

hold, he who guards Israel will not sleep.
And so, you too must keep watch *with fear and*

Cf. Ph 2:12.
Cf. 2 M 14:35.
Cf. 2 Co 5:10.

trembling,[3] *working out your salvation* in the
knowledge that the Lord of the universe, who
shall reward all flesh for whatever it does, ap-
peared after his resurrection only to his apostles,

and said to Peter, the prince of the apostles, *Simon,* [son] *of John, do you love me more than these? He answered: Lord, you know I love you. He said to him: Feed my lambs. He asked him a second time: Simon,* [son] *of John, do you love me? He answered: Yes, Lord, you know I love you. He said to him: Feed my sheep.* And he ordered him to feed his sheep a third time, and in Peter he enjoined this office on all of us,[4] diligently to feed the sheep of the Lord, that on the *day of his visitation* we may, for our toil and watchfulness, receive what he promised us in the Gospel, saying, *Father, I wish that where I am, these may be with me.* And again [he says], *Where I am, there also shall be my minister.* Let us look to the promises and the rewards; then in an attitude of faith we will more easily stand all our pains, *walking as the Lord himself walked,* who is the one promising the rewards.

18. And you too, the seconds of the individual houses, strive after humility and modesty, and consider the various commands of the elders[1] as a norm of common life, that in observing them you may save your souls and be like the man who said: *My soul is always in my hands.* May *the son glorify his father,*[2] and may you rejoice in your fruits. For, *without works* and fruits no man shall rejoice in the Lord's company. When you bear fruit in the Lord, you will enjoy him as *heir and coheir.*[3]

19. But also all of you, my brothers, who, each according to his rank,[1] are subject to a free servitude,[2] *have your loins girt and burning lamps in your hands, like servants waiting for their master to return from the wedding feast, so that, when he comes and knocks, they may open to him at*

Jn 21:15-17.

Cf. 1 P 5:2.
Is 10:3.

Jn 17:24.
Jn 12:26.

Cf. 1 Jn 2:6.

Admonition to the 'seconds' of the houses

Cf. Jr 48:6.
Ps 119(118):109.
Cf. Ml 1:6.
Jm 2:24.

Cf. Rm 8:17.

Admonition to all the brothers: obedience

once.³ *Happy the servants whom the master finds*

Lk 12:35-37. *awake when he comes.* It shall be like that for
you, too, if long labor does not fill you with weariness. You shall be called to the heavenly banquet,

Cf. Mt 4:11. and angels shall wait on you. These are the things
promised in return for keeping the command-
ments of God, and these are the rewards of the
life to come.

Ph 4:4.
Cf Eph 6:1. *Rejoice in the Lord. I repeat, rejoice.* Be subject to [the] fathers in all obedience, *without
murmuring or wavering thoughts,*⁴ bringing *sim-*

Cf. Ph 2:14-15. *plicity* of heart to your good deeds, that, filled
with virtues and the fear of God, you may be

Cf. Rm 8:23;
Ga 4:5. made worthy of his adoption. *Take up the shield
of faith, upon which you can extinguish all the
burning arrows of the devil. Take up the sword of*

Eph 6:16-17. *the Spirit, which is the word of God.*⁵ *Be wise as*
Mt 10:16. *serpents and simple as doves.*⁶ Listen to Paul
Col 3:20. speaking, *Sons, be obedient to your parents,* and
receive the salvation of your souls through those
who are set over you. And in another place it is
written, *Obey your superiors and be subject to
them for they are keeping watch over your souls
and give an account for you.* And always stand in

Heb 13:17. awe of what the same Paul says, *You are God's
temple, and the Spirit of God dwells in you. Now
if anybody should profane the temple of God,*

1 Co 3:16-17. *God will destroy him.* And again, *Do not grieve
the Holy Spirit of God with whom you have been*

Eph 4:30. *sealed for the day of redemption*⁷ [by] *the just*
2 Th 1:5. *judgement of God.*⁸

Chastity   20. Preserve the chastity of your body,¹ that
you may be like *a garden enclosed and a fountain*

Sg 4:12. *sealed.*² For *he who is born of God does not sin,*
1 Jn 3:9. *because His seed abides in him.*³ This same John

says, *I write to you, young men, because you are strong, and God's word abides in you, and you have overcome the Evil One.* When you, too, have overcome the enemy with God's help, then He himself will say, *I will save them from hell and rescue them from death. Death, where is your strife? Death, where is your sting?* If we swallow death, we shall overcome it, and we shall hear: *Death shall never have dominion over them,* for the death *by which we died to sin once for all has died in us,* and by the life whereby we live in Christ, we shall always live.* For, *when a man dies in the flesh, he is freed from sin.†* Let us no longer live *according to human desires, but let us spend the rest of our life according to the will of God.‡*

You who fear the Lord, arm yourselves with chastity, that you may deserve to hear, *You are not in the flesh but in the spirit.*⁴ And know that perfect things are given to the perfect, and that useless things are given to the useless, according to the Gospel saying, *The man who has shall receive, and he shall have in abundance. But the man who has not, even what he seems to have shall be taken away from him.* Let us imitate the wise virgins who were worthy to enter the bridal chamber with the bridegroom and had the oil of good works in their jars and lamps. Then the foolish virgins found the door of the bridal chamber closed; they had been unwilling to prepare oil for themselves before the wedding feast.⁵ *These things happened to them as a warning; they were written down to be a lesson for us,* that we may avoid what happened in the past and keep the precepts of the wise man who said, *My son, if your heart is wise, you shall gladden my own*

1 Jn 2:14.

Ho 13:14.
1 Co 15:55.
Cf. 1 Co 15:55.
Rm 6:9.

Cf. Rm 6:2.
*Cf. Rm 5:2;
    6:6–11;
    1 Co 15:22.
†Rm 6:7;
 Cf. 1 P 4:1.
‡Cf. 1 P 4:2.

Ps 135(134):20;
Si 2:8.

Cf. Rm 8:9.

Mt 25:29;
Lk 8:18.

Cf. Mt 25:4-12.

1 Co 10:11.

heart; and my lips shall linger on your words, if
Pr 23:15-16.   *only they be upright.* And again, *Do not let your*
                    heart be envious of sinners, but stand in fear of
Pr 23:17.   *God all day long*[6] and continually attend to his
Nb 3:7.   worship.

Detachment   21. Let us be even more vigilant, in the know-
                    ledge that God has granted us, through our fa-
                    ther Pachomius, the great grace to renounce the
                    world[1] and consider as nothing all the worries of
                    the world and the cares of worldly affairs. What
                    opportunity has been left to us to have anything
Gn 14:23.   as our own, *from a thread to a shoe strap,*[2] since
1 Co 2:3;   we have masters who *with fear and trembling* are
Cf. Tb 13:6;   so solicitous on our behalf both for food and cloth-
   Eph 6:5.   ing and during ill health,[3] if it should occur, that
                    we need not worry about anything and thereby
                    lose the soul's benefits for the sake of the flesh?
                    We are free; we have cast from our necks the yoke
                    of enslavement to the world. Why do we want to
Pr 26:11 =   go back to our vomit, to have something to worry
2 P 2:22.   about and to be afraid of losing? For what use
                    would an extra cloak serve, or fancier food, or a
                    better bed, when everything is provided in com-
                    mon,[4] and when nothing is harder than the Cross
                    of Christ? It is by living according to this [Cross]
                    that our fathers erected us *on the foundation of*
                    the apostles and prophets and on the discipline of
                    the Gospels, which is held fast *by the cornerstone,*
Eph 2:20.   *our Lord Jesus Christ.* Following him we descend
                    to life-giving humility, away from the pride that
                    causes death, exchanging wealth for poverty and
                    delicacies for simple food.

Never turn a   22. I beseech you not to forget the resolution
ministry to per-   you once took. And let us think of the traditions
sonal advantage   of our father as a ladder which leads to the king-

dom of heaven. Do not long for the things you once trampled underfoot. It is enough for us to have what is sufficient for any man: two tunics and another one which is worn out, a linen mantle, two hoods, a linen belt, shoes, a [goat]-skin and a staff.[1]

If the person to whom a ministry or the administration of the monastery is entrusted makes a profit out of it—that is, lays hold of something and turns it to his personal comfort—this must be considered a crime and a sacrilege. For by doing this he despises those who do not have[2] but are rich in blessed poverty. Not only is he lost, but he causes the rest to be lost.

Surely God has been pleased with those who have bent their neck and, with all humility and affliction, weep and mourn in this life.[3] When they leave the body, they shall be taken to recline with our holy fathers, Abraham, Isaac, and Jacob, the prophets and the apostles. They shall enjoy the consolation they deserve, just as Lazarus did in the bosom of Abraham.

But woe to those who lived in the *Koinonia*[4] and turned something from common to their own use. When they leave this body, they shall hear, *Remember that you received good things during your life,*[5] while your brothers were toiling in fasts, and in abstinence, and sweating from unceasing effort. Then look at those who, happy and cheerful, have forsaken the present life to obtain the life to come, while you are put in filth and torments and misery because you did not want to hear the word of the Gospel, and because you spurned the words of Isaiah, who said, *Behold, those who serve me shall eat, while you*

Cf. Gn 28:12.

Cf. 1 Co 11:22

Cf. Is 2:9.17;
Rm 11:10

Cf. Mt 8:11.

Cf. Lk 16:23.

Lk 16:25.

Cf. Mt 19:21;
Lk 12:33; 18:22.

go hungry. Behold, those who serve me shall drink, while you go thirsty. Behold, those who serve me shall rejoice, while you cry out on account of the anguish of your heart, and wail on
Is 65:13-14.
account of the grief of your spirit.[6] You have heard all the beatitudes of the Scriptures, and
Cf. Jr 5:3.
you have been unwilling to accept the discipline.

Uniformity in life-style

23. Therefore, brothers, let us be equal, from the least to the greatest, whether rich or poor, perfect in harmony and humility, that it can be said of us as well, *The man who* [gathered] *much, had nothing over; the man who* [gathered] *little*
Cf. 2 Co 8:15 = Ex 16:18.
did not go short. Let no one look after his own pleasure when he sees a brother living in poverty
Cf. 1 Jn 3:17; Dt 15:3.
and hardship;[1] let this saying of the prophet be told him, *Did one God not create* [all of] *you? Have you not all one father? Why has each of you abandoned his brother, thus profaning the covenant of your fathers? Judah has been forsaken,*
Ml 2:10, 11.
and abomination has been committed in Israel.[2]

Our Lord and Saviour gave his apostles this precept, *I give you a new commandment: Love one another, as I have loved you. By this you shall*
Jn 13:34-35.
truly be known as my disciples.[3] We should, therefore, love one another and show that we are truly the servants of our Lord Jesus Christ and sons of Pachomius and disciples of the *Koinonia.*[4]

Do not defend a brother

24. If a housemaster reprimands one of the brothers subject to him, instructing him in the fear of God and desiring to correct his error, and if another wishes to speak on his behalf and to defend him,[1] turning his heart astray, the one who does this sins against his own soul, because he led astray the person who could have been corrected; he threw to the ground the man who was rising,

and he deceived with evil persuasion the man who was tending to better things. Going astray himself, he leads others astray too. This saying can aptly be applied to him, *Woe to the man who gives to his neighbor a violent upheaval to drink and makes him drunk. Woe to the man who leads a blind man astray on the road.*[2] *It is better for the man who scandalizes any of those who believe in God to have a millstone hung around his neck and to be cast into the sea.* As we were saying, this is because he tripped a man who was rising; he turned over to pride someone who was obeying, and turned to bitterness a brother who was able to walk in the sweetness of charity; he corrupted with evil advice someone subject to the laws of the monastery and he brought him to hate and to be saddened against the one who was teaching him the Lord's discipline.[3] He has sown strife and discord among the brothers,[4] and did not fear what was written, *Who are you to judge another man's servant? He stands or falls for his own master. And he will stand because the Lord has the power to make him stand again.*[5] Consider what [Paul] said: It is the Lord who has the power to make him stand, not the man who disregards the Lord's words.

25. Therefore, brothers, let us especially avoid subverting the mind of anyone against his teacher and admonisher. Let us recall [the passage of] Scripture which says, *Free your heart from wickedness that you may be saved.* Let us not sow pride and stubborness in the place of obedience in each other's hearts. For, anyone who fears the Lord, if he sees his brother going astray and falling, ought rather to show him the things that are

Cf. 2 Tm 3:13.

Hab 2:15 (LXX).
Dt 27:18.

Mt 18:6.

Rm 14:4.

Do not undermine the superior's authority

Jr 4:14.

holy and point out to him the right way that, advancing with all chastity and the fear of God, he may carry out the saying of Solomon, *Rescue those being led away to death; and do not cease*

Pr 24:11.

delivering them from slaughter. And do not say, I do not know this man. Rest assured, *the Lord*

Pr 24:12(LXX);
Lk 16:15;
Ac 15:8.
Jude 23.

knows the hearts of all. And Jude says in his letter, *Snatching them from the fire and hating the soiled garment of the flesh.*[1] Let us beware of this kind of garment and *put on instead God's armor so as to be able to resist the devil's snares. For our fight is not against flesh and blood but against principalities and powers, against the rulers of darkness, and against the spirits of wickedness in*

Eph 6:11–12.

the heavens.

Do not dispose of anything as your own

26. Special precaution must be taken that no one consign anything in another house or in another's cell. This is against the discipline of the monastery.[1] The man who does this is not among the number of the brothers, but is a hireling and a stranger. He is not to eat the Passover of the

Cf. Ex 12:43.

Lord with the holy ones,[2] because he has become

Is 8:14 =
1 P 2:8
*Jr 50:26.

a stumbling-stone in the monastery. And this can be said of him, *Cast the stones out of my way.**
For if we do not have the right to keep our tunics with us until evening when we wash them and they are still wet—but we give them to the [house-] master who has charge over us or to the person in charge of the storeroom, that he may carry them to the place where everyone's clothing is kept together, and in the morning get them back to spread out in the sun and, when they are dry, do not keep them in our possession, but return them to be kept in common, according to the precepts of the elders[3]—how much more so then, if you

entrust to another or wish to have at your own disposal the things which you seem to have as your own, do you sin against the discipline of the monastery,[4] failing to understand Paul, who says to you, *You were called to liberty. Only do not abuse that liberty as an opportunity for the flesh, but serve one another in love.*[5] And again, *The Lord is near. Do not worry but be intent on prayer and supplications.* As for the one who takes something on consignment from another, thinking that he is doing a good deed and helping his brother, let him know that he sins against his own soul, undermining the rules of the monastery. Foolish man, your soul is entrusted to your [house]master; shall the one who guards your soul and body be considered unworthy of keeping perishable things? Let us love justice, that we may be justified. For we read: Mercy comes to meet those who live by the truth.

27. This must also be noted. Let no one, deceived by a foolish idea or, rather, netted in the *snares of the devil,* say in his heart, 'when I die, I will give what I have to my brothers'. Most foolish of men, where have you found this written? Did not all the saints and those who served God put down the whole load of the world at once? In the Acts of the Apostles, did they not bring everything they owned to the feet of the apostles? Or how will you be able to put on *the garment of justice*[1] after your death, if you did not earn it while you were alive? Why have you forgotten what is written, *A man shall reap what he sows?* And, *Each shall receive according to his deeds.*[2] And, *He will reward each one according to his works.* And again, *I, the Lord, search the hearts and*

Ga 5:13.

Ph 4:5-6.

Cf. Ps 85(84):11.

Not to retain
ownership until
death
Cf. Eph 6:11;
    1Tm 3:7;
    1Tm 6:9;
    2Tm 2:26.

Cf. Ac 4:34-35.

Is 61:10.

Ga 6:7.
Eph 6:8.
Mt 16:27;
Rm 2:6.

*probe the loins, to reward each man according to
his ways³ and the fruit of his actions.*

Jr 17:10.

While you are still alive and in the flesh, why
do you not listen to David saying, *He gathers
treasure and does not know for whom he gathers
it,* and that saying of the Gospel which rebukes
the avaricious rich man, *Fool, tonight the de-
mand will be made for your soul; who shall inherit the things you have stored up?*⁴ And again,
On that day all their thoughts shall perish. Fool,
why are you unwilling to hear the Lord exhorting
you: *Go, sell all you have and give it to the poor,
and take up your cross, and come, follow me?*
When the young man heard this, he turned away,
for his heart was not right. * Therefore, he was
unable to put down the heavy load of his wealth.⁵
He had the desire for a perfect life, as Scripture
testifies, and he was attracted by the luster of virtues in order to be praised, but wealth held him
back in his course. And he was unable to hear the
Saviour's teaching because he was still thinking
about the delights of the world. Thus, the Saviour says, *It is difficult for those who have riches
to enter the kingdom of heaven.* And again, *No
one can serve two masters. He will either hate one
and love the other, or he will obey one and despise the other. You cannot serve God and mam-
mon. The pharisees, however, since they were avaricious, heard these things and laughed.* * Let us
avoid their unbelief and not ridicule those who
challenge us. Let us renounce the world that, as
perfect men, we may follow Jesus, who is perfect.
To those whose soul is possessed by avarice, poverty for Christ's sake seems foolish. But *devotion with
a sufficiency is a great profit.* For, *we brought*

Ps 39(38):6.

Lk 12:20.
Ps 146(145):4.

Mt 19:21; 16:24;
Mk 10:21;
Lk 18:22.
*Ps 78(77):37.

Cf. Mt 19:21.

Mt 19:23;
Mk 10:23;
Lk 18:24.

Mt 6:24;
Lk 16:13.
*Lk 16:14.

Mt 5:48; 19:21.

nothing into the world, and we can take nothing
out of it. Let us be satisfied if we have food and
*clothing.*⁶ *People who wish to become rich fall in-*
to temptation and the snare, into many frivolous
and harmful desires that plunge men into ruin
and perdition. Avarice is the root of all evil.

1 Tm 6:6-10.

28. To this day Elijah admonishes Israel, saying, *How long will you go limping along? If God*
exists, go and follow him. And we are told: If
these are the commandments of God, which he
handed down to us through our father, and, if by
following them, we are able to come to the kingdom of heaven, then let us fulfill these same commandments with our whole will. But if we are following our own thoughts and our will reaches out
to something else, then why do we not simply admit our mistake and show ourselves to be what we
are ashamed to seem, lest perhaps we too may be
asked, Why have you defiled my holy place? And,
I will drive them out of my house.*¹ For the monastic communities² are indeed the house of God
and the vineyard of the saints;³ as we read, *Sol-*
omon had a vineyard in the place called Baal-
hamon. He entrusted it to overseers and each one
brings for its fruit a thousand pieces of silver. My
vineyard is before me, one thousand pieces of sil-
ver for Solomon and two hundred for those who
*oversee its fruit.*⁴ Let us not be cast out for defil-
ing it, as we read in the Gospel they were who sold
cattle and sheep in the temple. *Coming in, the*
Lord and Saviour made himself a whip of cords
and drove the money-changers out of the temple.
He scattered the money and the tables of the mer-
chants, and said to the pigeon sellers, Take all
these things out of here, and stop turning my Fa-

The monastery
is God's
vineyard
1 K 18:21.

Cf. Nb 15:39.

Cf. Lv 21:12;
Ez 23:38.
*Ho 9:15.

Cf. Ps 80(79):9,
15; Is 5:7.

Sg 8:11-12.

Jn 2:14-16.

*Mk 11:17;
Is 56:7; Jr 7:11.
†Rm 2:24;
cf. Is 52:5.

Warning against irregularity

1 Co 11:20-22.

1 Co 11:34.

Ez 20:8.

Ez 20:13.
Lm 3:42.

*Ez 20:25.
†Ho 10:13.
‡Is 2:8.

Is 2:6.

Fidelity to our vocation

Ho 12:8.

Ho 12:8.

ther's house into a house of business. [5] *For it is written, My house will be called a house of prayer for all the nations; but you have turned it into a robbers' den.* And in another place, *Because of you, my name is blasphemed among the pagans.* [6]

29. I beseech you, brothers, may this not be said of us as well, *One person goes hungry while another is drunk. Do you not have houses for eating and drinking in? Or do you despise the Church of God and put to shame those who have nothing?* [1] And they are told, *If anyone is hungry, he should eat at home, and then your assembly will not bring you condemnation.* Do not let our house [receive] an alien name, lest this statement be aptly applied to us, *They did not give up the works of Egypt.* And again, *They did not walk according to my commandments; they defiled my sabbaths. Therefore, when they call upon me, I will not listen to them. Let us not persist in hardness of heart and provoke God to anger,* lest he become our enemy and say, *I will give them precepts that are not good and observances by which they cannot live,* for they ate the fruit of lying,† and *adored the works of their own hands.*‡ From the beginning their land was filled with soothsaying, just like the land of the pagans.

30. And, after we have renounced the world and have undertaken to follow the banner of the Cross, let us not return to the things behind and seek temporal repose, [1] imitating Ephraim who says, [2] *I became rich and found rest for myself.* May we not hear what he deserved to hear, *All his works shall be lost, because of the iniquities by which he sinned.* And may this not be fulfilled in us, *You began in the Spirit, and you are now end-*

*ing in the flesh. Have you endured such things for
nothing?* And may this sentence not be uttered
against us, *The law has passed from the priest
and counsel from the elders, and the hands of the
people are unnerved. The elders have deserted
the gate, and the chosen ones have given up their
psalms.* And again, *Because of you, my name is
blasphemed among the gentiles.*[3] Let it not be
that we despise the institutions of our Father, that
forgetfulness creep in, and that, through our own
fault, we neglect the mediator of God[4] and of his
saints.

31. For what fruit or what sign of the precepts
of God is found in us? How do we show we are living up to our profession?[1] *Have we not left everything,* and are we not still subject to avarice? And
we are asked, *Whence these wars and battles?* Are
they not the result of avarice? Because each man
seeks[2] his own advantage and not that of his neighbor,[3] Ezekiel, alive to this day, reprimands us
with his prophetic word, saying, *Barterers were
among you.** Son dishonors father,†[4] and father
upbraids son.* What shall we answer on judgement day? Or what excuse shall we be able to offer in our defence on the last day? All these things
happened to us, because *the priests clapped their
hands and the people loved it.* For, *like people,
like priest.* Therefore, He says, *I will repay him
according to his ways and pay him off for his designs.*

32. I do not say these things about all of you
but about those who despise the precepts of the
elders. *It was much better for them not to have
known the way of justice than, knowing it, to
have turned aside from the holy commandment*

Ga 3:3-4.

Ez 7:26-27.

Lm 5:14.
Rm 2:24;
cf. Is 52:5.

Warning against
decadence

Mk 10:28.
Jm 4:1.

Cf. 1 Co 10:24.

*Cf. Ez 27:36.
†Mi 7:6.

Jr 5:31.

Ho 4:9.

This warning
is not for all

that was handed down to them. Of this kind of men, Jeremiah laments and writes, *My eyes are wasted away with weeping, my stomach is troubled, my glory is spilled on the ground because of the ruin of the daughter of my people; for the child and the suckling have fainted in the squares of the City.*[1] *They asked their mothers, 'Where is wheat and wine?' as they fainted like wounded men in the squares of the City, as they poured out their souls on their mother's breast.* We know that *God has no interest in the strength of a horse, nor does he take pleasure in a man's legs.*

33. Therefore, *let us return to the Lord our God,** and whenever we pray,† He, who daily urges us *to pause and get to know him,*‡[1] will hear us. And in another place he says, *Return to me and I will return to you.* And again, *Return to me, my backsliding sons, and I will rule over you.* Ezechiel likewise calls upon us, saying, *Why will you die, O house of Israel?*[2] *I want not the death of the sinner, only that he turn from his evil ways and live.*[3] The most merciful Lord and source of all goodness cries out to us in the Gospel and declares, *Come to me all you who labor and are overburdened, and I will give you rest.*[4] *Carry my yoke upon you and learn of me, for I am gentle and humble of heart,*[5] *and you will find rest for your souls.** Let us consider that *the goodness of God calls us to repentance,*†[6] and holy men encourage us to salvation. *Let us not harden our hearts and collect against ourselves a store of divine anger for the day of wrath; then shall be revealed the just judgement of God who will repay each one according to his deeds.** But *let us return to the Lord with our whole heart;*†[7] accord-

ing to the words of Moses, who reminds us, *If you return to the Lord with your whole heart, he will purify your heart and the heart of your descendants.*

Dt 30:2.6.

34. Let us *labor like good soldiers of Christ,** and let us be mindful of what is written, *No soldier of God gets himself involved in the affairs of this life,*[1] *that he may please Him under whom he serves. Even someone contending in an athletic struggle is not crowned unless he has fought according to the rules.*[2] *The farmer who does the work should get the first share of the produce.* It is written, *All the nations shall walk, each in its own way. We, however, shall glory in the name of the Lord our God. These became ensnared and fell. We have got up and stand erect.*

Labor like good soldiers
*2 Tm 2:3.

2 Tm 2:4-6.

Mi 4:5.

Ps 20(19):7-8.

35. *Whoever walks in daytime does not stumble, but whoever walks at nighttime does, because there is no light in him.* But we, as the Apostle said, *are not the sons of the transgression which leads to damnation, but of faith, for the salvation of our souls.* And in another place he said, *You are all sons of light and sons of the day; we are not sons of night or darkness.* Now if we are the sons of light, we ought to know what belongs to light, and bear *the fruits of light* in every good work. *What is revealed is light.*

Walk in the light

Jn 11:9.

Heb 10:39.

1 Th 5:5.

Eph 5:9.
Eph 5:14.

If we *return to the Lord with our whole heart,* and turn ourselves *with simplicity of heart* to the precepts of his saints and of our Father, *we shall abound in every good work.* But, if we are overcome by the pleasures of the flesh, *we shall grope along the wall in broad daylight, as if it were the dead of night,* and we shall *not find the way to the city of our dwelling;* of which it is said, *Out of*

Cf. Dt 30:2.
1 P 1:22.

Cf. 2 Co 9:8.

Jb 5:14.

Ps 107(106):4.

Ps 107(106):5.

*Cf. Ps 107(106):
11.
†Heb 3:18-19.

Be watchful

Rm 11:21.

Ho 7:13.

Jr 2:13.

Jr 6:17.

Ho 13:4 (LXX).

Dt 4:19.

hunger and thirst, their soul fainted within them because they despised the law given to them by God and did not listen to the voice of the prophets.* *Because of this they were unable to reach the promised rest.*†

36. Let us keep watch and be on our guard. *If he did not spare the natural branches, neither will he spare you.*[1] I am not talking about everybody but about the negligent. This lament can rightly be applied to them, *Woe to those who have strayed from me.* It has been made manifest that they have acted impiously against me: *They have abandoned me, the fountain of living water, and have dug for themselves broken cisterns that cannot hold water.* And, because they have not listened to his judges, let them hear God saying, *I have set watchmen over you. Listen to the sound of the trumpet. And they said, We will not listen.*

Where does this unbelief come from? Is it not because they got familiar with strangers and did not resist them? In yet another place, the Holy Spirit says through the prophet, *I am the Lord your God who fashioned heaven and created earth, whose hands formed all the heavenly host. I did not show you these things so you could walk after them.* And he gave the same admonition through Moses, saying, *When you look up to heaven and see the sun and the moon and the stars and all the array of heaven, do not let yourself be misled into adoring them. For I am God who led you out of Egypt; and you know no God but me. And there is no one who can save besides me. I am the one who fed you in the wilderness, in an uninhabitable land. And they were filled to satiety, and their hearts grew proud. So they for-*

got me, * and I will disperse them through all the
kingdoms.†

37. When we hear these things, let us wake up
as from a deep sleep, and let us prove that we are
worthy of the Lord's service, that he may take
pity on us and say to us, *Call upon me and I will
listen to you.* For he himself says, *He who scattered Israel will gather him.* And in another place,
he said, *I will not act according to the anger of
my rage, nor will I so desert Ephraim as to blot
him out.* And again, *I will not punish you forever, nor will I always be angry with you. For the
Spirit shall go forth from me, and everything that
he inspires I have made.* And in the same place
he adds, *I have given them true comfort, peace
upon peace, to those who were near and to those
who were afar. And the Lord said, I will heal
them.* That we may understand his mercy fully,
the word of Jeremiah teaches us, saying, *Even if
heaven is raised on high, and the foundation of
the earth is lowered, I will not reject the race of
Israel for all that they have done.*[1]

38. And since the kindness of our Lord and
Saviour is so great that he calls us forth to salvation, *let us turn our hearts to him.* * *For now is the
time to wake up from sleep.*[1] *Night has passed
and day approaches. Let us therefore give up the
works of darkness and put on the armor of light.*[2]
*And let us conduct ourselves honorably, as in the
day.* My little children, first let us love God with
our whole heart; then let us love one another.[3]
Keep in mind the precepts of our God and Saviour, in which he says, *My peace I give to you, my
peace I leave you. I do not give you peace as the
world does.* Now, *on these two commandments
the whole law and the prophets depend.*

*Ho 13:4-6.
†Jr 34:17.

Trust in
God's mercy

Is 58:9.
Jr 31:10.

Ho 11:9.

Is 57:16.

Is 57:18-19.

Jr 31:37(38:35).
Love of God and
of neighbor
*Dt 30:2.

Rm 13:11-13.
Cf. 1 Jn 4:7-8;
Mt 22:37-39;
Mk 12:30-31;
Lk 10:27.

Jn 14:27.

Mt 22:40.

Do not receive
personal gifts

39. If anyone living under a [house-] master in a house of the monastery, and lacking none of the things he is allowed to have in the monastery,[1] has a father and brother and a close friend, he is not to receive anything at all from them, neither tunic nor mantle nor anything else. But if it is proved that he has less than what is prescribed,[2] the entire fault and punishment shall fall on the [house-] master.

Responsibility of
the superiors to
provide for all
the brothers'
needs

40. Therefore, you who are the fathers of the monasteries, if you see that any [brothers] lack something and are hard pressed, do not neglect them,[1] knowing that you shall render an account for *all the flock over which the Holy Spirit has placed you, to watch over and to shepherd the Church of God, which he bought with his own*

Ac 20:28.

blood. Therefore, *we who are stronger should bear the infirmities of those who are weaker, and should not please ourselves but our neighbor, for the sake of his good and edification. For Christ did not please himself, but, as it is written, The*

Ps 69(68):9;
Rm 15:1-3.

1 Co 10:33.

taunts of those who insulted you fell on me. And again, *I do not seek my own advantage but that of all, that they may be saved.*[2]

Beware of
scandals

Rm 13:11.

41. Now, if our Lord and Saviour so ordained, and if the saints so lived, and if our fathers so taught us, then, *let us arise from sleep* and do what has been prescribed for us. For, *everything that was written was written for our instruction, that through patience and the consolation of the*

Rm 15:4.

Scriptures we might have hope. May none of us be the cause of another's failure, and may we not envy

Ps 37(36):7.

those who prosper in their way. After they have acquired all the things necessary for the body, they will not carry anything with them when they die.

The children of this age put their confidence in
this age, since they are from the world, and the
world loves its own. Those who are God's children,   Cf. Jn 15:19.
however, should remember this word of the Gos-
pel, *If the world hates you, know that it hated me
first.*[1] And again, *Whoever wants to be a friend of*   Jn 15:18.
this world, becomes an enemy of God. And again,   Jm 4:4.
*You will have tribulations but be brave; I have
overcome the world.* And again, *Happy those who*   Jn 16:33.
mourn, for they shall be comforted.[2] *Happy those
who hunger and thirst for righteousness, for they
shall be satisfied. Happy those who suffer persecu-*   Mt 5:5-6.
*tion for the sake of righteousness, for theirs is the
kingdom of heaven.* On the other hand, what is   Mt 5:10.
said about the *sons of night?* Is it not this? *Woe to*   1 Th 5:5.
*you who are rich, for you have received your con-
solation. Woe to you who are full now, for you
shall go hungry. Woe to you who laugh now, for
you shall mourn and weep.*[3]   Lk 6:24-25.

42. Let us, therefore, avoid the friendship of   **Separation from**
the world,*[1] that we may deserve to hear, *Weep-*   **the world**
ing shall linger through the evening, and joy   *Cf. Jm 4:4.
[shall come] *in the morning. The Lord heard and*   Ps 30(29):5.
*took pity on me. You have stripped off my sack-
cloth and wrapped me in gladness.*[2] Which one of   Ps 30(29):10-11.
the saints passed over the road of this world with-
out mourning and sadness? Jeremiah said, *I did
not sit in scoffers' company but trembled before
your hand. I sat alone, because I was filled with
bitterness.*[3] David, too, writes, *As one mourn-*   Jr 15:17.
ing and sorrowful, so was I brought low. Walking   Ps 35(34):14.
in their footsteps, we [shall] understand that *our
salvation is in a time of tribulation,*[4] and that the Is 33:2.
promise of the prophet is fulfilled, who said,
Those who are in distress for a time shall not be

Is 8:22.

Cf. Ps 126(125):5.

Cf. 2 P 2:9.

Avoid bad company
*Is 64:7(8)
Is 33:22.

Is 57:13.

*Cf. Jr 7:3;
26:13.
†Is 57:14.

Pr 22:10.

Pr 17:15.

1 M 6:24.

Is 3:16.

Is 1:21.

Ho 4:14.

Ps 119(118):162.

Ps 119(118):103.

abandoned. If tribulation is for a while and shall not last forever, let us *sow in tears*, that we may *reap in joy*, not growing weak, for we know that *the Lord rescues his worshippers from trial*.

43. *The Lord is our father.* * *The Lord is our judge. The Lord is our ruler. The Lord is our king. The Lord himself shall save us.*[1] If we neglect his precepts, we shall remain in distress. For he himself says, *Those who follow me shall possess the land and inherit my holy mountain*. We too shall possess this mountain, if we fulfill his law and listen to what is said, *Make your ways clean before him.* * And again, *Remove the obstacles from the way of my people.*† And in another place, *Expel the corrupt one from* the council *and strife shall go out with him. The man who calls a just man unjust, and the man who declares an unjust man just, both are unclean in the sight of God.*[2] Let us be on our guard that this is not said about us too: *Their sons have been estranged from them.* And this, *The daughters of Zion were haughty and walked with an outstretched neck and proud eyes, their dresses trailing at their feet, dancing in unison with their feet.* And again the word of the prophet serves for our correction, saying, *How has Zion, the faithful city that was full of judgement, become a harlot? Where justice is asleep, there are now thieves.* And, *The people, who knew* [the truth], *had commerce with a harlot; and you Israel, shall not go unnoticed.*

If we recite the divine [words], we will be able to say what David did, *I will rejoice in your words, like someone on finding a vast treasure.*[3] And, *How sweet to my palate are your words, sweeter than honey and honeycomb to my mouth.*

*Your judgements were the theme of my song in the
land of my sojourn.* And in another place he said, *Ps 119(118)54.*
*I have not placed any wicked thing before my eyes,
and I hated those who did evil.*[4] And, *The perverse* *Ps 101(100):3.*
*heart did not stay close to me, and I gave no recog-
nition to the wicked, as they parted company with
me. I persecuted the man who secretly slandered
his neighbor.*[5] *I did not eat with the man of
haughty eye and insatiable heart. My eyes were set
on the faithful of the land, to have them sit with
me.* *Ps 101(100):4-6.*

44. Let us imitate the example of all these men, **Show love**
that *there may be peace and righteousness in our* **for God through**
days,* and that what we read in another place **conversion**
may not happen to us: *Thorns and briars shall* *Cf. Ps 85(84):10;
spring up on the soil of my people. Rather, let us *Is 32:13.*
clean the fallow ground for ourselves *and not sow*
among thorns. *Jr 4:3;*
And, once we have kept the commandments cf. Ho 10:12.
which were given to us, it will be manifest that we
love God, as divine Scripture testifies in another
place, *He who hears my commandments and
keeps them is the one who loves me. And he who
loves me is loved by my Father, and I shall love
him. And my Father and I shall come and make
our dwelling with him, and I shall show myself to
him.*[1] And, *You are my friends, if you do what I* *Jn 14:21.23.*
command you. Let us take many words with us *Jn 15:14.*
and return to the Lord our God and say to him,
You are able to forgive [*our*] *sins, that we may receive good things. Let us offer him the fruit of our* *Ho 14:3.
lips. * *Then, our soul will rejoice within us.*† †Ps 35(34):9.

45. Would that we might repent of our error **Another call to**
and negligence, and, brought back to our former **conversion**
[ways], might say, *Assur will not save us. We will*

*not ride horses, and we will not say any more,
Our gods are the works of our hands. God, who is
within you, shall take pity on the people. I will*

Ho 14:4-5.

restore their dwellings. Then, he shall say about
us once again, *I will love them openly and turn
my anger from them. I will be like dew. Israel
shall bloom like the lily and thrust out his roots
like Lebanon. His branches will spread out, and
he will be like a fruitful olive tree, and his fragrance like incense. They will come back and sit,
each one in his tent. They will live and be strengthened with wheat. Their fame shall flourish like a
vine; Ephraim, like the fragrance of incense.
What has he to do with idols? I have brought him
low, now I will comfort him. I am like a thick
juniper, his fruit was produced from me. Who is
wise and understands these things, who under-*

Ho 14:5-10.

stands and knows them? And would that we too
might be able to bear fruit from him, for without

Cf. Jn 15:5.

him no good work is possible.

For Pachomius' sake

46. Let us return to the Lord, that he may say
of us too, *I will no longer remember their sins and*

Is 43:25.

iniquity. Let us not abandon the law of God,
which our father received from Him and handed
down to us.[1] And let us not value his commandments cheaply, lest this lamentation be made
over us: *How has gold become tarnished and
good silver changed; how have sacred stones been*

Lm 4:1.

scattered at the corner of every street? After the
many labors our Father undertook for our salvation, offering himself as a model of virtue, boasting over us among the saints with these words,
'These are my sons and my people; they are my
sons and they will not deny me' — after such a testimony, let us not lose the confidence of a good

conscience, being despoiled of the garments in
which he clothed us. He led us into the contest to
fight according to the rules, let us not be overcome by our enemies.[2] And once we have reached
the time for us to leave the body, let us not become enemies of our Father for serving [earthly]
treasures in such a way that we who ought to at-
tain freedom of soul through fasting and affliction of the body would dedicate ourselves to the
flesh and to pleasures, to fancier clothing and
softer bedding.[3] Then not only would we ourselves be lost; we would lead to ruin others who
could have profited from our example. This was
written about them, *You have not received the
spirit of servitude again in fear, but the spirit of
fortitude and love and purity.* Again, *Food does
not make us pleasing to God;* for, neither *if we
eat, shall we gain more; nor if we do not eat, shall
we lose something. Because the kingdom of God
is not food and drink but righteousness, peace
and joy in the Holy Spirit. The man who serves
Christ in this way pleases God and is approved by
men.* Isaiah also says, *Those who wait for the Lord
shall renew their strength. They shall put on wings
like eagles. They shall run without growing weary.
They shall walk without getting hungry.* Therefore, *he shall raise up a sign for the nations and assemble the fugitives of Israel. Know this: They
shall come swiftly; they shall not grow hungry or
sleepy. They shall not sleep, nor shall they remove
the belts from their waists or undo the straps of
their sandals. Their arrows are sharp and their
bows bent. Their feet are like the firmest rock; the
wheels of their chariots, like a whirlwind. They
shall attack like lions; they shall stand ready like
lion cubs.*

Cf. Heb 13:18.

Cf. 2 Tm 2:5.

Rm 8:15.
2 Tm 1:7.
Cf. 2 Tm 1:7.

1 Co 8:8.

Rm 14:17-18.

Is 40:31.

Is 11:12.

Is 5:26-29.

Cf. Lk 8:16.

Cf. Rm 8:16.
Cf. Mt 25:35.

*Cf. Mt 25:35.
†Cf. Is 25:4.
‡Cf. Mt 25:36.

Is 5:3-4.
Is 5:7.

Cf. Is 5:8-23.

Ho 12:2(1).
Ps 106(105):35.
Ga 5:13.

47. Therefore, let us be imitators of the saints and not forget the formation that our Father gave us while he was still alive. Let us not extinguish the burning lamp he placed above our heads. Walking [in] this world by the light of this [lamp],[1] let us remember that it is through his zeal that God has received us into his household. He gave a hospice to wayfarers, he showed a harbor of peace to those on a storm-tossed sea. [He provided] bread in hunger,* shade in heat,† clothing in nakedness.‡ He instructed the ignorant by spiritual precepts. He encircled with chastity those enslaved by vices and joined to himself those from afar.

And now, after his death, let us not forget such great kindness and everlasting benefits, and let us not turn judgement into rage and the fruits of righteousness into bitterness, so that he would say against us, *Judge between me and my vineyard. I expected it to yield fruit,* but *it yielded iniquity, not righteousness but a shout.*[2] Then that curse which follows in the prophetic text will fall on us.[3] It is a curse we should flee and avoid with utter zeal, by following the way of life[4] of those who have gone before us in the Lord, our fathers and brothers alike, who renounced the world[5] and made their way to the Lord at an uninterrupted pace and are now in possession of his inheritance, which I am afraid we may lose through our slothfulness. And so to us would that prophetic passage be applied, which says of Ephraim, *He carries on an oil trade with Egypt. They mingled with the pagans and learned their practices.*

After *we had receivd our call to freedom*[6] and we have been gathered from separate places to

form the one people of God—as it is written, *I*　　Cf. Jr 29:14.
will take them, one man from a people, and two
from a family, and I will bring you to Zion, and I
will give you shepherds after my own heart who
shall feed you with discipline—after that, let us　　Jr 3:14-15.
not break the bonds of charity, lest it be said of
us, *A son honors his father, and a servant his*
master. If I am a father, where is my honor? If I
am a master, where is my fear?[7]　　Ml 1:6.

48. Therefore, let our heart cry out to the　　**Salutary grief**
Lord. *May the walls of Zion flow with tears like a*
torrent day and night.[1] *Give yourself no relief,*
grant the apple of your eye no rest. Rise and give
praise in the night, at the beginning of your
watches. Pour out your heart like water before
the Lord. Stretch out your hands to him for the
lives of your children, who have fainted at the
mouth of every exit.[2] May this not be uttered　　Lm 2:18-19.
against us, *The earth mourned and was corrupt-*
ed; the heights of the land mourned. The land
sinned because of its inhabitants. For they aban-
doned the law and violated my precepts, my ever-
lasting covenant. Therefore, a curse shall con-
sume the land because its inhabitants sinned and
few men shall be left.[3] May *our wine and our*　　Is 24:5-6.
vines not mourn too. And may *those who earlier*
rejoiced with their whole heart not sigh. And this　　Is 24:7.
could be said of us, *They invented madness in the*
house [of God], *and were corrupted as* [on] *the*
days of the hill. And this, *The booty comes from*　　Ho 9:8-9.
you. And, *For you said it: you have made a cov-*　　Jr 37:17(LXX).
enant with hell and a pact with death.　　Is 28:15.

Avoiding these words, we believe instead that in
his own time *a star shall rise from Jacob and a man*

shall spring up from Israel who will strike the
Nb 24:17. *princes of Moab and destroy the sons of Sheth.* [4]
Let there not be an infuriating sting and a pain-
Ez 28:24. *ful thorn in the house of Israel; for Jacob was
made the Lord's portion, and Israel, the measur-
Dt 32:9. ing line of his inheritance.* [5] Jeremiah says elsewhere, *If this law passes away from my presence,
Jr 31:36. then the race of Israel could pass away.* And
again, *I will give the fruit of their toil to the just,
and I will establish with them an everlasting covenant. Their seed and descendants will be known
among the nations. Everyone who sees them will
know that they are a seed blessed by God* [6] *and
Is 61:8-10. they thoroughly enjoy the gladness of the Lord.* [7]

Call to
watchfulness
*Lm 3:40.
†2 Co 2:14.
‡Cf. Ps 119(118):11.
*Cf. Ps 119(118):1.

49. Let us then *examine our paths** [1] and ponder our own steps. Let us follow *the fragrance of
knowledge,*† ever concealing His words within
our hearts,‡ that we may be *blameless on our way
and walk in the law of the Lord.* * And may frailty
of body and prolonged effort not frighten us
away. *Our fathers and the prophets, where are
they? Shall they,* as it is written, *live forever?
Receive my words and my ordinances, which I
commanded through my Spirit to my servants,
Zc 1:5-6. the prophets, who were with your fathers.* May we
experience *the unspeakable kindness of our God,
Rm 2:4. who,* to this day, *urges us to repentance,* [2] saying,
*Shall the man who falls not stand up again, or the
man who strays not return? Why have my people
turned away in stubborn revolt? They clung to
Jr 8:4-5. their pleasures and they refused to come back.*

If we come back to him, he shall build us up
with his Spirit, as it is written, *The Lord builds
Ps 147(146):2. up Jerusalem, gathering Israel's exiles.* [3]

A community
of love

50. The Apostle taught us that our community, the communion by which we are joined to

one another, springs from God, when he said, *Do not forget good works and communion, for God takes pleasure in such sacrifices.*[1] We read the same thing in the Acts of the Apostles: *For the multitude of believers had one heart and soul, and no one called anything his own. They held everything in common.*[2] *And the apostles gave witness to the resurrection of the Lord Jesus with great power.* The psalmist is in agreement with these words when he says, *Behold, how good and how delightful it is for brothers to live together.* And let us who live together in the *Koinonia,*[3] and who are united to one another in mutual charity, so apply ourselves that, just as we deserved fellowship with the holy fathers in this life, we may also be their companions in the life to come. We know that the cross of our life is also the foundation of our doctrine,[4] and that *we must share Christ's sufferings,* and we must realize that without trials and difficulties no man attains victory. *Happy the man who endures trial,*[5] *for when he has proved himself, he shall receive the crown of life.* And again, *He toiled in the world, he shall live forever—provided we share his sufferings so as to share his glory.* For, [Paul] says, *I consider the sufferings of the present not worth comparing to the glory that shall be revealed in us.*[6] And elsewhere it is written, *I considered how I might understand this, hard though it is for me.* And again, *Following you was no toil for me, and I did not consider the day of men.* And in another place, *Many are the trials of the righteous, but the Lord will rescue them from all of them.* And our Lord says in the Gospel, *The one who perseveres to the end will be saved.* And elsewhere, *This is the book of the command-*

Heb 13:16.

Ac 4:32-33.

Ps 133(132):1.

Rm 8:17.

Cf. Ac 14:22.

Jm 1:12.
Ps 49(48):8.

Rm 8:17-18.

Ps 73(72):16.

Jr 17:16.

Ps 34(33):19.
Mt 10:22.

*ments and the law written forever. All who ob-
serve it shall live; those who desert it shall die.
Turn back, Jacob, seize it and walk in the radi-
ance of its light. Do not give your glory to another
and the things that befit you to a foreign nation.
We are happy, O Israel, that what pleases our
God has been revealed to us. Have trust, my peo-*

Ba 4:1-5.   *ple, O memorial of Israel.*[7] And again Isaiah
speaks, *Rejoice, O Israel,*[8] *make a feast, all you
who love him. Rejoice, you who trust in him, that
you may be suckled and be filled from the breasts*

Is 66:10-11.   *of his consolation.*

Recite God's
Scriptures   51. Let us devote ourselves to reading and
learning the Scriptures, reciting them continual-
ly, aware of the text, *A man shall be filled with*

Pr 13:2.   *the fruit of his own mouth, and he will be paid*
Ws 10:17.   *the price of his labors.* These are the [words]
which lead us to eternal life, the [words] our fa-
ther handed down to us and commanded us continually to recite,[1] that what was written might be
fulfilled in us: *The words which I command you
today shall be in your heart and in your soul. You
shall teach them to your sons. You shall talk
about them, whether sitting at home or walking
abroad, lying down or rising. You shall write
them as a sign on your hand, and they shall be
permanently before your eyes. You shall also
write them on the doorposts and thresholds of*

Dt 11:18-20.   *your houses, that you may learn to fear the Lord*
Dt 4:10.   *all the days of your life.* And Solomon, indicat-
Pr 3:3.   ing the same, says, *Write them across your heart.*

Admonition to
the young   52. Consider by how many testimonies the
word of the Lord urges us to recite the holy Scriptures that we may possess through faith what we
have repeated with our mouth.[1] *It is good for a*

man to bear the yoke from his youth. ² He shall sit
alone and be silent because he shall lift the yoke
upon himself. He shall offer his cheek to the strik-   Lm 3:27-28.
er, and be covered with insults, for the Lord will
not cast him off forever. ³ And elsewhere it is writ   Lm 3:30-31.
ten, *I remembered the mercy of your youth. And*   Jr 2:2.
again, *Young man, rejoice in your youth. Let
your heart be glad in the days of your youth. And
walk in the ways of your heart without blemish,
following the direction of your eyes. And know
that the Lord will bring you to judgement for all
these things. Remove anger from your heart and
evil from your flesh, for youth and foolishness are
vain. And remember your Creator in the days of*   Qo 11:9-10.
*your youth, before evil days come and the years
approach when you will say: They do not please
me; before the sun and the light, the moon and
the stars grow dark, and clouds return after the
rain, in the day when the guards of the house
tremble and men of courage are overthrown;
when the women cease grinding, because they are
reduced to a few; when women who look through
the windows are kept in darkness and the street
doors are shut; when the voice of the woman who
is grinding becomes weak; and men jump at the
chirp of the sparrow, and all the daughters of
song are brought low. They shall look from a
height and see terror on the way. The almond
tree blossoms, the locusts grow fat, and the caper
bush is cut down; for a man has gone to his everlasting home, and the mourners go about in the
street, before the silver cord has snapped, and the
golden trinket is broken, and the pitcher is shattered at the fountain⁴ or the pulley stopped at the
well and dust returns to the earth as it was, and
the spirit goes back to the Lord who gave it.*   Qo 12:1-7.

It is likewise written in the Gospel, *Children,
have you any food? Cast to the right of the ship
and you will find some.* And again, *Every boy
and little child who today does not know good
from evil shall enter the good land.* And again,
*Every male that opens the womb shall be called
holy.* And in the Gospel, *And the boy went on
growing and he made progress before God and
man.** Joshua also, the servant of Moses, was a
youth, and did not leave the tent of God.† We
read also what is written about David, *A boy of
fair color, with fine eyes.* Timothy, too, while still
a boy and a young man, was taught sacred Scriptures that he might come by way of their path to
faith in the Lord and Saviour.* And, because he
was instructed,† we read of Daniel that he was
called *a man of desires.*‡⁵ Joseph was the most
beloved of his father,⁶ because he kept his commands, and, when he was only seventeen years
old, he considered his father's orders the law of
his life.

53. I have unfolded all these things that, con-
sidering the lives of holy men, *we may not be
tossed about by every wind of doctrine,**¹ but that
we might struggle on and set their way of life as
the model for our own life, so as to be *God's special people. And let us not grieve the Holy Spirit
with whom we have been sealed for the day of re-
demption.² Let us not quench him* in ourselves
*nor treat the prophecies with contempt,*³ lest we
fail to provide a place for the Spirit who wishes to
dwell in us.* Let us fear no one but God,† who is
the avenger and judge of every deed. *He is holy
with the holy, and innocent with the innocent
man.* And he says, *I love those who love me. Those*

Jn 21:5-6.

Dt 1:39.

Ex 13:2.12.15;
Lk 2:23.

*Lk 2:52;
Cf. 1 S 2:26.
†Ex 33:11.

1 S 16:12.

*Cf. 2 Tm 3:15.
†Cf. Dn 1:4.
‡Dn 9:23;
   10:11.19.

Cf. Gn 37:2.
   3.14.

Final recom-
mendations.
The example of
the saints
*Eph 4:14.

Dt 7:6; 14:2;
   26:18.

Eph 4:30.

1 Th 5:19-20.

*Cf. Rm 8:11.
†Pr 7:1.

Cf. Ps 18(17):25.

who look for me shall find joy. And he says elsewhere, *If you walk perversely against me, I will
walk perversely against you.*

54. Let us not be angry with one another.*
Even if anger overcomes us, we do not sin by our
anger,† if we repent[1] it before sunset.‡ Let us
remember that we were commanded how many
times we must forgive the man who sins against
us,*[2] and *to leave our offering before the altar,*†
for it will never be received unless it is made acceptable by reconciliation. Then we will be able
to say, *Forgive us our debts as we forgive those
who are in debt to us.*[3] And the Apostle ordered,
*If anyone has a complaint against someone, let
him forgive him as Christ forgave us.* Let us be
disciples of the meekness practised by all the
saints, especially by David, of whom it was written, *Lord, remember David and all his meekness;*
and Moses, of whom we read, *he was the meekest
man on the whole earth.* And the Lord speaks
about the meek and the gentle in the Gospel,
Happy the gentle, for they shall possess the earth.
It is a sign of great wisdom to possess meekness
and to hear, *Be wise, my son, that my heart may
be glad.* And again, *Be imitators of God like very
loving sons.* And *Be perfect just as your heavenly
Father who is in heaven is perfect.* And elsewhere,
Be holy because I am holy, says the Lord.

55. Reading these testimonies, let us sow justice for ourselves, that we may reap the fruit of
life. Let us light the lamp of wisdom, for it is time
to get to know God, until the *fruit of justice* is
given to us. *Behold, now is the favorable time
and the day of salvation.*[1] And truly, according to
what is written, *Love is the fulness of the law.*[2]

Pr 8:17.

Lv 26:23-24.

**Mutual
forgiveness
and meekness**
*Cf. Qo 7:9.
†Cf. Ps 4:5.
‡Cf. Eph 4:26.

*Cf. Mt 18:21-
22;
Lk 17:4.
†Mt 5:23-24.

Mt 6:12.

Col 3:13.

Ps 132(131):1.

Cf. Nb 12:3.

Mt 5:4.

Pr 27:11.
Eph 5:1.
Mt 5:48.
Lv 11:44; 19:2.

Brotherly love
Cf. Pr 11:18.

Jm 3:18.

2 Co 6:2.
Rm 13:10.

2 Jn 4-5.
1 Jn 4:21.

*1 Jn 3:12-14.
†1 Jn 4:7.
Epilogue
*Rm 15:15.

Ac 20:31.
1 Th 4:1.
Ac 20:20.27.

Ac 20:32.

2 Tm 4:6-8.

John joins in agreement with this, *We have received this commandment from the Father, that we love one another.* And, *The man who loves God, loves his brother. Not like Cain, who was from the evil one and killed his brother. And why did he kill him? Because his works were evil, while his brother's were good. Let us not be surprised, brothers, if the world hates us. We know that we have passed from death to life, because we love the brothers.* Therefore, let us love one another.†³*

56. I will tell you something more daringly,* my dearest sons, since God has entrusted me with the flock following your way of life, the holy *Koinonia. I have not ceased to admonish and teach each of you with tears,¹ that you might be pleasing to God. And I have not held back from saying anything I considered useful for you.² And now I commend you to God and to the word of his grace;* [to God] *who has power to build you up and to give you an inheritance among the saints.³* Be vigilant. Strive with all your might and attention, that you not forget your resolution, but fulfill what you know you have promised. *I will soon be offered up, and the time for my dissolution is at hand.⁴ I have, for* [my] *part fought the good fight, I have finished the course. I have kept the faith. As for the rest, the crown of righteousness has been reserved for me, which the Lord, the righteous Judge, will give to me on that day—not only to me, but to all those who have loved his righteousness⁵* and have carried out all the commandments of [our] father. *The end of the discourse; listen to all of it. Fear God and keep his commandments, for this is* [the duty of] *every*

man, because he will bring every deed to judge-
ment in everything which was neglected, whether
good or evil.[6]   Qo 12:13-14.

Notes to the Testament of Horsiesios

(Hors. Test.)

Hors. Test. 1 [1]This sentence is quoted by Pachomius in Pach. Instr. 1: 16.

Hors. Test. 2 [1]This sentence is quoted again below, ¶20.
[2]The same expression: 'fathers and brothers' is found again below, ¶¶3 and 47.

Hors. Test. 3 [1]This is an allusion to Paul's handling of a case of incest at Corinth.
[2]According to Draguet Fragm. 1: 6, Pachomius established the rule that a sinner should not be expelled from the monastery, lest he 'be abandoned into the hands of the devil'.

Hors. Test. 4 [1]The same quotation from Lm 3:40-41 is found (with slight variants) in Pach. Letter 10: 1; Theod. Instr. 3: 38; and below, ¶49.
[2]The text is applied to Pachomius.
[3]'... poma sollicita germinans' does not correspond either to the Vulgate (non erit sollicitum, nec aliquando desinet facere fructum) or to the Septuagint (οὐχὶ ... ξηρανθήσεται; σὺν τῷ βόλῳ ἀνατολῆς αὐτῆς ξηρανθήσεται). It must be a mistake by either Horsiesios or Jerome.
[4]The Latin text: 'Graue cor in omnibus, et homo est' hardly makes any sense. H. Bacht (Das Vermächtnis, p. 65) notes that the copists had some problems with this text, as we can see from the variant 'hominis' instead of 'in omnibus'. Jerome's (or Horsiesios') misinterpretation is found also in the Septuagint and Symmachus, as well as in the Itala and the Syriac versions. On the basis of a false vocalization they all read enosch (man) instead of anosch (perverse). The meaning of the Hebrew text is: 'The heart is more devious than any thing, perverse too.'
[5]Jer. 17:10 is quoted again below, ¶27.

Hors. Test. 5 [1]The expression 'our father' obviously means Pachomius, as does *Apa* or Ἀββᾶ in the Coptic or Greek texts when used without any person's name.
[2]We find the same recommendation in Theod. Instr. 3: 5. See also Am. Letter 34.
[3]Ps 19(18):7-8 is quoted also in Hors. Letter 4: 5.

Hors. Test. 6 [1]The same text from Rm 13:11 is quoted again below, ¶¶38-41 and by Pachomius in the *Proemium* of Jud.
[2]Horsiesios quotes 1 P 5:8-9 very freely. 1 P 5:8 is also quoted in an Instruction by Theodore in G¹ 135, and there are clear allusions to it in Pach Instr. 1: 10 and 28; Pach. Fragm. 1: 2; and Theod. Instr. 3: 19.
[3]This theme of the imitation of the saints is important in pachomian spirituality. See P. Tamburrino, 'Les saints de l'Ancien Testament dans la Ière catéchèse de saint Pachôme', in *Melto* 4 (1968) 33-44.

⁴The curious expression: 'Let us understand the hair of our head on the way' is a direct quotation of Pach. Letter 1: 3.
⁵'... that there may be ... written' is a quotation from Pach. Letter 5: 2. Actually, in his sentence 'Let us understand ... written', Horsiesios combines a quotation from Pach. Letter 1: 3 ('And you, as a wise son, know the hair of your head on the journey ...') with one from Pach. Letter 5: 2 ('If you hold the hair of your head and find the ointment running down your beard to the collar of your robes you will be able to accomplish all that has been written').

Hors. Test. 7   ¹In the expression '*duces et praepositi monasteriorum ac domorum*' the word *monasteriorum* relates to *duces* and the word *domorum* to *praepositi*. The meaning is: '*duces monasteriorum et praepositi domorum*'. ¶¶7–18 are directed to various groups of superiors. See B. Steidle, 'Der "Obern-Spiegel" im "Testament" des Abtes Horsiesi'.
²We have here an indirect witness to the use of a secret alphabet or a code language among the Pachomians. As H. Quecke has noted (*Die Briefe Pachoms. Griechiescher Text*, pp. 28–29) if the characters we have here really mean groups of monks, Horsiesios' use of the characters is closer to that of the *Historia Lausiaca* than to that of Pachomius' letters. R. Weijenberg, in his review of H. Bacht's *Das Vermächtnis* (*Antonianum* 49 (1974) 394ff; quoted by H. Quecke, *Die Briefe*, p. 28, n. 4) thinks that the characters have to be understood as figures: 'twenty, ten or five or one'. This seems to us improbable since the expression 'to say it in plain language' (*ut in commune dicam*) obviously refers to a mysterious mode of speaking.
³The same quotation is found again below, ¶16, as well as in S² 7 and Inst. 18.

Hors. Test. 8   ¹This seems to us to be the meaning of: *Sunt aliqui attendentes semetipsos ut uiuentes iuxta mandatum Dei ...* ; but the text is not entirely clear and H. Bacht finds a different meaning: 'Manche [Obere] sind zwar für ihre eigene Person darauf bedacht, nach Gottes Gebot zu leben; aber ... (*Das Vermächtnis*, p. 75).
²With H. Bacht (*Das Vermächtnis*, p. 75, n. 27), we read *lanis operimini* instead of *lanis operemini* (Boon, p. 113, 10). So did Benedict of Aniane, *Codex Regularum*, PL 103: 455D.
³We find clear allusions to this text of Ezechiel in S¹ 25 and in Pach. Instr. 1: 2.
⁴The original meaning of Is 3:12 in the Hebrew Bible is quite different: 'Your rulers mislead you and destroy the road you walk on'.
⁵'... et principes tui in tempore comedunt in fortitudine': the meaning is not entirely clear.

Hors. Test. 9   ¹This text is quoted again below, ¶13.
²'*Sedentes in locis humilioribus, in quibus pater noster praecepit penitus non sedendum, caueant praepositi domorum, ne ...*' We translate literally, although the meaning of the sentence remains obscure. It is not clear what the *loci humiliores* are. O. Schuler (in B. Steidle and O. Schuler, 'Der "Obern-Spiegel" im "Testament" des Abtes Horsiesi, p. 32) understands by this expression the storeroom or cellar, and refers to Inst. 18 (Boon p. 58, 10); but his translation ('Die Vorstehere der Haüser sollen sich hüten, in Vorratsraum zu sitzen ...) does not respect the structure of the Latin sentence.
³Cf. same idea in Theod. Instr. 3: 11.

[4]This text is quoted again below, ¶54 and in Draguet Fragm. 1: 5.

[5]The same text is quoted twice by Pachomius, in Pach. Instr. 1: 6 and Pach. Letter 3: 13.

Hors. Test. 10 [1]We find the same eschatological perspective in Pachomius; see Pach. Instr. 1: 49-60 and his third, fourth and fifth letters.

[2]Theodore uses this text three times; see G[1] 132 and Theod. Instr. 3: 10 and 20.

[3]This text, which is the conclusion of the Book of Qohelet, is used by Horsiesios to end his Testament (see below, ¶56) and to end one of his letters (see Hors. Letter 1: 6). The expression: *'in omnibus quae neglecta sunt'* that we have here in Jerome's translation corresponds to the Coptic text in Hors. Letter 1: 6: *etbehôb nim eauolšou eroou.*

[4]2 Co 5:10 and the very similar text of Rm14:10 are used or alluded to very often; see below, ¶¶17 and 21 and Hors. Reg. 5 and 31; see also Pach. Instr. 1: 26 and 38.

[5]Cf. Inst. 13 and 17.

Hors. Test. 11 [1]See above, ¶10, n. 4. We have here a combination of Rm 14:10 (*'We must* all appear before the tribunal of Christ') and 2 Co 5:10 ('We shall all have *to stand before* the tribunal of Christ'). We find the same combination in Hors. Reg. 5.

[2]This seems to us to be an accurate—if not the most literal—translation of *'fratribus qui reputantur in plebem'.*

[3]Gal 6:2 is quoted also in Am. Letter 3 and in Pach. Letter 5: 11.

[4]*'Et nos habemus depositum a Deo traditum, conuersationem fratrum'.* The expression *conuersatio,* so important in the Rule of S. Benedict (v.g. in chapter 58) is often found in the *Pachomiana latina*: Pr., title; Inst. 18; Leg. 12 and 14; Theod. Letter 1; and below in Hors. Test. ¶¶47, 53 and 56 (see Boon, pp. 13,3; 60,3; 73,10; 74,3; 105,20; 140,17; 145,23 and 147,10. It is difficult to say what was the Greek or Coptic word used in the original text. Only in one of the cases mentioned do we have the Coptic parallel, where we read *sooun* (knowledge).

Hors. Test. 12 [1]The expression *opus Dei* means monastic life in general, or the whole of the ascetic effort of the monk, as in all the early monastic writings. It does not yet have the meaning of 'Divine Office' it will have in the Rule of S. Benedict. See I. Hausherr, *'Opus Dei'* in *Miscellanea Guillaume de Jerphanion I,* OCP-13 (1947) 195-218.

[2]*'Pater noster qui primus instituit coenobia':* About Pachomius considered the founder of the *Koinonia,* and for a justification of our translation of *coenobia* by *Koinonia,* see Theod. Letter 1: 2, n. 4.

[3]The assimilation of Pachomius to s. Paul is found also in Theod. Letter 1: 2.

Hors. Test. 13 [1]Ps 107:41 is quoted again by Horsiesios in Hors. Letter 1: 3 and 4: 5. See also Theod. Letter 1: 4.

[2]Same quotation below, ¶56.

[3]The same text is quoted in different words below, ¶56.

[4]The same expression of s. Paul ('weak with those who are weak') is found in Am. Letter, 21).

[5]Cf. above, ¶10 and Inst. 13: 'When a sin is committed among the men in

one of the houses, if the housemaster, seeing the fault does not notify the steward, it shall be done to him according to their canon'.

Hors. Test. 14   [1]Cf. Theod. Instr. 3: 30: 'Let us fear greatly lest for negligence a soul be brought to destruction which could have been saved.' See also *ibidem*, n. 2.
    [2]We find the same combination of Mt 24:45 and 49 quoted in a similar context in Pach. Letter 3: 3. There is also an allusion to Mt 24:51 in Pach. Instr. 1: 55.
    [3]Horsiesios ends one of his Instructions (Hors. Instr. 4: 2) with this quotation, used in the same manner. See also SBo 114, where this text is applied to Pachomius.

Hors. Test. 15   [1]Horsiesios replaces 'hope' by 'faith' in the text of 1 P 3:15.
    [2]1 Th 5:14 is quoted also in S[1] 25; the expression 'comfort the weak' is found also in Hors. Letter 3: 5.
    [3]'Do not drive your children to anger' is used by Pachomius in Pach. Letter 5: 10.
    [4]1 Co 10:33 is quoted again below, ¶40, and in Hors. Letter 3: 1.

Hors. Test. 16   [1]Cf. above, ¶9.
    [2]This text was quoted above, ¶7.
    [3]We find another allusion to 1 P 1:17 in Pach. Fragm. 3: 3.
    [4]'... anything mortal or shameful' probably refers to sexual sins, against which the pachomian monks were warned.
    [5]Cf. Inst. 13 and 17. See also above, ¶¶10 and 13.

Hors. Test. 17   [1]The Good Shepherd is given as a model to superiors in Theod. Instr. 3: 30. In G[1] 54 Pachomius is said to visit the monasteries day and night 'as a servant of the Good Shepherd'.
    [2]This verse is quoted by Pachomius in Pach. Letter 3: 4.
    [3]Same expression in SBo 26 and Paral. 41.
    [4]We find the same application of Jn 21:15-16 made by Theodore in G[1] 135. It is interesting to see how Horsiesios relates the role and the authority of the superior of a monastic community to the mission given to Peter by the risen Lord; see P. Tamburrino, 'Koinonia', pp. 13-18 and A. de Vogüé, 'Le Monastère', p. 34.

Hors. Test. 18   [1]'... *praecepta maiorum*': it can mean either 'the precepts of the elders' or 'the precepts of the superiors'. We often find this ambiguous meaning of *maiores* in the *Pachomiana latina*.
    [2]The same quotation occurs below, ¶47.
    [3]This expression from Rm 8:17 is quoted by Theodore in SBo 186 (= G[1] 142).

Hors. Test. 19   [1]The rank (*ordo*) in the community was important, and the Rule often stresses its respect; see Pr 13, 20, 63, 65, 131, 136, 137. See also F. van Beneden, 'Ordo. Über dem Ursprung einer kirchlicher Terminologie', in *Vigiliae Christianae* 22 (1969) 161-179.
    [2]The expression '*libera servitus*' is probably inspired by 1 Co 7:22 which is quoted in Hors. Letter 3: 1 and in Theod. Instr. 3: 19.
    [3]The same text is quoted again by Horsiesios in Hors. Letter 3: 1. See also Theod. Letter 1: 2 with n. 1.

⁴'...*sine murmuratione et cogitationibus uariis*'. These *cogitationes uariae* (cf. Ph 2:14: χωρὶς ... διαλογισμῶν; Vulgate: *sine* ... *haesitationibus*) played an important role in the ascetic psychology of the early monks. See H. Bacht, 'Die frühmonastischen Grundlagen Ignatianischer Frömmigkeit. Zu einigen Grundbegriffen der Exerzitien', in F. Wulf, *Ignatius von Loyola. Seine geistliche Gestalt und sein Vermächtnis*, (Würzburg, 1956) pp. 239-246; J.-C. Guy, 'Un dialogue monastique inédit περὶ λογισμῶν', in RAM 33 (1957) 171-188.

⁵We find the two members of this quotation in an inverted order in Theod. Instr. 3: 4; and an allusion to the same text, *ibidem*, ¶30. There is another mention of the 'arrows of the devil' in SBo 14.

⁶Same quotation in Pach. Instr. 1: 22.

⁷The same text occurs below, ¶53. We find a similar recommendation not to grieve the Spirit, in Pach. Instr. 1: 45. See also SBo 101 and Am. Letter 23.

⁸Same expression from 1 Th 1:4 in SBo 107.

Hors. Test. 20 ¹Note the depth of this doctrine on chastity, based on a belief in God's presence in our bodies.

²The same quotation occurs in Am. Letter 3.

³The same quotation occurs in S² 7.

⁴The same quotation occurs in SBo 194.

⁵Horsiesios makes reference more than once to this parable; see Hors. Reg. 3; Hors. Letter 3: 1; 4: 4; Hors. Test. 20. There is also a reference to it in SBo 118 and another in Pach. Instr. 1: 51.

⁶This text is used by Theodore in SBo 187.

Hors. Test. 21 ¹On the importance of renunciation in pachomian spirituality, see Pach. Instr. 1: 41, n. 1.

²This expression from Gn 14:23 is used with the same meaning in Pach. Instr. 1: 53. It is used also, but with a different meaning (nothing should be neglected) in Hors. Reg. 30.

³See Pr. 38; 40; 41; 42; 43; 53; 81; 105. The expression *languor corpusculi* is found also in Pr. 5 and Inst. 12. On the care for the sick brothers, see Pr. 40-47; 92; 105 and 129; Pach. Letter 5: 2 and Hors. Reg. 24. See also B. Steidle, '"Ich war krank, und ihr habt mich besucht" (Mt 25,26)', in *EuA* 40 (1964) 443-468; 41 (1965) 36-46; 99-113; 189-206.

⁴Cf. P. 87-88; Inst. 18. See also below, ¶46 ('let us not ... dedicate ourselves ... to fancier clothing and softer bedding').

Hors. Test. 22 ¹Cf. Pr. 81.

²1 Co 11:22 is quoted below, ¶29.

³Cf. Pach. Instr. 1: 59; Hors. Instr. 1: 3.

⁴'In coenobio': see above, ¶12, n. 2 and Theod. Letter 1: 2, n. 4.

⁵The same example of the rich man is given as a warning by Pachomius in G¹ 91.

⁶Part of this text is quoted in a different context in Theod. Letter 2: 1.

Hors. Test. 23 ¹Dt 15:3 is quoted also by Theodore in Theod. Letter 2: 4.

²Horsiesios often assimilates the community to the chosen people of Israel.

³We follow the punctuation proposed by H. Bacht (*Das Vermächtnis*, p. 121, n. 112): in Boon's text, a comma should replace the period after '*estis*' (p. 125,9). The '*quaproper*' of line six begins a sentence that is finished by

'*nos invicem amare debemus* . . . '. Jn 13:35 is quoted again in Hors. Letter 3: 5 and 4: 8.

⁴'*discipuli coenobiorum*': cf. similar expressions in Theod. Instr. 3: 20: ' . . . while making it plain to all who see them: "We are sons of the holy vocation of the *Koinonia*"'; and Theod. Instr. 3: 27: 'We have surrounded ourselves with a saving rampart, which is love for God's law and for the vocation of the *Koinonia* . . . so that all . . . may know that we are disciples of Christ, so as to love one another without hypocrisy.' On the translation of *coenobia* by *Koinonia*, see above, ¶22, n. 4; ¶12, n. 2 and Theod. Letter 1: 2, n. 4.

Hors. Test. 24 ¹Cf. Jud. 16: 'If someone agrees with sinners and defends someone else who has committed a fault, he shall be accursed before God and men, and shall be very severely rebuked.'

²Same quotation in Pach. Letter 3: 6, where it is also related to drunkenness.

³Cf. Leg. 14.

⁴Cf. Jud. 10.

⁵Rm 14:4 is also partly quoted in Pach. Instr. 1: 12.

Hors. Test. 25 ¹This is a very free quotation of Jude 23. The original text is: 'When there are some to be saved from the fire, pull them out; but there are others to whom you must be kind with great caution, keeping your distance even from outside clothing which is contaminated by vice'.

Hors. Test. 26 ¹Cf. Pr. 113: 'No one shall take anything on trust from another man, not even from his own brother.' See also Pr. 98 and Leg. 7.

²It is not clear whether what is meant is an excommunication from the eucharistic celebration (of which we have a few examples in the Life) or from the celebration of the *Passover* at Easter time (of which no case is mentioned in pachomian sources).

³See Pr. 70 and Leg. 15. We find something similar in G¹ 59, where the last redactor of G¹ complements his source borrowing directly from the Rule. G¹ 110 where Pachomius himself is described following these regulations faithfully is also a paragraph without any parallel in SBo and inspired by the Rule.

⁴See Pr. 113.

⁵Ga 5:13 is quoted again by Horsiesios in Hors. Letter 3: 1, and the same call to liberty is expressed here below, ¶47. See also SBo 105 and 107, and Pach. Letter 7: 1.

Hors. Test. 27 ¹Cf. Hors. Instr. 4: 1, n. 1.

²This theme of the reward according to each one's work is frequent; see Pach. Letter 5: 12, n. 2.

³Jr 17:10 was already quoted above, ¶4.

⁴Pachomius also quotes Ps 39(38):6 and Lk 12:20 together, and in a similar context, but in an inverted order: Pach. Instr. 1: 52.

⁵'*diuitiarum sarcinam*': compare this with the beginning of this same ¶ where 'all the saints and those who served God' are said to have 'put down the whole load of the world' (*saeculi sarcinam*).

⁶With H. Bacht (*Das Vermächtnis*, p. 135, n. 136) we read '*contenti simus*' instead of '*contenti sumus*'.

Hors. Test. 28 [1]Same quotation in SBo 108.

[2]'*conciliabula monachorum*': the expression is somewhat surprising. But Jerome makes great use of diminutive forms of words. See examples in H. Bacht, *Das Vermächtnis*, p. 117, n. 105.

[3]The pachomian *Koinonia* is called the vineyard of the Lord also in SBo 104 and in Pach. Instr. 1: 37. See also below, ¶47 and Hors. Reg. 4.

[4]Sg 8:11 is quoted again by Horsiesios in Hors. Instr. 3: 2.

[5]There is a clear reference to Jn 2:15 in Theod. Letter 2: 1.

[6]The same quotation occurs below, ¶30.

Hors. Test. 29 [1]Another clear allusion to this text above, ¶22.

Hors. Test. 30 [1]'*Refrigerium*'; concerning the use of this word (also above, ¶14), see Jer. Pref. 1, n. 6.

[2]Read '*imitantes Ephraim dicentem*' and not '*docentem*' which is a lapsus made by Boon (and copied by Bacht). MS M has *dicentem* (for this information we are indebted to A. de Vogüé)

[3]See above ¶28, n. 6.

[4]On Pachomius as 'mediator', see Theod. Letter 2: 4, n. 4.

Hors. Test. 31 [1]We follow the French translation of the monks of Solesmes, which seems to be the best approximation of a Latin phrase that hardly makes any sense: '. . .*aut in qua professione impleamus arreptam?*'

[2]'*Nam quia unusquisque quaerit* . . .': The word *quaerit* should be added to Boon's printed text.

[3]1 Co 10:24 is quoted again by Horsiesios in Hors. Letter 3: 1.

[4]Same complaint in Pach. Instr. 1: 49.

Hors. Test. 32 [1]We correct '*qui defecit paruulus* . . .' to '*quia defecit paruulus* . . .' as H. Bacht (*Das Vermächtnis*, p. 142) did.

Hors. Test. 33 [1]The same quotation occurs in Pach. Letter 3: 7 and 9.

[2]The same quotation is in Pach. Letter 3: 9.

[3]Ez 33:11 is quoted also in G[1] 85 and Paral. 11.

[4]This verse is quoted in G[1] 25 and 99.

[5]This verse is quoted in G[1] 9.

[6]The same quotation occurs below, ¶49.

[7]'Let us return to the Lord with our whole heart' is a kind of leitmotiv of the whole book. See below, ¶¶35 and 38.

Hors. Test. 34 [1]The same quotation is in Pach. Fragm. 4: 1.

[2]2 Tm 2:5 is quoted by Theodore in G[1] 132: see also below, ¶46.

Hors. Test. 36 [1]The same idea, with same quotation, is found above, ¶2.

Hors. Test. 37 [1]The same quotation occurs in Theod. Letter 2: 2.

Hors. Test. 38 [1]The same quotation occurs above, ¶6 and below, ¶41.

[2]Horsiesios quotes the same verse in Hors. Letter 4: 3.

[3]See the same Johannine recommendation below, ¶55.

Hors. Test. 39 [1]See above, ¶22.

[2]See Pr. 81.

Hors. Test. 40   ¹Cf. above, ¶13. See Pr. 41–42.
    ²See above, ¶15, n. 4.

Hors. Test. 41   ¹This text is quoted by Theodore in Theod. Instr. 3: 32.
    ²This text is quoted by Theodore in Theod. Instr. 3: 8.
    ³Lk 6:25 is quoted in Am. Letter 23.

Hors. Test. 42   ¹An allusion to Jm 4:4, quoted above, ¶41.
    ²The same quotation occurs in Am. Letter 28 and Theod. Instr. 3: 28.
    ³This text is quoted also in Am. Letter 23.
    ⁴The same quotation occurs in Theod. Instr. 3: 3 and 5.

Hors. Test. 43   ¹The same text is quoted also in Theod. Instr. 3: 5 and in SBo
    101. In Theod. Instr. 3:5 the text from Is 33:22 is preceded, just like here, by
    'The Lord is our father', which is from Is 64:8. In SBo 101 it starts with 'The
    Lord is our God, which actually is not in Is 33:22.
    ²There is a reference to Pr 17:15 in Inst. 18.
    ³The same quotation is in Hors. Letter 4: 5.
    ⁴The same quotation is in Pach. Instr. 1: 33.
    ⁵This sentence from Ps 101(100) is quoted in Pach. Fragm. 2: 2.

Hors. Test. 44   ¹The same promise is quoted in SBo 183, G¹ 112 and S² 7.

Hors. Test. 46   ¹See above, ¶28: 'If these are the commandments of God, which
    he handed down to us through our father . . .'.
    ²2 Tm 2:5 is quoted above, ¶34 and by Theodore in G¹ 132; with H. Bacht
    (*Das Vermächtnis*, p. 162), we read '*non superemur ab inimicis nostris*' in-
    stead of '*non superemus . . .*'.
    ³See above ¶21; Pr. 81; and Inst. 18.

Hors. Test. 47   ¹It is difficult to make sense out of '*Ad cuius lumen huius saeculi
    incedentes*'. We follow H. Bacht (*Das Vermächtnis*, p. 167, n. 209) who
    understands ' . . . ad cujus [*lucernae*] *lumen huius saeculi incedentes* . . .'.
    ²See above, ¶28, note 3.
    ³One of these curses is quoted by Hors. in Hors. Letter 4: 3.
    ⁴' . . . way of life (= *conuersationem*)'. On the meaning of *conuersatio*, see
    above ¶11, n. 4.
    ⁵On the importance of renunciation in pachomian spirituality, see above,
    ¶21, n. 1 and Pach. Instr. 1: 41, n. 1.
    ⁶The same quotation occurs above, ¶26.
    ⁷The beginning of this text is quoted above, ¶18; the rest is quoted in Pach.
    Instr. 1: 41.

Hors. Test. 48   ¹Lm 2:18 is quoted also in Pach. Letter 5: 3.
    ²At the end of the quotation: '*in capite uniuersorum gressuum*' is obscure.
    Jerome probably wrote *egressuum*, which would correspond to the ἐπ' ἀρχῆς
    πασῶν ἐξόδων of the Septuagint.
    ³'*et dereliquerunt homines pauci*', at the end of the quotation, is probably
    a copist's mistake for '*et derelinquentur homines pauci*', which would corres-
    pond to the καταλειφθήσονται ἄνθρωποι ὀλίγοι of the Septuagint and to
    the '*relinquentur*' of the Vulgate.
    ⁴The same quotation occurs in Hors. Letter 2.
    ⁵The same quotation occurs in Theod. Letter 2: 1.

⁶This sentence is quoted in Theod. Instr. 3: 8.
⁷See a more literal quotation of Is 61:10 in Hors. Instr. 4: 1.

Hors. Test. 49 ¹See above, ¶4, n. 1.
²See the same quotation above, ¶33.
³The same quotation is in Hors. Letter 2.

Hors. Test. 50 ¹The same quotation of Heb 13:16, in connection with Ac 4:32-33 (as here) is found also in S¹ 11 (according to the recension of S³). See S¹ 11, n. 4.
²This text of Ac 4:32, so important for the theology of cenobitic life, is quoted in S¹ 11; Theod. Instr. 3: 23 and Hors. Reg. 51. See also SBo 194.
³'in the *Koinonia*' translates '*in coenobiis*'; see Theod. Letter 1: 2, n. 4.
⁴The text should read: '*scientes quod crux uitae nostrae doctrinae quoque principium sit . . .*'. This is the text of MS M, as A. de Vogüé has confirmed to us. Boon has written '. . . *uitae nostra doctrinae . . .*' by mistake. Hoste, in PL 103: 473B, has reproduced *nostrae* correctly, but has arbitrarily corrected *quoque* into *-que*.
⁵There is an allusion to this text in G¹ 113.
⁶The same quotation is in Theod. Instr. 3: 5; see also above, in this ¶.
⁷Horsiesios uses this text from Baruch very often. See Hors. Letter 3: 2, n. 3.
⁸In Isaiah we read '*Jerusalem*' instead of '*Israel*'.

Hors. Test. 51 ¹See Pr. 3; 6; 11; 28; 36; 59; 60; etc.

Hors. Test. 52 ¹Against Boon, we prefer the reading of MS M (uoluimus [read *voluimus* rather than *voluimus*]) to that of MS E (*uolumus*).
²The same quotation occurs in Pach. Letter 3: 13.
³The same quotation of Lm 3:27-28.30 (without v. 29) occurs in Am. Letter 3.
⁴The sentence 'before . . . the pitcher is shattered at the fountain' (Qo 12:6) is quoted also in Inst. 18.
⁵'*uir desideriorum*' (= Jerome's Vulgate) corresponds to the ἀνὴρ ἐπιθυμιῶν of the Septuagint. The same text is quoted in Hors. Letter 1: 3, according to the Sahidic Bible: *rôme n̄šouašƒ:* 'a man worthy to be loved'.
⁶Pachomius mentions Jacob's special love for Joseph in Pach. Letter 3: 8.

Hors. Test. 53 ¹The same warning is quoted by Pachomius in two different letters: Pach. Letter 4: 6 and 5: 5.
²The same quotation occurs above, ¶19; SBo 101; and Am Letter 23. See also a similar exhortation not to grieve the Holy Spirit, in Pach. Instr. 1: 45.
³The same quotation occurs in Hors. Letter 4: 4.

Hors. Test. 54 ¹The text should read: '. . . *solis occubitum paenitentia praevenientes*'. Contrarily to Boon's *apparatus*, MS M has *penitentia* and not *penitentiae*.
²Mt 18:21 is quoted in Draguet Fragm. 1: 5; Mt 18:22 in Pach. Instr. 1: 59.
³This text is quoted above, ¶9 and in Draguet Fragm. 1: 5.

Hors. Test. 55 ¹The same quotation occurs in Paral. 9.
²The Prologue of the *Praecepta atque Judicia* begins with this text.
³The same quotation occurs above, ¶38.

Hors. Test. 56   [1]The same text is quoted differently above, ¶13.

    [2]Cf. *ibidem*.

    [3]The same quotation is in Theod. Instr. 3: 35.

    [4]This sentence seems to indicate that this book was written by Horsiesios at the end of his life.

    [5]We find several allusions to 2 Tm 4:6-8 in pachomian documents. See Theod. Instr. 3: 6 (end of the struggle); Pach. Instr. 1: 50 (the crown prepared for the winner); G[1] 49 and Pach. Fragm. 3: 3 (the righteous judge).

    [6]See above, ¶10, n. 3, and Hors. Letter 1: 6. The words 'for this is the duty of every man' are not quoted in Hors. Letter 1: 6.

ANALYTICAL INDEX

INDEX OF PERSONS

This Index contains only the names of persons found in the pa-chomian texts, not those found in the notes or the introductions. References are to the volumes and the pages where they occur.

INDEX OF PLACES

This Index contains only the names of places found in the pachomian texts, not those found in the notes or the introductions.
References are to the volumes and the pages where they occur.

235

BIBLICAL INDEX

The present Index contains all the biblical references found in the pachomian documents translated in our three volumes, but not other biblical references that may occur in the Introductions or in the Notes. The entries in italics indicate a simple allusion to a biblical text; all the other entries indicate either a literal quotation of a biblical passage or an explicit reference to it. The Index shows first the document in which the reference is found, with the number of the paragraph of that document, then the volume and the page of our translation.

23:35	Pach. Letter 3: 6	III 55
24:11	Hors. Test. 25	III 190
12	Pach. Fragm. 2: 3	III 86
	Hors. Test. 25	III 190
16	Hors. Test. 5	III 174
22	Hors. Test. 9	III 177
30–31	Am. Letter 24	II 94
31	G¹ 49	I 331
25:16	Pach. Letter 4: 6	III 62
25	*SBo 69*	*I 92*
	G¹ 77	*I 350*
	Pach. Letter 9b	III 74
26:11	*Hors. Test. 21*	*III 186*
27	Hors. Letter 4: 4	III 163
27:5,6	Hors. Letter 4: 7	III 165
7	SBo 13	I 35
11	Hors. Test. 54	III 213
13	Pach. Letter 11a (bis)	III 75, 76
23	Am. Letter 16	II 83
28:13	SBo 142	I 202
17	Hors. Letter 4: 4	III 163
29:8	Pach. Instr. 1: 32	III 27
21	S¹⁰ 2	I 451
24	Pach. Letter 4: 6	III 61
	Hors. Letter 4: 4	III 163
30:1	Hors. Reg. 10	II 200
17	Hors. Letter 1: 4	III 155
31:13	*Pach. Instr. 2: 2*	*III 47*
16	*Pach. Instr. 2: 2*	*III 47*
20	SBo 35	I 60
21	Hors. Letter 1: 2	III 153
29	Hors. Letter 1: 1 (bis)	III 153
30	Hors. Letter 1: 2	III 153
31	*Pach. Instr. 2: 2*	*III 47*

QOHELETH

1:7	Pach. Letter 11a	III 75
2:2	Am. Letter 23	II 92
6	*Hors. Instr. 3: 3*	*III 140*
14	Pach. Letter 11a	III 75
5:1	*Theod. Fragm. 2*	*III 133*
7:3	Am. Letter 23	II 92
6	Am. Letter 23	II 92
	Hors. Instr. 7: 10	III 149
9	*Hors. Test. 54*	*III 213*
11	Hors. Instr. 7: 8	III 148
12	Pach. Letter 3: 7	III 55
29	SBo 6, *107* (ter)	I 26, *153*

7:29	G¹ 3	I 299
8:5	Hors. Letter 1: 4	III 154
9:2	SBo 82	I 109
8	Hors. Instr. 4: 1	III 141
10:8	SBo 141	I 198
	Hors. Letter 4: 4	III 163
9	Hors. Letter 4: 4	III 163
10	Pach. Letter 3: 4	III 54
11	*Pach. Letter 4: 5*	*III 61*
17	Hors. Test. 8	III 176
18	Pach. Letter 3: 5	III 54
19	Hors. Reg. 40	II 210
11:3	Hors. Letter 3: 3	III 160
9-10	Hors. Test. 52	III 211
12:1-7	Hors. Test. 52	III 211
6	Inst. 18	II 174
13-14	Hors. Letter 1: 6	III 156
	Hors. Test. 56	III 215
14	Hors. Test. 10	III 177

SONG OF SONGS

2:3	*Pach. Letter 9b*	*III 73*
8	Hors. Instr. 3: 3	III 140
11	Pach. Letter 4: 6	III 62
3:2	*SBo 94*	*I 128*
4:12	Am. Letter 3	II 72
	Hors. Test. 20	III 84
7:11-13	*Pach. Instr. 1: 20*	*III 20*
8:11-12	Hors. Test. 28	III 193
11	Hors. Instr. 3: 2	III 140
14	Hors. Instr. 3: 3	III 140

WISDOM

1:7	*Am. Letter 18*	*II 85*
2:23	*SBo 107*	*I 153*
4:7	*Hors. Letter 4: 5*	*III 163*
19	*SBo 186*	*I 225*
	G¹ 140	*I 398*
5:9	Paral. 19	II 42
18	Pach. Letter 3: 4	III 54
6:7	Hors. Reg. 33	II 209
17	Pach. Letter 3: 8	III 56
10:4	Pach. Letter 3: 8, 10	III 55, 57
8	Pach. Letter 3: 8	III 56
17	Hors. Test. 51	III 210
11:24 (25)	Paral. 39	II 63

SIRACH

1:10	SBo 67	I 88
2:8	Hors. Test. 20	III 185
3:29 (31)	Pach. Letter 3: 10	III 56
	Pach. Letter 11a	III 76
5:2	*Inst. 18*	*II 173*
	Pach. Instr. 1: 19	*III 20*
	Pach. Letter 3: 9	III 56
6:16	*Pach. Instr. 1: 42*	*III 33*
23	*Pach. Instr. 1: 1*	*III 13*
7:4	*Pach. Instr. 1: 33*	*III 27*
16-17	*SBo 96*	*I 134*
	G¹ 113	I 377
9:8	*Pach. Instr. 1: 35*	*III 29*
10:9	*Paral. 19*	*II 42*
	Pach. Instr. 1: 24	*III 23*
12-13	*Paral. 1*	*II 20*
27	Pach. Letter 3: 3	III 53
13:24	Pach. Instr. 1: 13	III 16
16:24	*Pach. Instr. 1: 2*	*III 13*
17:25	Pach. Instr. 1: 20	*III 20*
31	*S¹ 16*	*I 434*
32	*Pach. Instr. 1: 24*	*III 23*
18:25	Pach. Instr. 1: 53	III·38
19:2	*Inst. 18* (bis)	*II 172, 174*
	Pach. Instr. 1: 45	*III 34*
	Pach. Letter 3: 4, 7	*III 55*
20:22	*Inst. 18*	*II 173*
21:2	G¹ 31	I 318
25	*Pach. Fragm. 2: 3*	*III 86*
22:1-2	Hors. Reg. 17	*II 202*
9	Hors. Instr. 7: 13	III 151
25:3,17	*Pach. Instr. 1: 33*	*III 27, 28*
31:28	*Pach. Instr. 1: 45*	*III 35*
29-30	*Pach. Instr. 1: 45*	*III 34*
34:4	Pach. Instr. 1: 36	III 29
38:6	*SBo 110*	*I 163*
39:28	*SBo 88*	*I 115*
40:29	*Inst. 18*	*II 173*
42:12	*Pach. Instr. 1: 35*	*III 28*
44:16	Pach. Instr. 1: 25	III 24
46:1	Paral. 41	II 66
48:9	Pach. Instr. 1: 25	III 24

ISAIAH

1:21	Hors. Test. 43	III 202
2:6,8	Hors. Test. 29	III 194
9	*Hors. Test. 22*	*III 187*

32:13	Hors. Test. 44	III 203
33:2	Theod. Instr. 3: 3, 5	III 94, 95
	Hors. Test. 42	III 201
16	G¹ 17	I 308
18	S¹⁰ 4	I 453
22	SBo 101	I 139
	Theod. Instr. 3: 5	III 95
	Hors. Test. 43	III 202
35:10	SBo 2	I 24
	G¹ 2	I 298
37:1	Paral. 10	II 32
40:10	*Paral. 39*	*II 64*
17	*SBo 142*	*I 200*
31	Hors. Test. 46	III 205
43:2	Pach. Instr. 1: 25 (bis)	III 23
25	Hors. Test. 46	III 204
47:6	Hors. Test. 11	III 178
14	Pach. Letter 3: 13	III 58
48:18	*Pach. Instr. 1: 54*	*III 38*
21	Pach. Letter 4: 5	III 61
49:13	Pach. Letter 9b	III 74
15	Theod. Instr. 3: 33	III 113
50:6	Pach. Instr. 1: 31	III 27
11	SBo 2	I 24
	G¹ 2	I 298
51:2	S¹ 2	I 425
52:1	Hors. Letter 3: 2	III 158
5	*Hors. Test. 28, 30*	*III 194, 195*
6	Paral. 39, 40	II 63, 65
53:3	Theod. Instr. 3: 19	III 104
4	*SBo 142*	*I 201*
	Pach. Letter 5: 11	III 66
	Hors. Test. 13	*III 179*
5	Pach. Instr. 2: 4	III 48
7	*Pach. Instr. 1: 25*	*III 23*
10	SBo 142	I 201
	G¹ 56	I 337
	Pach. Instr. 1: 31	III 27
54:4	Theod. Instr. 3: 7	III 97
13	*Theod. Instr. 3: 43*	*III 118*
17	G¹ 113	I 378
55:6-7	Theod. Instr. 3: 38	III 115
56:7	Hors. Test. 28	III 194
57:13	Hors. Test. 43	III 202
14	Hors. Test. 43	III 202
15	SBo 67	I 88
	G¹ 72	I 347
16	Hors. Test. 37	III 199

19:27	Theod. Instr. 2: 1	III 91
20:8	SBo 145	I 207
11-12	Hors. Reg. 48	II 215
15	Hors. Reg. 48	II 215
26,28	SBo 98	I 135
21:33	*SBo 104*	*I 145*
22:1-13	Hors. Reg. 2	II 197
4	SBo 145	I 208
11-12	*Pach. Instr. 1: 41*	*III 32*
13	Hors. Reg. 2	II 197
	Pach. Instr. 1: 41	III 32
37-39	S¹⁰ 2	I 452
	Hors. Test. 38	*III 199*
37	SBo 70, *204*	I 92, *255*
	G¹ 78	I 351
40	Hors. Test. 38	III 199
23:4	Hors. Test. 7	III 175
8	Theod. Instr. 3: 17	III 103
9	*G¹ 108*	*I 374*
	S¹ 2	I 425
12	SBo 97	I 134
	Pach. Instr. 1: 17	III 19
16	G¹ 57	I 338
23	Inst. 18	II 174
26	Hors. Reg. 54	II 217
27	G¹ 57	I 338
24:3	Am. Letter 6 (bis)	II 75
22	Pach. Instr. 1: 49	III 36
35	Theod. Letter 2: 2	III 128
41	Pach. Letter 11b	III 78
44	*Hors. Letter 3: 1*	*III 158*
45	Pach. Letter 3: 3	III 53
	Hors. Test. 14	III 180
46-47	Pach. Instr. 1: 20	III 20
49-51	Hors. Test. 14	III 180
49	Pach. Letter 3: 3	III 53
51	*Pach. Instr. 1: 55*	*III 39*
25:1-13	Hors. Reg. 3	II 197
	Pach. Instr. 1: 51	*III 37*
4-12	*Hors. Test. 20*	*III 185*
6	Hors. Letter 3: 1	III 158
7	*Hors. Letter 4: 4*	*III 163*
10-12	*Hors. Letter 3: 1*	*III 158*
12	Hors. Reg. 3	II 197
13	SBo 118	I 173
15	*Hors. Reg. 56*	*II 218*
20	Am. Letter 14	II 81
	Hors. Instr. 4: 2	III 142

18:2-3	G¹ 141	I 399
9	Hors. Test. 13	III 180
19:5	*Pach. Instr. 1: 4*	*III 48*
20:28	G¹ 56	I 337
29	Theod. Instr. 1: 1	III 91
21:5-6	Hors. Test. 52	III 212
15-17	Hors. Test. 17	III 183
15,16	G¹ 135	I 394
20	Theod. Instr. 1: 2	III 91
	Theod. Instr. 3: 9	III 98
25	S² 5	I 446

ACTS

1:24	*SBo 198*	*I 245*
2:11	Am. Letter 18 (bis)	II 86
3:20	Hors. Test. 14	III 180
4:32-33	Hors. Test. 50	III 209
32	SBo 194	I 237
	S¹ 11	I 431
	Hors. Reg. 51	II 216
	Theod. Instr. 3: 23	III 107
34-35	Hors. Test. 27	III 191
5:1-11	Draguet 2: 2	II 115
41	Pach. Instr. 1: 22, 59	III 22, 40
	Theod. Instr. 3: 5	*III 95*
7:9-10	G¹ 126	I 387
22	*SBo 135*	*I 193*
	Pach. Instr. 1: 55	*III 38*
36	Paral. 38	II 62
42	Pach. Letter 3: 7	III 55
55	Am. Letter 9, 12	II 77, 80
	Pach. Instr. 2: 4	III 48
56	S² 5	I 446
8:23	Am. Letter 16	II 83
32	*Pach. Instr. 1: 25*	*III 23*
9:15	G¹ 123	I 385
	Am. Letter 9	II 77
34	*Am. Letter 27*	*II 97*
10:4	*Hors. Letter 3: 2*	*III 158*
13	*Paral. 18*	*II 40*
42	*SBo 198*	*I 245*
11:8	*Hors. Letter 3: 2*	*III 158*
12:7-8	*SBo 184*	III 219
	Am. Letter 14	*II 81*
14:8-10	Am. Letter 16	II 83
14	Pach. Instr. 1: 22	III 22
17	SBo 101	I 139
22	*Hors. Test. 50*	*III 209*

6:4	Hors. Test. 15	III 181
5	Hors. Test. 21	III 186
8	Hors. Test. 27	III 191
11-13	*Pach. Instr. 1: 42*	*III 33*
11-12	Hors. Test. 25	III 190
11	*Pach. Instr. 1: 47*	*III 35*
	Theod. Instr. 3: 26	*III 108*
	Hors. Test. 27	*III 191*
12	*S² 1*	*I 444*
	Am. Letter 3	II 73
	Pach. Instr. 1: 54	*III 38*
14	Pach. Letter 3: 4	III 54
15	Theod. Letter 1: 2	III 123
16-17	Hors. Test. 19	III 184
16	*SBo 14*	*I 36*
	Theod. Instr. 3: 4 (bis)	III 94
	Theod. Instr. 3: 30	*III 110*

PHILIPPIANS

1:11	*S¹ 16*	*I 436*
17	Am. Letter 5	II 74
28	*Theod. Instr. 3: 26*	*III 108*
29	Am. Letter 34	II 103
	Theod. Instr. 3: 5	III 95
	Hors. Test. 5	III 173
2:8	SBo 30	I 55
	Paral. 1	II 20
	Pach. Instr. 1: 47	*III 35*
12	SBo 26	I 49
	Paral. 41	II 66
	Hors. Test. 17	III 182
13	Hors. Letter 2	III 157
14-15	*Hors. Test. 19*	*III 184*
15	Theod. Instr. 3: 8	III 97
3:6	*Theod. Instr. 3: 19*	*III 104*
13	SBo 19	I 43
	G¹ 15, 49	I 307, 331
19-20	*S¹ 2*	*I 426*
21	Theod. Instr. 3: 9	III 98
4:3	SBo 2. 194	I 24, 239
	G¹ 2	I 298
4	Hors. Test. 19	III 184
5-6	Hors. Test. 26	III 191
7	Pach. Letter 4: 6	III 62
8-9	*S¹ 2*	*I 426*
8	Hors. Instr. 7: 3	III 146
12-13	Hors. Reg. 50	III 216
13	Theod. Instr. 3: 5	III 95

1 PETER

1:13	Am. Letter 14	II 81
17	Pach. Fragm. 3: 3	III 87
	Hors. Test. 16	III 181
19	*Hors. Instr. 5*	*III 143*
22	Hors. Test. 35	III 197
2:1	*S² 14*	*I 449*
5	S¹ 1	I 425
8	Hors. Test. 26	III 190
9	SBo 3	I 25
	G¹ 2	I 299
12	Pach. Letter 3: 2	III 53
13-14	SBo 125	I 181
21-24	Pach. Instr. 1: 59	III 40
21-22	S¹ 8	I 429
21	*Hors. Test. 3*	*III 172*
23	G¹ 57 (ter)	I 337, 338
	S¹ 8	I 429
24	Pach. Instr. 2: 4	III 48
25	*Pach. Instr. 1: 37*	*III 30*
3:7	Pr 52, 119	II 154, 164
8	Theod. Instr. 3: 23	III 107
9	Pach. Letter 7: 3	III 70
	Hors. Instr. 4: 2	*III 141*
10	*Theod. Fragm. 4*	*III 134*
15	Hors. Test. 15	III 180
16	*Theod. Instr. 3: 5*	*III 95*
4:1	*Hors. Test. 20*	*III 185*
2	*Hors. Test. 20*	*III 185*
5	Theod. Instr. 3: 23	III 106
7	*Pach. Instr. 1: 10*	*III 15*
8	Pach. Instr. 1: 38	III 31
13	*Theod. Instr. 2: 1*	*III 91*
	Theod. Instr. 3: 41	*III 116*
5:2	*Hors. Test. 17*	*III 183*
3	*Hors. Test. 13*	*III 179*
4	Pach. Instr. 1: 7	III 14
7	*Theod. Instr. 3: 41*	*III 116*
8-9	Hors. Test. 6	III 174
8	G¹ 135	I 394
	Pach. Instr. 1: 10, 28	*III 15, 26*
	Pach. Fragm. 1: 2	*III 85*
	Theod. Instr. 3: 19	*III 105*
9	*Pach. Instr. 1: 61*	*III 41*
	Theod. Instr. 3: 31	III 112

ABBREVIATIONS
of names of periodicals and series

ADMG	*Annales du Musée Guimet*, Paris.
AnBoll	*Analecta Bollandiana*, Brussels.
BKV	*Bibliothek der Kirchenväter*, Kempten.
BM	*Benediktinische Monatschrift* (later: *Erbe und Auftrag*), Beuron.
ChE	*Chronique d'Egypte*, Brussels.
CSCO	*Corpus scriptorum Christianorum orientalium*, Louvain.
DACL	*Dictionnaire d'archéologie chrétienne et de liturgie*, Paris.
EuA	*Erbe und Auftrag* (formerly *Benediktinische Monatschrift*), Beuron.
GuL	*Geist und Leben. Zeitschrift für Aszese und Mystik*, Würzburg.
HJ	*Historisches Jahrbuch*, Munich-Freiburg.
JEH	*The Journal of Ecclesiastical History*, London.
LTK	*Lexikon für Theologie und Kirche*, Freiburg.
LuM	*Liturgie und Mönchtum. Laacher Hefte*, Maria Laach.
Muséon	*Le Muséon*, Louvain.
NGG	*Nachrichten der Gesellschaft der Wissenschaften zu Göttingen*, Göttingen.
OCP	*Orientalia Christiana Periodica*, Rome.
OGL	*Ons geestelijk leven.*
Orientalia	*Orientalia. Commentarii Periodici Pontificii Instituti Biblici*, Rome.
OstKSt	*Ostkirchliche Studien*, Würzburg.
PG	*Patrologia Graeca* of Migne, Paris.

PL	*Patrologia Latina* of Migne, Paris.
PO	*Patrologia Orientalis*, Paris.
RAM	*Revue d'ascétique et de mystique*, Toulouse.
RBén	*Revue bénédictine*, Maredsous.
RHE	*Revue d'histoire ecclésiastique*, Louvain.
RHR	*Revue de l'histoire des religions*, Paris.
RHS	*Revue d'Histoire de la Spiritualité*, Toulouse.
RMab	*Revue Mabillon*, Liguqé.
SA	*Studia Anselmiana*, Rome.
Sal	*Salesianum*, (Rome) Turin.
StMon	*Studia Monastica*, Montserrat.
TGL	*Tijdschrift voor geestelijk leven*, Nijmegen.
TSK	*Theologische Studien und Kritiken*, (Hamburg) Gotha.
TU	*Texte und Untersuchungen zur Geschichte der altchristlichen Literatur.* Archiv für die griechisch-christlichen Schriftsteller der ersten drei Jahrhunderte, Leipzig-Berlin.
VS	*La Vie Spirituelle*, Paris.
ZDMG	*Zeitschrift der deutschen morgenländischen Gesellschaft*, Leipzig.
ZKT	*Zeitschrift für katholische Theologie*, (Innsbruck) Vienna.

PACHOMIAN BIBLIOGRAPHY

Amand de Mendieta, A. 'Le système cénobitique basilien comparé au système cénobitique pachômien,' *RHR* 152 (1957) 31-80.

Amélineau, E. 'Etude historique sur St. Pachôme et le cénobitisme primitif dans la Haute-Egypte,' *Bulletin de l'Institut d'Egypte*, series 2,7 (1886) 306-309.

Bacht, H. 'Pakhome—der grosse "Adler",' *GuL* 22 (1949) 367-382.

————. 'Ein Wort zur Ehrenrettung der ältesten Mönchsregel,' *ZKT* 72 (1950) 350-359.

————. 'L'importance de l'idéal monastique de s. Pacôme pour l'histoire du monachisme chrétien,' *RAM* 26 (1950) 308-326.

————. 'Heimweh nach der Urkirche. Zur Wesensdeutung des frühchristlichen Mönchtums.' *LuM* 7 (1950) 64-78.

————. 'Vom gemeinsamen Leben. Die Bedeutung des christlichen Mönchideals für die Geschichte des christlichen Mönchtums,' *LuM* 11 (1952) 91-110.

————. '"Meditatio" in den ältesten Mönchsquellen,' *GuL* 28 (1955) 360-373.

————. 'Antonius und Pachomius. Von der Anachorese zum Cönobitentum,' in B. Steidle, *Antonius Magnus Eremita, SA* 38; Rome, 1956 Pp. 66-107.

————. 'Studien zum "Liber Orsiesii".'*HJ* 77 (1958) 98-124

————. 'Mönchtum und Kirche. Eine Studie zur Spiritualität des Pachomius,' in J. Daniélou and H. Vorgrimler, *Sentire Ecclesiam, Das Bewusstsein von der Kirche als gestaltende Kraft der Frömmigkeit.*Freiburg, 1961. Pp. 113-133.

————. 'Pakhôme et ses disciples,' in *Théologie de la vie monastique, Théologie* 49. Paris, 1961. Pp. 39-71.

————. 'La loi du "retour aux sources". (De quelques aspects de l'idéal monastique pachômien),' *RMab* 51 (1961) 6-25.

————. 'Ein verkanntes Fragment des koptischen Pachomiusregel,' *Muséon* 75 (1962) 5-18.

————. 'Pachomius der Jüngere,' in *LTK*, 7^2 (1962) Col. 1331.

————. 'Zur Typologie des koptischen Mönchtums. Pachomius und Evagrius.' In *Christentum am Nil (Internationale*

Arbeitstagung zur Ausstellung 'koptische Kunst'). Recklinghausen, 1964. Pp. 142-157.

_____. 'Vom Umgang mit der Bibel im ältesten Mönchtum,' *Theologie und Philosophie* 41 (1966) 557-566.

_____. '...Vexillum crucis sequi (Horsiesius). Mönchtum als Kreuzesnachfolge,' *Martyria. —Leiturgia—Diakonia. Festschrift für H. Volk, Bischof von Mainz, zum 65. Geburtstag*, Mainz, 1968. Pp. 149-162.

_____. *Das Vermächtnis des Ursprungs (Studien zum Frühen Mönchtum I)*. Würzburg, 1972.

_____. 'Agrypnia. Die Motive des Schlafentzugs im frühen Mönchtum,' *Bibliothek—Buch—Geschichte (Kurt Köster zum 65. Geburtstag; herausgegeben von Günther Pflug, Brita Eckert und Heinz Friesenhahn)*. Frankfurt am Main, 1977. Pp. 353-369.

Batlle, C.M. 'La vida religiosa comunitària a l'Egipte del segle IV.' Un nou plantejament des de les bases. *StMon* 12 (1970) 181-194.

Biedermann, H.M. 'Die Regel des Pachomius und die evangelischen Räte,' *OstKSt* 9 (1960) 241-253.

Büchler, B., *Die Armut der Armen. Über den ursprünglichen Sinn der mönchischen Armut.* Kösel, 1980.

Chitty, D.J. 'Pachomian Sources Reconsidered,' *JEH* 5 (1954) 38-77.

_____. 'A Note on the Chronology of Pachomian Foundations,' *Studia Patristica*, Vol. II, *TU* 64. Berlin, 1957. Pp. 379-385.

_____. 'Some Notes, mainly Lexical on the Sources for the Life of Pachomius,' *Studia Patristica*, V, *TU* 80. Berlin, 1962. Pp. 266-269.

_____. 'Pachomian Sources once more,' *Studia Patristica*, X. Berlin, 1970. Pp. 54-64.

Crum, W.E. *Theological Texts from Coptic Papyri edited with an Appendix upon the Arabic and Coptic Versions of the Life of Pachomius, Anecdota Oxoniensia, Semitic series* 12). Oxford, 1913.

_____. *Der Papyruscodex saec. VI-VII der Phillipsbibliothek in Cheltenham. Koptische theologische Schriften. Mit einem Beitrag von A. Ehrhard. Schriften der Wissenschaftlichen Gesellschaft in Strassburg* 18. Strasbourg, 1915.

De Clercq, D. 'L'influence de la Règle de saint Pachôme en Occident,' *Mélanges d'Histoire du Moyen Age dédiés à la mémoire de Louis Halphen.* Paris, 1951. Pp. 169-176.

Delhougne, H. 'Autorité et participation chez les Pères du cénobitisme,' *RAM* 45 (1969) 369-394; 46 (1970) 3-32.

Deseille, P. *L'esprit du monachisme pachômien, suivi de la traduction française des Pachomiana latina par les moines de Solesmes, Spiritualité orientale* 2. Bellefontaine, 1968.

Draguet, R. 'Le chapitre de HL sur les Tabennésiotes dérive-t-il d'une source copte?' *Muséon* 57 (1944) 53-145; 58 (1945) 15-95.

Ehrhard, A. 'Zur literarhistorischen und theologischen Würdigung der Texte,' W.E. Crum, *Der Papyruscodex....* Pp. 129-171. [Concerns the letter of Theophilos to Horsiesios].

Gindele, C. 'Die Schriftlesung im Pachomiuskloster,' *EuA*, 41 (1965) 114-122.

Gnolfo, P. 'Pedagogia Pacomiana,' *Sal* 10 (1948) 569-596.

Gribomont, J. 'Pachomios der Ältere,' *LTK* 7² (1962) Col. 1330-1331.

Grützmacher, O. *Pachomios und das älteste Klosterleben.* Freiburg, 1896.

Halkin, F. 'Les Vies grecques de S. Pacôme.' *AnBoll* 47 (1929) 376-388.

——————. 'L'Histoire Lausiaque et les Vies grecques de S. Pacôme,' *AnBoll* 48 (1930) 257-301.

Hedrick, C.W., 'Gnostic Proclivities in the Greek *Life of Pachomius* and the *Sitz im Leben* of the Nag Hammadi Library,' *Novum Testamentum* 22 (1980) 78-94.

Hengstenberg, W. 'Pachomiana (mit einem Anhang über die Liturgie von Alexandrien),' in A.M. Königer, *Beiträge zur Geschichte des christlichen Altertums und der Byzantinischen Literatur. Festgabe Albert Ehrhard.* Bonn and Leipzig, 1922. Pp. 228-252.

Heussi, K. 'Pachomios,' in Pauly-Wissowa, *Realencyklopädie der classischen Altertumswissenschaft,* 18 (1942) Col. 2070 ff.

Ladeuze, P. 'Les diverses recensions de la vie de S. Pakhôme et leurs dépendances mutuelles,' *Muséon* (1897) 148-171; (1898) 145-168; 269-286; 378-395.

——————. *Etude sur le cénobitisme pakhômien pendant le IVe*

siècle et la première moitié du Ve. Louvain and Paris, 1898; rpt. 1962.

Leclercq, H. 'Pachôme, in *DACL* XIII/1 (1937) Col. 499-510.

Lefort, L.T. 'Théodore de Tabennêsi et la lettre pascale de S. Athanase sur le canon de la Bible,' *Muséon* 29 (1910) 205-216.

_____. 'Un texte original de la règle de saint Pachôme,' *Comptes rendus de l'Académie des Inscriptions et Belles-Lettres*, 1919. Pp. 341-348.

_____. 'La Règle de S. Pachôme (étude d'approche),' *Muséon* 34 (1921) 61-70.

_____. 'La Règle de S. Pachôme (2ᵉ étude d'approche),' *Muséon* 37 (1924) 1-28.

_____. 'La Règle de S. Pachôme (Nouveaux documents),' *Muséon* 40 (1927) 31-64.

_____. 'S. Pachôme et Amen-em-ope,' *Muséon* 49 (1927) 65-74.

_____. 'Littérature bohaïrique,' *Muséon* 44 (1931) 115-135.

_____. 'S. Athanase écrivain copte,' *Muséon* 46 (1933) 1-33.

_____. 'La Règle de S. Pachôme (nouveaux fragments coptes),' *Muséon* 48 (1935) 75-80.

_____. 'Les premiers monastères pachômiens. Exploration topographique,' *Muséon* 52 (1939) 379-408.

_____. 'Les sources coptes pachômiennes,' *Muséon* 67 (1954) 217-229.

Lehmann, K. 'Die Entstehung der Freiheitsstrafe in den Klöstern des heiligen Pachomius,' *Z. d. Savigny-Stift. f. Rechtsgesch., Kan. Abt.* 37 (1951). Pp. 1-94.

Leipoldt, J. 'Pachom,' *Bulletin de la Société de l'Archéologie Copte* 16 (1961-62) 191-229.

_____. 'Pachom,' *Koptologische Studien in der DDR. Wissenschaftliche Zeitschrift der Martin-Luther-Universität Halle-Wittenberg.* Sonderheft 1965, 236-249.

Levis, A. 'Koinonia e comunidade no monacato pacomiano,' *Claretianum* 15 (1975) 269-327.

Lozano, J.M. 'La comunità pacomiana: dalla comunione all'istituzione,' *Claretianum* 15 (1975) 237-267.

Monachino, V. 'Pacomio,' *Enciclopedia Cattolica* 9 (1952) Col. 511-514.

Morson, J. 'The sixteenth Centenary of St. Pachomius.' *Pax* 38 (1948) 65-74

Orlandi, T. 'Nuovi Testi copti pacomiani,' *Commandements du Seigneur et Libération évangélique, SA* 70. Rome, 1977. Pp. 241-243.

Peeters, P. 'A propos de la Vie sahidique de S. Pacôme.' *AnBoll* 52 (1934) 286-320.

————. 'L'édition critique des Vies coptes de S. Pacôme par le Prof. Lefort,' *Muséon* 59 (1946) 17-34.

————. 'Le dossier copte de S. Pacôme et ses rapports avec la tradition grecque,' *AnBoll* 64 (1946) 258-277.

————. 'Un feuillet d'une Vie arabe de saint Pacôme,' *Muséon* 59 (1946) 399-412.

Philaret, Brother. 'The Pachomian Origin of Christian Cenobitism' in *Diakonia* 9 (1974) 118-125, 216-233.

Pietschmann, R. 'Theodorus Tabennesiota und die sahidische Übersetzung des Osterfestbriefs des Athanasius vom Jahre 367,: *NGG* (1889) I, 87-104.

Quecke, H. 'Ein Pachomiuszitat bei Schenute,' *Probleme der koptischen Literatur. Wissenschaftliche Beiträge der Univ. Halle-Wittenberg.* 1968. Pp. 155-171.

————. 'Briefe Pachoms in koptischer Sprache. Neue deutsche Übersetzung,' *Zetesis* (*Festschrift E. de Strycker*). Antwerp and Utrecht, 1973. Pp. 655-664.

————. 'Ein neues Fragment der Pachombriefe in koptischer Sprache,' *Orientalia* 43 (1974) 66-82.

————. 'Die Briefe Pachoms,' *ZDMG*, Supp. II (1974) 96-108.

————. 'Die griechische Übersetzung der Pachombriefe,' *Studia Papyrologica* 15 (1976) 153-159.

————. 'Eine Handvoll Pachomianischer Texte,' *ZDMG*, Supp. III, 1 (1977) 221-229.

Revillout, E. 'Funérailles des moines égyptiens au temps de Saint Antoine et de Saint Pacome,' *Académie Delphinale*, Bull. s. 2,1 (1856-60) 374-386.

Řezáč, I. 'De forma unionis monasteriorum Sancti Pachomii,' *OCP* 23 (1957) 381-414.

Ruppert, F. *Das Pachomianische Mönchtum und die Anfänge klösterlichen Gehorsams. Münsterschwarzacher Studien* 20. Münsterschwarzach, 1971.

————. 'Arbeit und geistliches Leben im pachomianischen Mönchtum,' *OstKSt* 24 (1975) 3-14.

Samir, K. 'Témoins arabes de la catéchèse de Pachôme "A propos d'un moine rancunier". (CPG 2354.1),' *OCP* 42 (1976) 494-508.

Schiwietz, S. 'Geschichte und Organisation der pachomianischen Klöster im vierten Jahrhundert,' *Archiv für kathol. Kirchenrecht* 81 (1901) 461-490; 630-649.

Steidle, B. '"Der Zweite" im Pachomiuskloster,' *BM* 24 (1948) 97-104; 174-179.

————, and O. Schuler, 'Der "Obern-Spiegel" im "Testament" des Abtes Horsiesi († nach 387),' *EuA* 43 (1967) 22-38.

Steidle, B. 'Der Osterbrief unseres Vaters Theodor an alle Klöster. Zur 1600. Wiederkehr des Todesjahres (368-1968),' *EuA* 44 (1968) 104-119.

————. 'Der heilige Abt. Theodor von Tabennesi. Zur 1600. Wiederkehr des Todesjahres (368-1968),' *EuA* 44 (1968) 91-103.

Tamburrino, P. 'Koinonia. Die Beziehung "Monasterium"-"Kirche" im frühen pachomianischen Mönchtum,' *EuA* 43 (1967) 5-21.

————. 'Bibbia e vita spirituale negli scritti di Orsiesi,' in C. Vagaggini, ed., *Bibbia e spiritualità, Biblioteca di cultura religiosa* 79. Rome, 1967. Pp. 85-119.

————. 'Les saints de l'Ancien Testament dans la Ière catéchèse de saint Pachôme,' *Melto* 4 (1968) 33-44.

————. 'Die Heiligen des Alten Testaments in der 1. Katechese des heiligen Pachomius,' *EuA* 45 (1969) 50-56.

Van Cranenburgh, H. 'La "Regula Angeli" dans la Vie latine de saint Pachôme,' *Muséon* 76 (1963) 165-194.

————. 'Nieuw licht op de oudste kloostercongregatie van de christenheid: de instelling van Sint-Pachomius,' *TGL* 19 (1963) 581-605; 665-690; and 20 (1964) 41-54.

————. 'Actualiteitswaarde van het pachomiaanse kloosterleven,' *TGL* 24 (1968) 233-257.

————. 'Valeur actuelle de la vie religieuse pachômienne,' *VS* 120 (1969) 400-422.

——— . 'Etude comparative des récits anciens de la vocation de saint Pachôme,' *RBén* 82 (1972) 280-308.

——— . 'Les noms de Dieu dans la prière de Pachôme et de ses frères,' *RHS* 52 (1976) 193-212.

Van Molle, M.M. 'Essai de classement chronologique des premières règles de vie commune en chrétienté,' *VS Supplément* 84 (1968) 108-127.

——— . ''Confrontation entre les Règles et la littérature pachômienne postérieure,' *VS Supplément* 86 (1968) 394-424.

——— . 'Aux origines de la vie communautaire chrétienne, quelques équivoques déterminantes pour l'avenir,' *VS Supplément* 88 (1969) 101-121.

——— . 'Vie commune et obéissance d'après les intuitions premières de Pachôme et Basile,' *VS Supplément* 93 (1970) 196-225.

Van Rijen, A. 'Een regel van Pachomius,' *Ons geestelijk leven* 48 (1971) 334-344.

Veilleux, A. 'Le problème des Vies de Saint Pachôme,' *RAM* 42 (1966) 287-305.

——— . *La liturgie dans le cénobitisme pachômien au quatrième siècle,* SA 57. Rome, 1968.

——— . 'San Pacomio, abate di Tabennesi,' *Bibliotheca Sanctorum,* Vol. X (1968) Col. 10-20.

——— . 'Pacomio il Giovane,' *Ibidem,* Col. 9-10.

——— . 'Teodoro di Tabennesi,' *Ibidem* Vol. XII (1969) Col. 270-272.

——— . 'Holy Scripture in the Pachomian Koinonia,' *Monastic Studies* 10 (1974) 143-153.

Vergote, J. 'L'oeuvre de L.T. Lefort,' *Muséon* 59 (1946) 41-62.

——— . 'En lisant "Les Vies de saint Pakhôme",' *ChE* 22 (1947) 389-415.

——— . 'La valeur des Vies grecques et coptes de S. Pakhôme,' *Orientalia Lovaniensia Periodica* 8 (1977) 175-186.

Vogüé, A. de. 'Points de contact du chapitre XXXII de l'Histoire Lausiaque avec les écrits d'Horsièse,' *StMon* 13 (1971) 291-294.

——— . 'Les pièces latines du dossier pachômien,' *RHE* 67 (1972) 26-67.

——— . 'L'Anecdote pachômienne du "Vaticanus graecus" 2091. Son origine et ses sources,' *RSH* 49 (1973) 401-419.

_____ . 'Le nom du Supérieur de monastère dans la Règle pachômienne. A propos d'un ouvrage récent,' *StMon* 15 (1973) 17-22.

_____ . 'La vie arabe de saint Pachôme et ses deux sources présumées,' *AnBoll* 91 (1973) 379-390.

_____ . 'Saint Pachôme et son oeuvre d'après plusieurs études récentes,' *RHE* 69 (1974) 425-453.

_____ . 'Sur la terminologie de la pénitence dans la Règle de saint Pachôme', *StMon* 17 (1975) 7-12.

_____ . 'Les noms de la porte et du portier dans la Règle de Pachôme,' *StMon* 17 (1975) 233-235.

Wirszycka, E. 'Les terres de la congrégation pachômienne dans une liste de payements pour les apora,' *Le monde grec. Pensée, littérature, histoire, documents. Hommage à Claire Préaux.* Brussels, 1975. Pp. 625-636.

Zananiri, G. 'Saint Pacôme et le monachisme.' *Revue Confér. Franc. Or.* Cairo, 1948, 178-185.

* * * *Pachomiana. Commémoration du XVIème Centenaire de St Pacôme l'Egyptien (348-1948).* (*Publications du Centre d'Etudes Orientales de la Custodie Franciscaine de Terre-Sainte, Coptica* 3). Cairo, 1955.

SOURCES
Editions and Translations

A: *EDITIONS*

Coptic

Lefort, L.T. *S. Pachomii vita bohairice scripta, CSCO* 89. Louvain, 1925; rpt. 1953.

————. *S. Pachomii vitae sahidice scriptae, CSCO* 99/100. Louvain, 1933/34; rpt. 1952.

————. 'Glanures pachômiennes,' *Muséon* 54 (1941) 111-138. [S¹⁹, S²⁰, and fragments of S³, S³ᶜ, and S⁴].

————. 'Vies de S. Pachôme (Nouveaux fragments),' *Muséon* 49 (1936) 219-230. [Fragments of S²].

————. *Oeuvres de s. Pachôme et de ses disciples, CSCO* 159. Louvain, 1956.

Quecke, Hans. *Die Briefe Pachoms. Griechischer Text der Handschrift W. 145 der Chester Beatty Library eingeleitet und herausgegeben von Hans Quecke. Anhang: Die koptischen Fragmente und Zitate der Pachombriefe. Textus Patristici et Liturgici* 11. Regensburg, 1975. [Coptic texts: pp. 111-118].

————. 'Ein Brief von einem Nachfolger Pachoms,' *Orientalia* 44 (1975) 426-433.

Greek

Halkin, F. *Sancti Pachomii Vitae Graecae, Subsidia hagiographica* 19. Brussels, 1932.

————. 'La vie abrégée de saint Pachôme dans le ménologe impérial (BHG 1401b),' *AnBoll* 96 (1978) 367-381.

————. 'Une vie inédite de saint Pachôme,' *AnBoll* 97 (1979) 5-55; 241-287.

Bousquet, J., and F. Nau. *Histoire de saint Pacôme (Une rédaction inédite des Ascetica) Texte grec des manuscrits Paris 881 et Chartres 1754 avec une traduction de la version syriaque et une analyse du manuscrit de Paris Suppl. grec. 480, PO* IV, 5. Paris, 1907.

Lefort, L.T. 'La Règle de S. Pachôme (2ᵉ étude d'approche),' *Muséon* 37 (1924) 1-28. [Text of the Greek *Excerpta* of the Rule of Pachomius. Rpt. in A. Boon, *Pachomiana latina. . . , p. 169-182*].

Draguet, R. 'Un morceau grec inédit des Vies de Pachôme apparié à un texte   d'Evagre en partie inconnu,' *Muséon* 70 (1957) 267-306.

_____ . 'Un Paralipomenon pachômien inconnu dans le Karakallou 251,' *Mélanges Eugène Tisserant*, Vol. II, *ST* 232. Vatican City, 1964. Pp. 55-61.

Quecke, Hans. *Die Briefe Pachoms. Griechischer Text der Handschrift W. 145 der Chester Beatty Library eingeleitet und herausgegeben von Hans Quecke. Anhang: Die koptischen Fragmente und Zitate der Pachombriefe, Textus Patristici et Liturgici* 11. Regensburg, 1975.

Latin

Boon, A. *Pachomiana latina. Règle et épîtres de s. Pachôme, épître de s. Théodore et 'Liber' de s. Orsiesius. Texte latin de s. Jérôme, Bibliothèque de la Revue d'histoire ecclésiastique* 7. Louvain, 1932.

Van Cranenburg, H. *La vie latine de saint Pachôme traduite du grec par Denys le Petit, édition critique, Subsidia hagiographica* 46. Brussels, 1969.

Arabic

Amélineau, E. *Monuments pour servir à l'histoire de l'Egypte chrétienne au IVᵉ siècle.—Histoire de Saint Pakhôme et de ses communautés. Documents coptes et arabe inédits, publiés et traduits par E. Amélineau, ADMG* 17, 2 Vol. Paris 1889. [Arabic text: Vol. II, pp. 337-711].

Syriac

Budge, E.A.W. *The Book of Paradise.* London, 1904. [Syriac version of the *Paralipomena*, which Budge erroneously calls the Rule of Pachomius].

Ethiopic

Dillmann, A. *Chrestomatia Aethiopica.* Leipzig, 1866; 1941², pp. 57-69. [Ethiopic version of the Rules of Pachomius].

Löfgren, O. 'Zur Textkritik der äthiopischen Pachomiusregeln I, II,' *Le Monde Oriental* 30 (1936) 171-187. [Critical *apparatus* to be added to Dillman's edition].

Arras, V. *Collectio Monastica*, CSCO 238. Louvain, 1963. Pp. 141-143. [Ethiopic translation of the Greek *Excerpta* of the Rule of Pachomius].

B: *TRANSLATIONS*

From Coptic

Lefort, L.T. *Sancti Pachomii vita bohairice scripta*, CSCO 107. Louvain, 1936. [Latin translation].

_____ . *Les Vies coptes de Saint Pachôme et de ses premiers successeurs*, Bibliothèque du Muséon 16. Louvain 1943; rpt. 1966.

_____ . *Oeuvres de s. Pachôme et de ses disciples*, CSCO 160. Louvain 1956.

Draguet, R. *Les Pères du désert*. Paris, 1949. Pp. 87-126. [French translation of a Life of Pachomius reconstructed from the Coptic fragments].

Gribomont, J. and F. Moscatelli. *Vita copta di S. Pacomio. A cura di Jean Gribomont. Traduzione, introduzione e note di Francesca Moscatelli*. Praglia 1981.

Quecke, H. 'Briefe Pachoms in koptischer Sprache. Neue deutsche Übersetzung,' *Zetesis. Festschrift E. de Strycker.* Antwerp/Utrecht, 1973. Pp. 655-664.

Vögué, A. de. 'Epîtres inédites d'Horsièse et de Théodore,' *Commandements du Seigneur et Libération évangélique, SA* 70. Rome, 1977. Pp. 244-257.

From Greek

Athanassakis, A.N. *The Life of Pachomius (Vita Prima Graeca). Translated by Apostolos N. Athanassakis. Introduction by Birger A. Pearson.* Missoula, MT, 1975.

Festugière, A.-J. *Les Moines d'Orient, T. IV/2: La première Vie grecque de saint Pachôme. Introduction critique et traduction.* Paris, 1965.

Mertel, H. *Leben des hl. Pachomius, BKV* 31. Kempten, 1917. [German translation of the second Greek Life and of a few fragments of the fourth Greek Life].

From Latin

D'Andilly, A. *Les Vies des Saints Pères des Déserts*, Lyon, 1663. Pp. 175-276. [French translation of the Latin Life].

Bacht, H. *Das Vermächtnis des Ursprungs, Studien zum Frühen Mönchtum* I. Würzburg, 1972. [German translation of the *Liber Orsiesii*].

De Elizalde, M. *Libro de nuestro Padre San Orsisio. Introducción, traducción y notas de Martín de Elizalde. Cuadernos monásticos*, Nos. 4-5 (1967) 173-244.

Deseille, P. *L'esprit du monachisme pachômien, suivi de la traduction française des Pachomiana latina par les moines de Solesmes, Spiritualité orientale 2.* Bellefontaine 1968.

Starowieyski, M. 'Regula św Pachomiusza', in *Starożytne Reguły Zakonne. (Pisma Starochrzescijanskich Pisarzy*, Tom. XXVI.) Warsaw, 1980 (A Polish translation of the Rule of Pachomius, from the *Pachomiana Latina*).

Steidle, B. and O. Schuler. 'Der "Obern-Spiegel" im "Testament" des Abtes Horsiesi († nach 387),' *EuA* 43 (1967) 5-21. [German translation of the chapters 7-18 and 39-40 of the *Liber Orsiesii*].

From Arabic

Amélineau, E. *Monuments pour servir....* [French translation under the Arabic text].

From Syriac

Budge, E.A.W. *The Book of Paradise.* London, 1904. [English translation of the Syriac version of the *Paralipomena*]. Rpt. in *The Paradise or Garden of the Holy Fathers.* London, 1907, Vol. 1, pp. 283-315; and again in *Stories of the Holy Fathers*, Oxford, 1934, pp. 373-416.

Nau, F., in Bousquet J. and F. Nau, *Histoire de saint Pacôme* (Cited above). [A French translation of the Syriac version of the *Paralipomena* is given in front of the text of the sixth Greek Life].

From Ethiopic

Arras, V. *Collectio Monastica, CSCO* 239. Louvain, 1963. Pp. 104-105. [Latin translation of the Ethiopic version of the Greek Excerpta of the Rule.].

Basset, R. *Les apocryphes éthiopiens traduits en français*, fasc. 8. Paris, 1896. Pp. 28-40. [Translation of the Ethiopic Rules]. Partly reprinted in *Règles des moines*, Edit. Jean-Pie Lapierre, Paris, 1982.

König, E. 'Die Regeln des Pachomius', *TSK* 51 (1878) 328-332.

Löfgren, O. 'Pakomius' etiopiska klosterregler. I svensk tokning.' *Kyrkohistorisk Årsskrift* 48 (1948) 163-184. [Swedish translation].

Schodde, G.H. 'The Rules of Pachomius translated from the Ethiopic,' *Presbyterian Review* 6 (1885) 678-689.

SIGLA

Ag	Arabic Life in Göttingen Ms.116.
Am	Arabic Life published by E. Amélineau.
Am. Letter	Letter of Bishop Ammon (*Epistula Ammonis*).
Apoph.	*Apophthegmata Patrum.*
Av	Arabic Life in Vatican Ms. 172.
Bo	Bohairic Life.
Den.	Latin Life translated by Denys (*Dionysius Exiguus*).
Draguet Fragm.	Fragment published by R. Draguet.
G¹, G², etc.	First Greek Life, Second Greek Life, etc.
H.L.	Lausiac History of Palladius (*Historia Lausiaca*).
H.M.A.	History of the Monks in Egypt (*Historia monachorum in Aegypto*).
Hors. Fragm.	Fragments from Horsiesios.
Hors. Instr.	Instruction of Horsiesios.
Hors. Letter	Letter of Horsiesios.
Hors. Reg.	Regulations of Horsiesios.
Hors. Test.	Testament of Horsiesios (*Liber Orsiesii*).
Inst.	Institutes (*Praecepta et Instituta*).
Jer. Pref.	Jerome's Preface to the *Pachomiana Latina.*
Jud.	Judgements (*Praecepta atque Judicia*).
Leg.	Laws (*Praecepta ac Leges*).
Pach. Fragm.	Fragments from Pachomius.
Pach. Instr.	Instruction of Pachomius.
Pach. Letter	Letter of Pachomius.
Paral.	*Paralipomena*

Pr.	Precepts (*Praecepta*).
S¹, S², etc.	First Sahidic Life, Second Sahidic Life, etc.
SBo	Recension of the Life represented by the group Bo, Av, S⁴, S⁵, S⁶, S⁷, etc.
Theod. Fragm.	Fragments from Theodore.
Theod. Instr.	Instruction of Theodore.
Theod. Letter	Letter of Theodore.
VB	L.-T. Lefort, *S. Pachomii vita bohairice scripta.*
VC	L.-T. Lefort, *Les vies coptes de saint Pachôme et de ses premiers successeurs.*
Vit. Ant.	Life of Antony by Athanasius (*Vita Antonii*).
VS	L.-T. Lefort, *S. Pachomii vitae sahidice scriptae.*

CISTERCIAN PUBLICATIONS, INC.
TITLES LISTINGS

CISTERCIAN TEXTS

THE WORKS OF BERNARD OF CLAIRVAUX

Apologia to Abbot William
Five Books on Consideration: Advice to a Pope
Grace and Free Choice
Homilies in Praise of the Blessed Virgin Mary
The Life and Death of Saint Malachy the Irishman
Love without Measure. Extracts from the Writings
    of St Bernard (Paul Diemier)
The Parables of Saint Bernard (Michael Casey)
Sermons for the Summer Season
Sermons on the Song of Songs I - IV
The Steps of Humility and Pride

THE WORKS OF WILLIAM OF SAINT THIERRY

The Enigma of Faith
Exposition on the Epistle to the Romans
Exposition on the Song of Songs
The Golden Epistle
The Mirror of Faith
The Nature and Dignity of Love

THE WORKS OF AELRED OF RIEVAULX

Dialogue on the Soul
The Mirror of Charity
Spiritual Friendship
Treatises I: On Jesus at the Age of Twelve, Rule for
    a Recluse, The Pastoral Prayer

THE WORKS OF JOHN OF FORD

Sermons on the Final Verses of the Song of
    Songs I - VII

THE WORKS OF GILBERT OF HOYLAND

Sermons on the Songs of Songs I-III
Treatises, Sermons and Epistles

OTHER EARLY CISTERCIAN WRITERS

The Letters of Adam of Perseigne I
Baldwin of Ford: Spiritual Tractates I - II
Gertrud the Great of Helfta: Spiritual Exercises
Gertrud the Great of Helfta: The Herald of God's
    Loving-Kindness
Guerric of Igny: Liturgical Sermons I - II
Idung of Prüfening: Cistercians and Cluniacs: The
    Case of Cîteaux
Isaac of Stella: Sermons on the Christian Year
The Life of Beatrice of Nazareth
Serlo of Wilton & Serlo of Savigny
Stephen of Lexington: Letters from Ireland
Stephen of Sawley: Treatises

MONASTIC TEXTS
EASTERN CHRISTIAN TRADITION

Besa: The Life of Shenoute
Cyril of Scythopolis: Lives of the Monks of Palestine
Dorotheos of Gaza: Discourses

Evagrius Ponticus:Praktikos and Chapters on Prayer
The Harlots of the Desert (Benedicta Ward)
John Moschos: The Spiritual Meadow
Iosif Volotsky: Monastic Rule
The Lives of the Desert Fathers
The Lives of Simeon Stylites (Robert Doran)
The Luminous Eye (Sebastian Brock)
Mena of Nikiou: Isaac of Alexandra &
    St Macrobius
Pachomian Koinonia I - III
Paphnutius: Histories of the Monks of Egypt
The Sayings of the Desert Fathers
Spiritual Direction in the Early Christian East (Irénée
    Hausherr)
The Syriac Fathers on Prayer and the Spiritual Life
    (Sebastian Brock)

WESTERN CHRISTIAN TRADITION

Anselm of Canterbury: Letters I - III
Bede: Commentary on the Seven Catholic Epistles
Bede: Commentary on the Acts of the Apostles
Bede: Gospel Homilies I - II
Bede: Homilies on the Gospels I - II
Cassian: Conferences I - III
Gregory the Great: Forty Gospel Homilies
Guigo II the Carthusian: Ladder of Monks and
    Twelve Mediations
Handmaids of the Lord: The Lives of Holy Women in
    Late Antiquity and the Early Middle Ages
Peter of Celle: Selected Works
The Letters of Armand-Jean de Rancé I - II
The Rule of the Master

CHRISTIAN SPIRITUALITY

Abba: Guides to Wholeness & Holiness East & West
A Cloud of Witnesses: The Development of
    Christian Doctrine (D.N. Bell)
Athirst for God: Spiritual Desire in Bernard of
    Clairvaux's Sermons on the Song of Songs
    (M. Casey)
Cistercian Way (André Louf)
Drinking from the Hidden Fountains: A Patristic
    Breviary (Tomas Spidlík)
Fathers Talking (Aelred Squire)
Friendship and Community (B. McGuire)
From Cloister to Classroom
Herald of Unity: The Life of Maria Gabrielle
    Sagheddu (M. Driscoll)
Life of St Mary Magdalene and of Her Sister
    St Martha (D. Mycoff)
The Name of Jesus (Irénée Hausherr)
Penthos: The Doctrine of Compunction in the
    Christian East (Irénée Hausherr)
Rancé and the Trappist Legacy (A.J. Krailsheimer)
The Roots of the Modern Christian Tradition
Russian Mystics (S. Bolshakoff)
The Spirituality of the Christian East (Tomas Spidlík)
Spirituality of the Medieval West
Tuning In To Grace (André Louf)

MONASTIC STUDIES

Community & Abbot in the Rule of St Benedict
    I - II (Adalbert De Vogüé)
Beatrice of Nazareth in Her Context (Roger
    De Ganck)
Consider Your Call: A Theology of the Monastic Life
    (Daniel Rees et al.)

TITLES LISTINGS

The Finances of the Cistercian Order in the Fourteenth Century (Peter King)
Fountains Abbey & Its Benefactors (Joan Wardrop)
The Hermit Monks of Grandmont (Carole A. Hutchison)
In the Unity of the Holy Spirit (Sighard Kleiner)
Monastic Practices (Charles Cummings)
The Occupation of Celtic Sites in Ireland by the Canons Regular of St Augustine and the Cistercians (Geraldine Carville)
The Rule of St Benedict: A Doctrinal and Spiritual Commentary (Adalbert de Vogüé)
The Rule of St Benedict (Br. Pinocchio)
Towards Unification with God (Beatrice of Nazareth in Her Context, II)
St Hugh of Lincoln (D.H. Farmer)
Serving God First (Sighard Kleiner)
With Greater Liberty: A Short History of Christian Monasticism and Religious Orders

CISTERCIAN STUDIES

A Difficult Saint (B. McGuire)
A Second Look at Saint Bernard (J. Leclercq)
Bernard of Clairvaux and the Cistercian Spirit (J. Leclercq)
Bernard of Clairvaux: Man, Monk, Mystic (M. Casey) Tapes and readings
Bernard of Clairvaux: Studies Presented to Dom Jean Leclercq
Bernardus Magister
Christ the Way: The Christology of Guerric of Igny (John Morson)
Cistercian Sign Language
The Cistercian Spirit
The Cistercians in Denmark (Brian McGuire)
The Cistercians in Scandinavia (James France)
The Eleventh-century Background of Cîteaux (Bede K. Lackner)
The Golden Chain: Theological Anthropology of Isaac of Stella (Bernard McGinn)
Image and Likeness: The Augustinian Spirituality of William of St Thierry (D. N. Bell)
An Index of Cistercian Works and Authors in the Libraries of Great Britain I (D.N. Bell)
The Mystical Theology of St Bernard (Étienne Gilson)
Nicolas Cotheret's Annals of Cîteaux (Louis J. Lekai)
The Spiritual Teachings of St Bernard of Clairvaux (J.R. Sommerfeldt)
Studiosorum Speculum
Wholly Animals: A Book of Beastly Tales (D.N.Bell)
William, Abbot of St Thierry
Women and St Bernard of Clairvaux (Jean Leclercq)

MEDIEVAL RELIGIOUS WOMEN
Lillian Thomas Shank and John A. Nichols, editors

Distant Echoes
Peace Weavers
Hidden Springs

STUDIES IN CISTERCIAN ART AND ARCHITECTURE
Meredith Parsons Lillich, editor

Volumes I, II, III, IV now available

THOMAS MERTON

The Climate of Monastic Prayer (T. Merton)
The Legacy of Thomas Merton (P. Hart)
The Message of Thomas Merton (P. Hart)

Thomas Merton: The Monastic Journey
Thomas Merton Monk (P. Hart)Thomas Merton Monk & Artist (Victor Kramer)
Thomas Merton on St Bernard
Thomas Merton the Monastic Journey
Toward an Integrated Humanity (M. Basil Pennington et al.)

CISTERCIAN LITURGICAL DOCUMENTS SERIES
Chrysogonus Waddell, ocso, editor

The Cadouin Breviary (two volumes)
Hymn Collection of the Abbey of the Paraclete
Two Early Cistercian *Libelli Missarum*
Molesme Summer-Season Breviary (4 volumes)
Institutiones nostrae: The Paraclete Statutes
Old French Ordinary and Breviary of the Abbey of the Paraclete: Text & Commentary (2 vol.)
The Twelfth-century Cistercian Psalter
The Twelfth-century Usages of the Cistercian Lay-brothers

STUDIA PATRISTICA
Papers of the 1983 Oxford patristics conference edited by Elizabeth A. Livingstone

XVIII/1 Historica-Theologica-Gnostica-Biblica
XVIII/2 Critica-Classica-Ascetica-Liturgica
XVIII/3 Second Century-Clement & Origen-Cappadocian Fathers
XVIII/4 *available from Peeters, Leuven*

Cistercian Publications is a non-profit corporation. Its publishing program is restricted to monastic texts in translation and books on the monastic tradition.

North American customers may order these books through booksellers or directly from the warehouse:
Cistercian Publications
St Joseph's Abbey
Spencer, Massachusetts 01562
(508) 885-7011
fax 508-885-4687

British and European customers may order these books through booksellers or from:
Brian Griffin
Storey House, White Cross
South Road, Lancaster LA1 4QX
England

Editorial queries and advance book information should be directed to the Editorial Offices:
Cistercian Publications
Institute of Cistercian Studies
Western Michigan University
Kalamazoo, Michigan 49008
(616) 387-8920
fax 616-387-8921

A complete catalogue of texts in translation and studies on early, medieval, and modern monasticism is available at no cost from Cistercian Publications.